The EU and the European Security Strategy

The European Security Strategy (ESS) has become an important reference framework for the EU since its inception in 2003. Without strategy an actor can only really be a 'reactor' to events and developments. In the ESS the EU now has a strategy, with which it has the potential of shifting boundaries and shaping the World.

The EU and the European Security Strategy explores this statement and examines the underlying concepts and implementation of the ESS as a judging tool of all the European Union's external actions. Contributors, closely involved in the early debate leading up to the ESS, assess questions such as how the strategy has shaped EU policy, how it relates to existing policies but also how it has added value to these policies and whether the strategy's objectives are sufficient to safeguard EU interests or whether they should be reviewed and added too.

The outline of the strategy itself is followed, addressing its historical and conceptual context, the threat assessment, the multilateral and regional policies of the EU, its military capabilities and its strategic partnerships. This book offers a comprehensive vision of how the EU can achieve the ambitious objectives of the European Security Strategy and become an effective global actor as the strategy helps to forge a global Europe.

This book will be of great interest to students and researchers of European politics and security studies.

Sven Biscop is a senior research fellow at Egmont – The Royal Institute for International Relations in Brussels and visiting professor at the College of Europe in Bruges.

Jan Joel Andersson is programme director at the Swedish Institute of International Affairs and teaches international relations at Stockholm University, Sweden.

Routledge Advances in European Politics

The EU and the European Security Strategy

Forging a global Europe

Edited by
Sven Biscop and **Jan Joel Andersson**

Routledge
Taylor & Francis Group

LONDON AND NEW YORK

First published 2008
by Routledge
2 Park Square, Milton Park, Abingdon, Oxon OX14 4RN

Simultaneously published in the USA and Canada
by Routledge
270 Madison Ave, New York, NY 10016

Routledge is an imprint of the Taylor & Francis Group, an informa business.

© 2008 Sven Biscop and Jan Joel Andersson

Typeset in Sabon by
Book Now Ltd, London
Printed and bound in Great Britain by
Biddles Ltd, King's Lynn

British Library Cataloguing in Publication Data
A catalogue record for this book is available from the British Library

Library of Congress Cataloging in Publication Data
The EU and the European security strategy: forging a global Europe/edited by Sven Biscop and Jan Joel Andersson.
      p. cm. – (Routledge advances in European politics; 49)
1. National security–European Union countries. 2. European Union.
3. European Union countries–Military policy. 4. European Union countries–Foreign relations. I. Biscop, Sven. II. Andersson, Jan Joel.

UA646.E866 2007
355'.03354–dc22   2007003398

ISBN10: 0–415–39317–5 (hbk)
ISBN10: 0–203–94558–1 (ebk)

ISBN13: 978–0–415–39317–1 (hbk)
ISBN13: 978–0–203–94558–2 (ebk)

'Mon père, ce héros au sourire si doux' (Victor Hugo, *Après la Bataille*)

To my father François Biscop (1944–2006)

Sven Biscop

To my daughter Stella Buus Andersson (born 2006)

Jan Joel Andersson

Contents

Contributors

Jan Joel Andersson is programme director and a research fellow at the Swedish Institute of International Affairs. He teaches international relations at Stockholm University and has published extensively on Swedish and European security and defence policy. A graduate of Uppsala University, Jan Joel received his MA and PhD in political science from the University of California at Berkeley.

Sven Biscop is a senior research fellow at Egmont – The Royal Institute for International Relations in Brussels and visiting professor at the College of Europe in Bruges. He is editor in chief of the journal *Studia Diplomatica* and sits on the Executive Academic Board of the European Security and Defence College. He co-organises the Higher Studies in Security and Defence with Belgium's Royal Defence College and has been a visiting professor at Carleton University in Ottawa and Renmin University in Beijing.

Roland Dannreuther is senior lecturer in international relations at the School of Social and Political Studies, University of Edinburgh. Recent publications include *International Security: the Contemporary Security Agenda* (Polity, 2007); *Security Strategy and Transatlantic Relations* (co-edited with John Peterson) (Routledge, 2006); and *European Union Foreign and Security Policy: Towards a Neighbourhood Strategy* (ed.) (Routledge, 2004).

Richard Gowan is the coordinator of the International Security Institution Programme at the Center on International Cooperation at New York University. He was formerly manager of the Europe Programme at the Foreign Policy Centre in London. He holds a BA in History and MPhil in International Relations from Cambridge University.

Jean-Yves Haine is Senior Fellow for Euro-Atlantic, regional and global security at the Stockholm International Peace Research Institute (SIPRI).

Jolyon Howorth has been visiting professor of political science at Yale University since 2002. His recent books include: *Security and Defence Policy in the European Union* (Palgrave, 2007); *Defending Europe: the EU, NATO and the Quest for European Autonomy* (edited with John Keeler) (Palgrave, 2003); and *European Integration and Defence: the Ultimate Challenge?* (WEU-ISS, 2000).

Catherine Kelleher is College Park Professor at the University of Maryland and senior fellow at the Watson Institute for International Studies at Brown University. Her government service includes service as President Clinton's deputy assistant secretary of defense for Russia, Ukraine and Eurasia, and the secretary of defense's representative to NATO in Brussels, and on President Carter's National Security Council staff. She is a former senior fellow of foreign policy studies at the Brookings Institution, and she directed the Aspen Institute, Berlin. Kelleher has taught and written extensively on conventional and nuclear arms control as well as on German, Russian, and European security issues. She has been decorated for her public service by both the American and German governments and received a DLitt from Mt. Holyoke College and a PhD from the Massachusetts Institute of Technology.

Roberto Menotti is a research fellow in the International Programs at Aspen Institute Italia, Rome, focusing on transatlantic relations. He has published in several specialised journals (including *Survival, Europe's World, Turkish Policy Quarterly*) and edited volumes, and is author of two books in Italian (1999, 2003, respectively) on NATO enlargement and international security. He has lectured extensively in Italy and abroad, and taught undergraduate courses at LUISS University and John Cabot University.

Maria Francesca Vencato joined the Katholieke Universiteit Leuven in 2002 as a researcher in post-Soviet and Asian studies while working for community programmes supporting the development of civil society in Eastern Europe and Central Asia. She is currently finalising her PhD at the Katholieke Universiteit Leuven on the impact of institution building in Central and Eastern Europe in the field of development cooperation on EU external governance. She holds a First-class Honours degree in Political Science and International Relations from LUISS University in Rome and an MA in European Studies from the College of Europe of Bruges, Belgium.

Acknowledgements

This volume grew out of our mutual fascination with the European Security Strategy (ESS) and its potential role in forging a Global Europe. The first draft of the ESS was presented by Javier Solana at the Thessaloniki European Council in June 2003. This draft was then discussed in an unusual European-wide consultation process at three seminars organised by the EU in the fall of 2003 in Rome (19 September), Paris (6–7 October) and Stockholm (20 October). Both of us had the privilege to participate in this process. Jan Joel Andersson of the Swedish Institute of International Affairs (SIIA) participated in all three events and was responsible for organising the Stockholm seminar and authored the seminar's discussion paper on Coherence and Capabilities (Andersson 2003a). Sven Biscop of Belgium's Egmont – The Royal Institute for International Relations took part in two of the seminars and co-authored a proposal for a security concept, which was presented to Solana at a conference on 26 November (Coolsaet and Biscop 2003). By the end of the consultation process and once the ESS had been adopted by the European Council in December 2003, we agreed that we should edit a volume on this remarkable document. To this end, we assembled a great team of colleagues of whom several also had participated in the consultation process on the draft ESS.

It has been a pleasure to serve as the editors of this volume. We appreciate the patience and endurance of our authors, who wrote their chapters with good humour – if not always with great speed. We have learned greatly from their efforts and have enjoyed ourselves in the process. We would also like to thank Harriet Brinton at Routledge, for her immense patience with us and for repeatedly extending our deadlines, as well as her colleague Amelia McLaurin, for the smooth transition after she took over our project from Harriet.

Jan Joel Andersson would also like to gratefully acknowledge financial support from the Swedish Ministry for Foreign Affairs and the European Foreign and Security Policy Studies Programme, jointly funded by the Riksbankens Jubileumsfond, Volkswagen Stiftung and Compagnia di San Paolo.

Abbreviations

AC	Arctic Council
ACO	Allied Command Operations
ACP	African, Caribbean and Pacific states
ACT	Allied Command Transformation
AEC	ASEAN Security Community/ASEAN Economic Community
APEC	Asia-Pacific Economic Cooperation
APRM	African Peer Review Mechanism
ARF	ASEAN Regional Forum
ASCC	ASEAN Socio-Cultural Community
ASEAN	Association of Southeast Asian Nations
ASEM	Asia-Europe Meeting
AVF	All-Volunteer Force
BEAC	Barents Euro Arctic Council
BG	Battlegroup
CBSS	Council of the Baltic Sea States
CFSP	Common Foreign and Security Policy
CIS	Commonwealth of Independent States
CJTF	Combined Joint Task Force
CRBN	Chemical, Radiological, Biological, Nuclear
CS	Combat Support
CSAP	Council for Security Cooperation in Asia-Pacific
CSCE	Conference on Security and Cooperation in Europe
CSS	Combat Service Support
DDR	Disarmament, Demobilisation and Reintegration
DRC	Democratic Republic of Congo
ECAP	European Capability Action Plan
ECE	East Central Europe
EDA	European Defence Agency
EDC	European Defence Community

EMP	Euro-Mediterranean Partnership
ENEC	European Network Enabling Capability
ENP	European Neighbourhood Policy
ENPI	European Neighbourhood Policy Instrument
EPC	European Political Cooperation
ESDC	European Security and Defence College
ESDI	European Security and Defence Identity
ESDP	European Security and Defence Policy
ESS	European Security Strategy
EU3	The governments of Britain, France and Germany
EUISS	European Union Institute for Security Studies
EUMM	European Monitoring Mission
EUSR	European Union Special Representative
GCC	Gulf Cooperation Council
GIA	Groupe Islamique Armé
GPG	Global Public Goods
GPS	Global Positioning System
HEU	High-Enriched Uranium
HGTF	Headline Goal Task Force
HHG	Helsinki Headline Goal
IAEA	International Atomic Energy Agency
ICC	International Criminal Court
ISTAR	Intelligence, Surveillance, Target Acquisition and Reconnaissance
MD	Mediterranean Dialogue
NAFTA	North American Free Trade Area
NEPAD	New Partnership for Africa's Development
NIS	Newly Independent States
NPT	Nuclear Non-Proliferation Treaty
NRF	NATO Response Force
NSS	National Security Strategy (of the US)
OSCE	Organisation for Security and Cooperation in Europe
PBC	Peacebuilding Commission
PCA	Partnership and Cooperation Agreement
PGMs	Precision-Guided Munitions
PSC	Political and Security Committee
ROE	Rules of Engagement
SEA	Single European Act
SHAPE	Supreme Headquarters Allied Powers Europe
SIIA	Swedish Institute of International Affairs
SSR	Security Sector Reform

TACIS	Technical Assistance to the Commonwealth of Independent States
TEU	Treaty on European Union
UAV/STA	Unmanned Aerial Vehicle/Surveillance, and Target Acquisition
WEU	Western European Union
WMD	Weapons of Mass Destruction

Introduction

Sven Biscop and Jan Joel Andersson

When the EU ministers of foreign affairs, meeting informally at Kastellorizo on the island of Rhodes on 2–3 May 2003 tasked Javier Solana, High Representative for the Common Foreign and Security Policy (CFSP) with the drafting of a strategic concept, this came as a complete surprise to most observers, or at least to the editors of this volume. Until then the adoption of anything like a strategy for the CFSP had been thought politically unfeasible in a European Union divided between 'Atlanticists' and 'Europeanists'. Academic publications calling for the adoption of a strategy had been laid aside as certainly interesting, perhaps even welcome, but in any case unrealistic proposals (Van Staden *et al.* 2000; Biscop 2002). But about a month later already, at the Thessalonica European Council on 19–20 June, Solana presented his first draft, which was subsequently discussed by those same observers, along with diplomats, the military, NGO representatives etc., at three seminars organised by the European Union for that purpose in the fall of 2003: Rome (19 September), Paris (6–7 October) and Stockholm (20 October).[1] On 12 December 2003 the European Council meeting in Brussels adopted the final document, *A Secure Europe in a Better World – European Security Strategy* (ESS) (European Council 2003a).

Perhaps the editors were not the only ones to be surprised at the suddenness and the magnitude of this move: the adoption of a strategic document covering in effect the whole of EU foreign policy, across the pillars, from aid and trade to diplomacy and the military. Rumour had it that not all participants in the Kastellorizo meeting were equally aware of the scope of the decision they had taken. By concentrating the drafting of the ESS in the hands of his own team and then seeking feedback from a broad audience, at the three seminars, Solana prevented Member States with second thoughts from blocking the process, although this implied that to some extent normal decision-making procedures were by-passed, to the detriment notably of the Political and Security Committee (PSC). Yet reluctant Member States could still hope, as a number of observers did expect as well, that soon after its adoption the ESS would disappear into some dusty drawer – the key of which some would probably have liked to present to NATO for safekeeping. There was indeed a risk that the adoption of the ESS, which was accompanied by the necessary pomp and circumstance, would be nothing more than a one-off demonstration of regained unity after the intra-European divide over Iraq, a step of high symbolic value but with little impact on actual policy-making. A stratagem rather than a strategy . . .

The ESS has certainly not disappeared, however. Quite the contrary, it is omnipresent in EU discourse. In many policy documents and decisions on different aspects of foreign policy, especially those relating to the CFSP and its military dimension, the European Security and Defence Policy (ESDP), the guidelines fixed by the ESS are constantly being referred to. They also serve as the connecting thread throughout the trainings organised by the European Security and Defence College (ESDC) for practitioners from the Member States. In the decision-making process, Member States as well as the European institutions make good tactical use of the ESS: the more convincingly a proposed initiative can be linked to it, the more difficult it is to oppose. This demonstrates that the ESS is more than 'a recipe for masterly inactivity' (Toje 2005: 132). Moreover, the ESS frequently appears on reading lists at colleges and universities around the world and is one of the most spread and read EU documents among the general public.

> On this initial evidence, the most pessimistic alternative view of the ESS as a mere 'piece of paper' can already be set aside. A suitable political and procedural transmission belt appears to have been found to translate specific desiderata from the ESS into more immediate operational requirements, and to make sure that the latter are followed up and reported on in good time.
>
> (Bailes 2005a: 22)

There are of course authors who insist that the ESS is not a strategy at all (Heisbourg 2004; Toje 2005). Too much influenced perhaps by the traditional strategic studies in the realist school, they associate strategy in the first place with the use of force. That is just one dimension of many which a foreign policy strategy has to cover, however. For that is what the ESS does: it covers not just security policy, as the title of the document indeed misleadingly – and perhaps mistakenly – suggests, but foreign policy as a whole. That does not mean that the European Union would not benefit from the adoption of a military doctrine or operational concept, outlining the conditions for and ways of utilising the military instrument (Bailes 2005a: 20).

Such a document could provide the link between the ESS and ESDP. What this book aims to do is to assess whether the ESS effectively functions as a strategy in the much broader sense of the term as it is understood in the context of public management, a definition which is not linked specifically to defence, security or even foreign policy, but can be applied to any policy field. A strategy is a policy-making tool which, on the basis of the values and interests of in this case the European Union, outlines the long-term overall policy objectives to be achieved and the basic categories of instruments to be applied to that end. It serves as a reference framework for day-to-day policy-making in a rapidly evolving and increasingly complex international environment and it guides the definition of the means – i.e. the civilian and military capabilities – that need to be developed (Biscop 2005: 1). A strategy thus obviously is not meant to be an operational document, another reason used to dismiss the strategic claims of the ESS (Maull 2005: 792–94), but has to be translated into sub-strategies for specific policy fields and then into concrete policies and actions. In a way, a strategy has an inspirational function *vis-à-vis* policy-making (Bailes 2005a: 14).

Given the omnipresence of the ESS, it can be argued that in this sense a strategic culture is developing at the EU level, i.e. the habit of automatically referring to the strategic framework of the ESS when taking decisions and the willingness to undertake the actions and commit the means required to achieve those strategic objectives. Just like strategy is a much broader concept than often thought, strategic culture as well must thus be judged by much more than the willingness to use force when necessary, even though admittedly this aspect of strategic culture is the most difficult to realise. European Union strategic culture may not be uniform or common enough, but it seems to be gradually becoming so (Baun 2005).

This emerging strategic culture is what this book aims to investigate. To what extent do the choices made in the ESS effectively function as a reference framework for day-to-day decision-making and shape EU policy? How do these choices relate to existing policies and what added value has the adoption of the strategic framework brought? Are the assumptions of the ESS still valid, are its objectives sufficient to safeguard EU interests and can they be achieved? Which additional actions, instruments and means could help achieving these objectives? Are there areas still to be covered by fundamental strategic reflection? Should the ESS be reviewed?

In order to address these questions, the book follows the outline of the ESS itself. In Chapter 1 Sven Biscop puts the ESS in its historical and conceptual context, focusing on the trend of comprehensive or holistic approaches to deal with the challenges of an ever more complex global environment. Jean-Yves Haine in Chapter 2 then analyses the EU assessment of that environment: how does Europe see the world? The ensuing chapters address the different strategic objectives which the European Union has arrived at on the basis of that worldview: 'effective multilateralism' at the global level (Chapter 3 by Richard Gowan); securing the EU's neighbourhood (Chapter 4 by Roland Dannreuther); building an effective military capacity (Chapter 5 by Jolyon Howorth); establishing strategic partnerships (Chapter 6 by Roberto Menotti and Maria Francesca Vencato); and increasing the coherence of EU foreign policy (Chapter 7 by Jan Joel Andersson). As the emergence of the European Union as a strategic actor automatically impacts on the transatlantic relationship, finally Chapter 8 will offer an American view of the ESS by Catherine Kelleher.

Without strategy any actor can really only be a 'reactor' to events and developments. Equipped with a clear strategy and endowed with a strong strategic culture, an actor can shape the world. Whether the ESS has succeeded in forging such a global Europe is the topic of this volume.

Note

1 The programmes, discussion papers and reports from the three working seminars on the draft European Security Strategy in Rome, Paris and Stockholm are available on the webpage of the EU Institute for Security Studies (www.iss-eu.org/solana/solanae.html).

1 The European Security Strategy in context

A comprehensive trend

Sven Biscop

If the task given to Javier Solana by the May 2003 informal Council meeting to draft a European strategic concept came as a surprise, it was because it happened at a time when the CFSP seemed to be in shambles as a result of the fierce intra-European debate over the American-led invasion of Iraq. Only a few months before, on 10 February, Belgium, France and Germany had provoked what seemed to be the worst crisis yet for both the CFSP and the transatlantic Alliance when they broke the 'silent procedure' introduced by NATO Secretary-General George Robertson to approve a number of US requests in the framework of the planned invasion. Although on 19 February consensus was reached on defensive measures to assist Turkey in the event of any Iraqi incursion, other proposed measures, including advance planning for a post-invasion NATO peacekeeping mission in Iraq, were silently removed from the agenda (Pailhe 2003). Seen to be too evidently framed in a war logic at a moment when they felt non-military options were still available, Belgium, France and Germany could not consent to such measures without betraying the principles of their own foreign policy. Fierce recriminations across the Atlantic as well as between EU member states were the result.

Yet a few months later these same member states agreed to have the first ever common European foreign policy strategy drafted, which on 12 December 2003 they duly adopted. How was it that at exactly the moment of what seemed to be the lowest point of the CFSP the European Union achieved what right up until then had been considered politically unfeasible?

Codification of a strategic orientation

It was of course evident from the beginning that the CFSP – as is not entirely uncommon in policy-making – did not follow the scientifically prescribed logic of first adopting a strategy and then designing specific policies and acquiring the required capabilities to implement it. The notion of strategy was not, however, completely absent either. The Amsterdam Treaty added the 'common strategies' to the range of CFSP instruments; these are strategies – now effectively sub-strategies *vis-à-vis* the ESS – on specific functional or geographical issues. Only three have ever been adopted by the European Council: on Russia, Ukraine (both 1999) and the Mediterranean (2000). Subsequently more documents of a similar scope have been adopted by the Council and European Council though, only in other legal formats, even if some carry the word 'strategy' in the title – which also holds true for the ESS itself. Examples are the *European Strategy Against the Proliferation of WMD* (2003b), the Council decision to launch the European Neighbourhood Policy (2004), and the *European Union Counter-Terrorism Strategy* (2005c). None of these amounts to a strategy for foreign policy as a whole. So if prior to 2003 the member states were familiar with the idea of strategies – plural – they probably also became aware of 'possible deficits in coherence and completeness among the strategies so far adopted on a piecemeal basis (and perhaps of a quality problem as well)' (Bailes 2005a: 8).

This strategic void became particularly evident after 1999, when the European Union started to build a military dimension, ESDP. Although the Petersberg-Tasks as included in the Amsterdam Treaty describe which types of operations the European Union can undertake – really anything but collective defence – without a foreign policy strategy it was far from clear in support of which political objectives forces were to be deployed under the EU flag. Member states were very much divided over the desired degree of autonomy of ESDP *vis-à-vis* NATO and the United States. In view of the perceived unfeasibility of achieving anything like a strategic consensus at the time, it was decided to push on with those elements on which agreement existed, i.e. the development of command and control structures and the making available of military capabilities to the European Union, assuming that the strategic debate would inevitably resurface at another, hopefully more suitable time. Again this is a tactic which is not uncommon in EU policy-making, nor is it necessarily an unwise one, for otherwise the window of opportunity to launch ESDP might have been missed. In 2001 the Belgian Presidency did propose to task the Paris-based EU Institute for Security Studies (EUISS) with the drafting of a strategic concept, but in the face of strong opposition from a number of member states the mandate was watered down to the elaboration of a number of scenarios with which the European Union might be confronted and an assessment of the required capabilities to deal with such situations. Eventually published in 2004 (EUISS 2004), this is a stimulating contribution to the debate on ESDP but nothing like a strategic concept.

It seems as if the intra-European crisis over Iraq finally provided the stimulus that made a breakthrough possible. On the one hand, the member states supporting the invasion would have been motivated to demonstrate that the European Union does care about the security threats perceived by the United States and that the transatlantic Alliance is viable still. Hence the similarity between the threat assessment in the ESS and the 2002 US *National Security Strategy* (NSS), which must be seen as a political message to Washington, and the strong emphasis in the ESS on transatlantic partnership. On the other hand, the member states opposing the invasion would have been equally eager to show that even though the threat assessment is to a large degree shared with the United States – be it perhaps not the perception of the intensity of the threat (see Chapter 2) – there are other options available to deal with these threats. In that light the heavy criticism of the NSS by many European observers, because of its emphasis on unilateralism and the – pre-emptive – use of force, is significant. The context of mid-2003 partially also favoured the adoption of the ESS (Bailes 2005a: 9–10): the successful conclusion of the European Convention and the grand and – then still – promising undertaking to draw up a Constitutional Treaty created a climate in which the elaboration of a strategy seemed more feasible than before. Prominent members of the Convention, such as Wim van Eekelen, former WEU Secretary-General, had explicitly called for the formulation of a strategic concept. The summer of 2003 also witnessed the first EU military operation without the use of NATO assets and outside of Europe: Operation Artemis in the DRC (12 June – 1 September).

The main reason why these partly contradictory motivations led to results is that the European Union was able to build on an extensive foreign policy *acquis*. Many of the strategic choices contained in the ESS were already evident as emerging strategic orientations in actual EU policies. Rather than adopting a fundamentally new orientation, to a large extent therefore the ESS must be seen as the codification of existing foreign policy guidelines. In other words, although the context of the Iraq crisis would suggest a deep division between member states, the ESS actually builds on a strong consensus on the basic orientations of EU foreign policy. Indeed, the real intra-European divide over Iraq did not concern the substance and principles of policy. Based on an assessment of past policies, it can safely be argued, e.g. that all member states agree that in principle the use of force is an instrument of last resort which requires a Security Council mandate. As in 1999, the real issue at stake was still the nature of the transatlantic partnership. If the United States reverts to the use of force in a situation in which the European Union in principle would not do so, or not yet, what then has priority for the European Union: steering an autonomous course, based on its own principles, or supporting its most important ally? Besides, it should not be forgotten that on a number of foreign policy issues the European Union had already unanimously taken positions contrary to those of the United States, e.g. on the ICC, on the Kyoto Protocol and on various trade issues.

If the motivation to effectively pursue this codification and draft the document was context-specific, the ESS itself thus is not. Because it builds on the past, on existing guidelines established during ten years of CFSP, and even before, the ESS has been able to transcend the context of its adoption. It thus has the potential to have a durable impact on the future of EU foreign policy-making, as is testified to by its omnipresence in EU foreign policy documents. A comparison can be made with the codification of European Political Cooperation (EPC), the predecessor of the CFSP, in the Single European Act (SEA) of 1986. The SEA did not really strengthen the informal mechanisms of EPC, but by giving them a legal basis did prevent them from weakening. Codification creates a framework from which it is afterwards more difficult to depart; it circumscribes the room for manoeuvre of future policy-making. In the same sense the ESS has consolidated the strategic orientations that were already emerging. To the extent that the ESS will now effectively function as a reference framework for daily decision-making in all fields of foreign policy, it will promote consistency and the emergence of a strong strategic culture. The fact that the ESS, as a European Council declaration instead of a 'common strategy' as defined in the Amsterdam Treaty, is politically rather than legally binding is of less importance in this context.

Naturally, the ESS is not perfect. It can only build on consensus in areas where that existed. On a number of issues it remains particularly vague because consensus was absent or not yet strong enough. Many issues are mentioned in the ESS, because not to do so would have invoked strong criticism, but no more than that: no real choices are made on notably the nature of the transatlantic partnership and the degree of autonomy of the European Union as an international actor. This divide remains a fundamental obstacle to a fully cohesive and resolute CFSP (Dassù and Menotti 2005: 107). Nevertheless, the ESS does contain a number of clear choices and thus certainly has the potential to serve as a strategic framework for EU foreign policy.

Building on a comprehensive *acquis*

The main characteristic of the foreign policy *acquis* on which the ESS builds is its comprehensive or holistic nature, i.e. the integration of all dimensions of foreign policy, from aid and trade to diplomacy and the military.

A holistic approach has been particularly characteristic of EU policy with regard to its neighbouring states, which it attempts to integrate in an encompassing network of relations, witness the Stability Pact for the Balkans, the Euro-Mediterranean Partnership (EMP), and the successful transition of Central and Eastern Europe, probably the most significant European achievement since the start of the European integration project itself. Under the heading of European Neighbourhood Policy (ENP) an enhanced framework for relations between the European Union and all of its neighbours has now been created, in the same period in which the ESS was drafted. In the bilateral ENP Action Plans with each individual neighbour an attempt is made to link all dimensions of relations through the mechanism of 'positive conditionality' (see Chapter 4). At the global level, the 2000 Cotonou Agreement with the ACP countries, replacing the 1975 Lomé Convention, has similarly become wider in scope, including notably an enhanced political dimension. The holistic approach was also evident in the adoption of the *EU Programme for the Prevention of Violent Conflicts* by the Göteborg European Council (15–16 June 2001), which called for the streamlining of short-term prevention and long-term stabilisation in EU policies across the pillars. The picture that emerges is what Keukeleire (2003) has dubbed the 'structural foreign policy' of the European Union and has been so well described by Bretherton and Vogler (2005): a European Union that is – perhaps not always too visibly – seeking to influence the international environment in the long term, attempting to use all the instruments at its disposal, across the pillars, in an integrated way.

This comprehensive approach can be conceptualised through the notion of global public goods (GPG), which emerged in the context of the UN at the end of the 1990s (Biscop 2005). GPG have traditionally been seen in the context of development, but currently the concept is being used more and more in more general political terms, e.g. by Joseph Nye (2002). The starting point of this approach is the assumption that there are a number of 'goods' that are global or universal in the sense that it is generally felt – at least in Europe – that every individual is entitled to them.[1] If to a certain extent the definition of the core GPG is a political and normative choice – Rotberg (2004) uses the term 'political goods' – many elements have been recognised as being universal beyond any doubt, notably in the field of human rights. Like in the 'human security' approach, the individual is the point of reference. These goods are public in the sense that their provision cannot be left to the market but should be supervised by government at the different levels of authority (local, national, regional and global). These core GPG can be grouped under four broad headings:

- physical security or 'freedom from fear';
- political participation, the rule of law and respect for human rights and fundamental freedoms;
- an open and inclusive economic order that provides for the wealth of everyone or 'freedom from want';
- social wellbeing in all of its aspects – access to health services, to education, to a clean and hazard-free environment etc.

These GPG are strongly interrelated: ultimately, one cannot be ensured or enjoyed without access to the other; the four categories are therefore equally important. Effective global governance means ensuring access to GPG; a system that fails to provide the core GPG lacks legitimacy. Global stability, and therefore the security of all states, depends on the availability of sufficient access to the core GPG. Rather than terrorism, weapons of mass destruction (WMD) or other military threats, the most important threat is the ever growing gap between haves and have-nots, a gap which can be best expressed in terms of access to the essential GPG. While this gap and the feelings of exclusion, marginalisation and frustration resulting from it certainly do not justify conflict, they do help to explain it, which is a prerequisite for prevention and resolution of conflicts. The gap between haves and have-nots is foremost among the challenges of the globalised world, because it is a threat of a systemic nature, i.e. it results from the malfunctioning of, and impacts on, the global order itself. For unless mechanisms of governance are created or rendered more effective that can alleviate this situation, at a certain level of inequality, the resulting political upheaval, extremism of all kinds, economic uncertainty and massive migration flows will become uncontrollable. Because of this interdependence GPG are non-exclusive, like true public goods: ultimately maintaining our access to GPG requires improving others' access. Since it denies access to core GPG to a large share of the world's population, the status quo is not an option.

Against this background, specific politico-military challenges do stand out. They include regions of chronic tension and long-standing disputes and conflicts, failed states and civil wars, proliferation of WMD and excessive militarisation, and terrorism. These challenges directly threaten people, states and regions. They have to be tackled head-on, but as they are symptoms of the 'dark side of globalization', effective global governance, improving access to GPG, must be pursued at the same time as the key to *preventing* such threats. 'Security is the precondition of development', the ESS states, but this works the other way around as well. Of course, the strength of the causal relationship between, on the one hand, the gap between haves and have-nots in the broadest sense and, on the other hand, specific politico-military issues differs from case to case. Nonetheless, in the long term no durable solution of politico-military problems can be achieved unless the stability of the world system itself is assured.

The keyword when implementing a comprehensive or holistic approach, based on the notion of GPG, is *integration*. Because the core GPG are inextricably linked together, action must be undertaken to address all of them simultaneously and in a coordinated fashion, by all relevant actors, in all fields of external policy, putting to use all the instruments at their disposal, including trade, development, the environment, police, intelligence and legal cooperation, diplomacy, and security and defence. In the words of the ESS:

> Spreading good governance, supporting social and political reform, dealing with corruption and abuse of power, establishing the rule of law and protecting human rights are the best means of strengthening the international order.

The same plea for a comprehensive approach could be found in the objectives of EU external action as formulated in the draft Constitutional Treaty (Article III-292), which put additional emphasis on aspects of global governance, such as sustainable economic, social and environmental development, the eradication of poverty, the integration of all countries into the world economy, and the abolition of trade restrictions. In its recent communications on development, the Commission has explicitly mentioned the provision of 'universal public goods' as a basic factor (European Commission 2005a) and has emphasised the link between security and development:

> Development is crucial for collective and individual long-term security: they are complementary agendas and neither is subordinate to the other. There cannot be sustainable development without peace and security, and sustainable development is the best structural response to the deep-rooted causes of violent conflicts and the rise of terrorism, often linked to poverty, bad governance and the deterioration and lack of access to natural resources.
>
> (European Commission 2005c: 8)

Although policies in all of these fields must be integrated under the same overall objective of increasing access to GPG, in order to avoid contradictory actions being undertaken, each policy should continue to operate according to its own rationale and dynamic. 'Securitisation', i.e. the instrumentalisation of non-military dimensions of external policy in function only of 'hard' security concerns or 'freedom from fear', must be avoided, for it ignores the intrinsic importance of the other GPG. Here a difference can be seen between the ESS and the NSS. The latter actually devotes more space to issues such as democracy, human rights and trade than the ESS, but these fields are all instrumentalised in function of the one near exclusive priority of US strategy: the 'war on terror'. An integrated approach deals with all GPG simultaneously, but does not require that all issues must be put under the label of security. On the contrary, although this may raise their importance in the eyes of states, it also blurs the distinctions between policy areas. Poverty or HIV/AIDS are of a different nature than terrorism, proliferation or conflict: they can be life-threatening but they do not imply a threat of violence and cannot be tackled by politico-military means. Accordingly, rather than including all challenges under the label of security, issues must not be dealt with as security threats unless they pose an effective threat of violence. In that sense, the ESS has perhaps not really been aptly named. It really is a foreign policy strategy rather than just a security strategy, a title which apparently has been chosen in reference to the NSS (Toje 2005: 120).

By thus addressing the root causes of conflict, a policy oriented on the core GPG emphasises *structural conflict prevention*. This presents a formidable challenge: it implies dealing with more issues, related to all the core GPG, at an earlier stage, before they become security threats. Effective prevention is much more than mere appeasement: it demands a proactive stance, aiming to change circumstances that induce instability and conflict. Mark Duffield analyses how structural prevention in effect amounts to the 'merging of development and security':

> [Development] is no longer concerned with promoting economic growth in the hope that development will follow. Today it is better described as an attempt, preferably through cooperative partnership arrangements, to change whole societies and the behaviour and attitudes of people within them.
>
> (Duffield 2002: 42)

In this broad sense, development 'not only leads to the reduction of poverty, more political freedom, and greater affirmation of human rights, but also lays the foundation for more durable peace and security' (Culpeper 2005: 4). In the terms of the Commission:

> The EU will treat security and development as complementary agendas, with the common aim of creating a secure environment and of breaking

the vicious circle of poverty, war, environmental degradation and failing economic, social and political structures.

(European Commission 2005b: 10)

A policy oriented on GPG will thus in fact be quite intrusive, which can
make it rather contentious with the target countries (Hurwitz and Peake
2004). But as it is in the very nature of GPG that pursuing them is in the
mutual interest of all concerned, it is at the same time a very positive
approach, contrary to other, threat-based strategies. 'For whom' rather than
'against whom' is the question that determines policy. The sincere pursuit of
GPG will bring greatly enhanced legitimacy. As Nye (2002: 143) advises the
United States: 'We gain doubly from such a strategy: from the public goods
themselves, and from the way they legitimize our power in the eyes of
others'.

As effective action in all policy fields concerned requires the cooperation
of a wide range of actors at many different levels, a GPG-oriented policy
implies *multilateralism*: an intricate web of states, regimes, treaties and
organisations, i.e. multi-level governance, implicating all levels of authority
in a coordinated effort to improve people's access to GPG. Although in the
spirit of human security the individual is taken as point of reference, the
state indeed remains a primary partner, for no effective arrangements can be
made with weak and failed states. In the words of the ESS: 'The best protection for our security is a world of well-governed democratic states'. Third
states must therefore be seen as partners for cooperation rather than as mere
subjects of EU policies; the aim is to influence rather than to coerce, to use
the carrot rather than the stick. There will be cases where the use of force is
inevitable, for not all actors are amenable to preventive initiatives and security threats will arise. But in the framework of multilateralism, the use of
force can only be a measure of last resort to be mandated by the Security
Council. In those cases, the legitimacy acquired through the pursuit of GPG
can be capitalised upon.

A comprehensive trend

The idea of a holistic approach is certainly not new. In the opening lines of
the UN Charter already the joint objectives of ensuring peace and security,
respect for human rights, and economic and social development were put
forward and they have remained the basis of the work of the UN ever since.
During the Cold War the CSCE, now the OSCE, promoted the idea of
comprehensive security, including politico-military issues, the protection
and promotion of human rights and fundamental freedoms, and economic

and environmental cooperation, which is reflected in its organisation into three baskets. In addition, the CSCE/OSCE stands for cooperative security: the idea that security is indivisible, hence states should cooperate to achieve security in Europe. It took the end of the Cold War, however, for the holistic approach to really come to the foreground. With the Warsaw Pact and the USSR disappeared the direct and vital military threat to Europe and therefore the almost exclusive focus on the politico-military dimension of foreign and security policy, while challenges in other areas gained prominence. Confronted with a drastically changed global environment and the increased interdependence in a globalised world, numerous states and organisations gradually developed new approaches.

This included the European Union itself, through the practice of the CFSP, but also the Western European Union (WEU), which under the Maastricht Treaty and until the creation of ESDP was the European Union's military arm. It was in the framework of WEU that the first attempt was made to draft a distinctive European strategic document. In the resulting *Common Concept*, adopted on 14 November 1995, the member states

> acknowledged that their security is indivisible, that a comprehensive approach should underlie the concept of security and that cooperative mechanisms should be applied in order to promote security and stability in the whole of the continent.

The document stressed 'Europe's new responsibilities in a strategic environment in which Europe's security is not confined to security in Europe', and described the security environment, highlighting the importance of 'the maintenance of international peace and order and the widest possible observance of generally recognised norms of conduct between States' and of 'democratic institutions, respect for human rights and fundamental freedoms and the rule of law', as well as the need to 'prevent economic imbalances from becoming a threat to our continent'. In terms of how to deal with this new environment, however, the document was limited to an assessment of Europe's military capabilities and the identification of partners for cooperation. At that time, drafting an effective strategy proved to be politically unfeasible because of divisions between the member states; furthermore the CFSP was then still in its infancy. Nevertheless, as the first official European document assessing the changing security environment, it was an important and all too easily forgotten step in the development of the European Union as an international actor.

The terrorist attacks of 11 September 2001 and the US-led invasion of Iraq in March 2003 provoked a major debate on global foreign and security policy as it had developed since the end of the Cold War. The perception by numerous governments and observers of a new threat, on a massive scale, of international terrorism led to a renewed focus on the politico-military dimension and on defence, including proactively, against external enemies. This was put into practice by the United States, by-passing the Security Council when it became clear no mandate was forthcoming and invading Iraq in the absence of any imminent threat, let alone any act of aggression. Proponents of the invasion condemned the collective security system of the UN as being obsolete and called for a major overhaul in order to adapt to the so-called new threats, while the EU member states opposing the invasion were blamed for what was dubbed their naïveté and aversion to the use of force.

In response, UN Secretary-General Kofi Annan created the High-Level Panel on Threats, Challenges and Change, tasked with an assessment of the global environment and the recommendation of measures to render the collective security system more effective. The Panel's report, *A More Secure World – Our Shared Responsibility* (2 December 2004) fed into Annan's own recommendations, *In Larger Freedom – Towards Development, Security and Human Rights for All* (21 March 2005), which formed the basis for discussions at the UN 2005 World Summit in September of that year (High-Level Panel 2004; Annan 2005). By the time the Summit adopted its *Outcome Document* (General Assembly 2005), the nature of the debate had changed, driven by developments on the ground. The lack of preparedness of the US-led coalition in Iraq for the post-intervention stabilisation and reconstruction phase; the rise of terrorism, inside and outside Iraq, which the invasion had provoked rather than its demise; and the impossibility of winning a 'war' on terror by military means as well as the excesses and human rights violations which it had led to, all combined into a powerful argument for a holistic approach, which not even the greatest proponents of the use of force could ignore. As a result, the UN reconfirmed its belief in the comprehensive approach and other states and organisations, which had so far been more reluctant, began to introduce elements of it in their policies and institutions.

For the foreign policy of the European Union, '9/11' did not constitute a turning point in the first place (nor did the terrorist attacks in Madrid in March 2004 and in London in July 2005). It rather served to confirm the European Union's view that a strategy focusing exclusively on the politico-military dimension cannot achieve durable results, hence the adoption of a comprehensive response to terrorism as opposed to declaring a one-dimensional 'war on terror'. The extraordinary European Council meeting of 21 September 2001 called for 'an in-depth political dialogue with those countries and regions of the world in which terrorism comes into being' and 'the integration of all countries into a fair world system of security, prosperity and improved development'. Because of the deep divide between the member states the European Union as such was absent from the debate on the invasion of Iraq, but the adoption of the ESS later that same year confirmed the unanimous preference of the member states for a long-term holistic approach. This conviction was expressed in the EU *Paper for Submission to the High-Level Panel on Threats, Challenges and Change,* which the Council approved for transferral to the Panel in May 2004. In this the European Union stressed the need for 'economic, political and legal instruments, as well as military instruments, and close cooperation between states as well as international organizations across a range of sectors'. It also advocated a gradual and comprehensive process of intervention in case of actual or threatened crisis, with military intervention as a last resort, to be mandated by the Security Council. The June 2005 European Council then expressed its strong support for the Secretary-General's recommendations. The European Union thus emerged as the single most ardent supporter of the collective security system and undoubtedly played a vital part in the World Summit and the debates leading up to it. Conceptually, its influence is undeniable; in a way, the European Union's assertion of a holistic strategy aided the UN to reconfirm what really are its own roots. Diplomatically, without the efforts of the European Union during the extremely difficult World Summit negotiations there would very likely never have been an *Outcome Document* at all (Hannay 2005).

From being absent from the Iraq debate, the European Union thus became a trend-setter or, perhaps more accurately, helped to clear the obstacles for the already existing trend towards a holistic approach to continue after the low point of the Iraq crisis. It was probably not so much the conceptual work or the adoption of the ESS that convinced others of the validity of the EU approach, as the success of its actual policies and the creation of effective integrated institutions, notably in the field of crisis management. The European Union has effectively taken the lead in building integrated civil–military structures, in which both the Commission and the General Secretariat of the Council are represented. In addition to the existing joint Situation Centre, the Civil–Military Cell, including an Operations Centre for the running of missions, became operational in 2005, the only civil–military headquarters available, and a concept for comprehensive civil–military planning has been elaborated. Operations have been launched in fields such as security sector reform (SSR), in Congo, and the rule of law, in Georgia. Having become the leading actor in the field of integrated missions, EU expertise is ever more in demand, e.g. for the mission in Aceh, which was launched on 15 September 2005 to monitor the implementation of the peace agreement between the government of Indonesia and the Free Aceh Movement. It has indeed been recognised, and illustrated by the failure to 'win the peace' in Iraq, that in effect all operations have to be civil–military from the start, even operations at the higher end of the scale of violence, in order to plan from the beginning for the civilian actions that inevitably have to follow on to every type of military intervention. The integrated deployable capabilities under ESDP come in addition to the existing instruments under the Commission. The challenge for the European Union now is to forge a close link between the pillars to achieve a fully coherent policy (see Chapter 7).

The comprehensive or holistic approach has thus come to the foreground again, witness efforts at different levels to develop integrated policies and institutions and the lively conceptual debate, in different guises, such as the 'security-development nexus' (DFID 2005).

At the UN level, the Outcome Document of the 2005 World Summit includes an unequivocal reconfirmation of the comprehensive approach:

> We therefore reaffirm our commitment to work towards a security consensus based on the recognition that many threats are interlinked, that development, peace, security and human rights are mutually reinforcing, that no State can best protect itself by acting entirely alone and that all States need an effective and efficient collective security system pursuant to the purposes and principles of the Charter.
>
> (General Assembly 2005: 21–22)

The UN as well has translated this into the creation of new institutions, next to reform of the existing bodies. The new Peacebuilding Commission is to bring together all UN and other actors that are present in the same country in the post-conflict phase, in order to stimulate coherence between them. Like the EU's ENP, this is a country-specific approach. A greater challenge is the integrated management of cross-border issues, for which the fragmentation of the multilateral architecture, with separate organisations for different policy fields, is a serious obstacle. EU support for the UN is not just rhetorical: a close partnership is developing, including regular high-level dialogue and staff-to-staff contacts as well as cooperation at the operational level (see Chapter 3).

NATO too has discovered the comprehensive approach or at least the need for civil–military operations. In their *Strategic Vision: The Military Challenge* the Alliance's two Strategic Commanders stress 'the need for a concerted and co-ordinated political, military, civil and economic approach' (NATO 2004). A broad range of interrelated challenges is identified:

> [. . .] globalisation, the increasing sophistication of asymmetric warfare, the effects of changing demography and environment, failing states, radical ideologies and unresolved conflicts. [. . .] Continuing globalisation will make the nations of the Alliance more dependent on broad stability elsewhere in the world. [. . .] Impoverishment and inequitable distribution of these resources fosters grievances, provokes extremists and offers an opportunity for organised crime to further threaten security. Poverty, hunger and disease prevail in much of the developing world and contribute to the increasing stress in the security environment.
>
> (NATO 2004: 2–3)

Faced with the necessity that even high-intensity military operations must incorporate a civil dimension from the start, to which is added the fact that many interventions currently in demand are of a primarily civilian nature, the Alliance has realised that it will need to adapt or risk obsolescence. The in itself very welcome relief operation in Pakistan following the earthquake of 8 October 2005, including airlifting supplies and deploying medical units and engineers from the NATO Response Force (NRF), must also be seen in this light. The same holds true for the NATO Katrina Support Operation in September 2005, following the hurricane that struck New Orleans, which also saw the deployment of NRF capabilities. NATO is limited, however, in what it can do in this area by its very nature, i.e. that of a military Alliance. Developing deployable civilian capabilities in fields such as police, the rule of law and human rights seems to be beyond its scope and would certainly not meet with the approval of all Allies. Hence the idea has been raised to create an arrangement that would give NATO access to the European Union's civilian capabilities, in particular the Civil–Military Cell and the deployable capabilities. This option has been rejected from the start by most EU member states, however, who do not want to relinquish control over civilian assets forming an integral part of the European Union to a military organisation. In any case, even if it were realised, it would not alter the basic fact that NATO covers only the politico-military dimension. Even if the Alliance were to be equipped with a civilian crisis management capacity, it could never acquire the development and trade instruments that are vital for the post-intervention stabilisation and reconstruction efforts. In that sense the trend seems to be for the centre of gravity to be shifting to the European Union (see Chapter 6).

Finally, many individual states are developing integrated concepts and institutions, such as the Post-Conflict Reconstruction Unit in the UK and the Office of the Coordinator for Reconstruction and Stabilisation in the United

States. Next to the conceptual or strategic debate, typical issues discussed at the national level are the coordination between ministries of foreign affairs, development and defence, and the question whether development funds can contribute to the financing of civil–military operations, e.g. via the setting up of joint budget lines. Another question is how to train and, in crisis situations, rapidly mobilise civilian experts for deployment abroad who in normal times are engaged full-time in domestic functions. The strategic debate is particularly vibrant in the United States, where critics of the NSS and the policies of the Bush administration call for a more holistic approach. Haass, for instance, finds that the principal threat to the United States is not a great power rival but the dark side of globalisation: 'terrorism, nuclear proliferation, infectious disease, trade protectionism and global climate change' (Haass 2005: 24). To meet those challenges he calls for a foreign policy strategy based on 'integration', working with partners for the 'positive commitments' of physical security, economic opportunity and political freedom. A similar plea for an alternative NSS based on integrated power has been put forward by the Center for American Progress (Korb and Boorstin 2005). Similarly, Cerny concludes that

> [. . .] what is needed is not so much a war on terror as a political, economic and social war on the causes of terror – uneven development, inequality, injustice, and, perhaps most importantly, the incredible frustrations engendered by the revolution of rising expectations in a globalizing world [. . .].
>
> (Cerny 2005: 30)

Conclusion

The strength of the ESS is that it builds on a strong foreign policy *acquis*. Its adoption coincided with the revival of the existing trend towards comprehensive policies which originated at the end of the Cold War. Not only did the European Union already form part of this trend, it is now in the vanguard of the reflection on, as well as the practice of, comprehensive strategy, its integrated institutions serving as a source of inspiration to many others. This fact only serves to strengthen the solidity of the strategic framework which the ESS offers and the consensus on the basic assumptions of the comprehensive approach on which it is based. This in turn constitutes a major stimulus for the development of a strong EU strategic culture. Of course, ultimately the political will of the member states determines whether the European Union will act as an effective global power or will remain a mere global actor. The following chapters will assess to which extent the

ESS already functions as a reference framework and which steps need to be taken to foster this strategic culture.

Note

1 GPG are sometimes defined more narrowly as comprising only those public goods which cannot be provided but through international cooperation, excluding public goods of which the state is or should be the main provider, such as education or political participation. See e.g. the International Task Force on Global Public Goods, www.gpgtaskforce.org (accessed 29 December 2005).

2 The European Security Strategy coping with threats

Is Europe secure?

Jean-Yves Haine

The crucial novelty of the European Security Strategy lies in the identification of threats, a première for the Union. It identifies five major threats: international terrorism, WMD proliferation, regional conflicts, failed states, and organised crime. Entitled 'A Secure Europe in a better world', the document focuses primarily on the 'better world' part, though it notes that the distinction between internal and external security is increasingly blurred. The document acknowledges that the traditional territorial form of defence, in a Cold War fashion, is a thing of the past. By underlining that 'the first line of defence now lies abroad', it implies a projection of power, soft and hard, that Europe was not used to exercising in a strategic fashion. Faced with a significantly deteriorated international environment, the Union cannot postpone its strategic dimension any longer; it cannot be a 'pole of indifference', especially when the 'pole of power', i.e. the United States, is engaged in a revolutionary agenda in world affairs (Wolfers 1962: 81–102). The spirit of the document is thus a tacit calling for a more extrovert and active role of the Union in the world. To undertake global responsibilities, unity in diplomacy and capabilities in defence are necessary conditions that the document duly reminds to all Member States, especially after the Iraqi fiasco and the too slow progress of the Helsinki Headline Goal.

The threats identified by the document are a mix of old and new threats, a combination of '11/9' unfinished crises, like the Balkans where the bulk of European troops are still deployed, and the '9/11' international terrorism agenda. They form a common ground between the inevitably divergent threat perceptions and strategic postures of the Member States. For example, the threat of international terrorism is differently perceived throughout the Union, and among those who rank it high on their security agenda, it is framed in distinct and sometimes divergent manners. Spain looks at terrorism through the prism of immigration, Poland through international crime, Italy keeps a close eye on the Balkans, France is focused on

Algeria . . . This disparity renders a common approach more difficult than it may seem. As for instability and failed states, the minimal consensus offers a fragile basis for action, especially with regard to peacekeeping operations in Africa. The two main directions of EU influence and power, i.e. the South and the East, are often mutually exclusive. For the foreseeable future, the Balkans will remain the theatre of necessity for European duties beyond its borders, and Africa the theatre of choice, with more specific and limited operations. Overall, however, the definition of these threats was pretty similar to those underlined by the US National Security Strategy of 2002. Of course, this was not a coincidence. Bridging the gap with Washington by underlining the common fundamentals of the assessment of the security environment was a key objective of the document. Yet, these threats are framed in a different perspective. As argued in a report by a Group of Personalities for the European Commission,

> These threats can evolve rapidly. They may or may not include a military dimension, are often asymmetric, and can threaten the security of Member States both from outside and inside EU territory. The distinction between external and internal security becomes increasingly blurred. [. . .] Military instruments can and do play a role, but in most cases intelligence, police, judicial, economic, financial, scientific and diplomatic means will be at least as important (Group of Personalities 2004).[1]

Because European vulnerabilities are inside as well as outside the continent, the European Union puts a premium on its soft power approach, far removed from the 'war on terror' mantra, the regime change project, and the pre-emptive strike doctrine promoted by the US National Security Strategy. For the European Union, the world appears to be more dangerous indeed, but it is also far more complex. And the international complexities are echoed internally in Europe. Rather than simple formulae, it thus underlines a comprehensive approach, long-term goals and implicit dilemmas.

The old risks

The ESS does not rank or prioritise the five above-mentioned security threats. The tone and content of subsequent initiatives and the scope of European engagement on the ground indicate, however, that old threats, i.e. failed states, regional conflicts and organised crime, remain prominent. If there is an implicit ranking in the threats defined by the ESS, these would come first, although from a strategic point of view, they are less directly threatening to 'European' interests than the new ones. Of course, it is always artificial to consider these risks separately and the interconnections between them may indeed represent the most dangerous situation. In large measure the new threats, i.e. international terrorism and WMD proliferation, have modified the acuity and the management of these risks. As was clear in Afghanistan, a failed state may become a base and a training camp for international terrorists. International crime may include trafficking in WMD material for terrorists. Instability inside can rapidly spill over outside. In European terminology, 'failed or failing' is preferred to 'rogue' state, partly to differentiate itself from the US 'axis of evil' rhetoric, partly to underline the comprehensive approach and the civilian component favoured by the European Union. State failure is thus an aggravating environment; it empowers non-state actors and increases security risks and threats, domestically as well as externally.

But to what extent does a failed state represent a threat to European security? As with every generic category, the term refers to widely diverging situations (Rotberg 2003). The basic idea behind state failure as a security risk is relatively straightforward when put in perspective. It refers to the notion that interstate conflicts, local rivalry between neighbours or global competition between great powers do not represent the most serious security risks. What is happening *inside* a state matters more in the current context of peaceful, even if uneasy, relationships between world powers in an increasingly globalised world. Globalisation unites people but it also creates tensions and conflicts. Economic crises, failed governance, ethnic violence and religious antagonism are amplified by the gap between haves and have-nots. These dividing lines cross the old geopolitical system based on territories and sovereignty. The latter sources of conflicts are not new, and not more numerous or bloodier than before, but their impact today is quite different. These two components of the international scene, globalisation and peace between the great powers, have transformed the issue of state sovereignty, i.e. the monopoly of the domestic and legitimate use of force, into a global strategic problem.[2] There is nothing specifically new in the globalisation of conflicts; this element was the basis behind Wilson's 14 points. A new layer in international security is now added to the classic Westphalian system. It does not erase it, since these groups are somehow located on a map, even elusively, but it renders the geopolitics of conflicts far more complex and multilayered. Despite their differences in nature, scope and consequences, state failures have become 'public bads' for the international community (Fearon and Laitin 2004). Without entering into the details about the types, sources, effects and remedies of state failure, three dimensions can be distinguished, from the least to the most threatening. For each instance, Europe has a broad strategy, at least on paper.

The first dimension is in essence an issue of human rights or human security (Kaldor 2004; Roland 2001). It refers to situations in which the domestic population is the first direct or indirect casualty of state collapse or abuse. As Europe painfully discovered from the Balkan wars in the early 1990s, human values need to be defended at home and protected abroad. The worst massacres in Europe since World War II triggered the entire ESDP effort, so that Europe could be more able, diplomatically and militarily, to prevent situations of genocide and mass murder. More broadly, the UN for the last 15 years has authorised and implemented an impressive number of peacekeeping and peace enforcement missions, from El Salvador to Cambodia, from Bosnia to Somalia, with mixed results. Successes in many instances were real, but the fiascos were also spectacular. In 2000, the Brahimi report took stock of a decade of interventions and suggested some fundamental reforms to improve them. Among the problems identified were the often inadequate mandates leading to vague and sometimes overambitious objectives, the lack of capabilities and commitments from the international community, and insufficient planning, coordination and management of operations on the ground. Yet, the most patent failures were the result of the absence of intervention: in Rwanda, Congo and Darfur the international community watched mass murder and genocide without serious attempts to stop them. This provoked a renewed effort, supported and promoted by the European Union, which led to the formal endorsement by the UN in September 2005 of the Responsibility to Protect populations from genocide, war crimes, ethnic cleansing and crimes against humanity.[3] The international community has acknowledged that it should act collectively, through the UN Security Council, if states fail to protect their populations from these violations. Yet the current passivity regarding Darfur illustrates the complexities and the difficulties of implementing this responsibility (International Crisis Group 2005). Duties beyond borders are costly, risky and not always popular at home. They demand a technical and military expertise that few countries do actually possess. In this context, Europe has developed a special partnership with the UN.[4] As Benita Ferrero-Waldner, the Commissioner for External Relations, pointed out in July 2006, there is a 'tradition to react positively, in general, to UN requests'. The European Union is a strong supporter of the new Peacebuilding Commission (PBC) but the experience in Bosnia of multiple and conflicting chains of command has left bitter memories in some Member States. The partnership is thus natural but at times uneasy. Overall, however, the European Union has deployed a significant number of forces abroad that surpasses its Helsinki Headline Goal of 60,000 troops (Giegerich and Wallace 2004). More than any other power, the European Union has demonstrated its UN credentials.

The second dimension of state failure is linked to the broader issue of governance. In this framework, the failed state has lost its ability to provide to its citizens positive political goods, such as the provision of an independent judicial system to adjudicate disputes, to enforce the rule of law and to protect the most fundamental civil and political rights, the right to participate in free and fair elections, the right to compete for office, freedom of speech etc. Such unstable situations can rapidly spill over to neighbouring countries. Collapse or discredit of state authority can rapidly lead to chaotic situations of civil unrest, economic crisis and international crime. In these situations, the European Union has developed a comprehensive and preventive approach based on civilian capabilities aimed at strengthening or restoring state authorities. As the European Union states, 'these risks can most effectively be addressed through early and determined multilateral engagement with the government or regime in question, initially on issues of governance, economic management and human rights' (Council of the European Union 2004c).

Several missions illustrate this approach. In December 2005, the European Union sent a team of police advisors to provide further support to the development of a professional police service in Macedonia. Specifically, the aim was to strengthen the Border Police, and to fight against corruption and organised crime. In the same vein, the EU Border Assistance Mission to Moldova/Ukraine, launched on 30 November 2005, has helped the Moldovan and Ukrainian authorities to tackle illegal trade, trafficking, smuggling, organised crime and corruption. Special attention was given to effective border control and surveillance in the context of the continuing Transnistrian dispute. These types of missions are not demanding in terms of personnel and resources, yet they could have a critical impact on the ground. According to Moldovan authorities, the EU involvement has significantly reduced organised crime and illegal trafficking of raw materials. In Georgia, the focus was on the criminal justice system, an area deemed critical to strengthen the 'Rose Revolution' in the short term and to build a secure public security environment in the long term, with mixed success, however (Helly 2006; Peters and Bittner 2006). These short-term missions are thus part of a broader framework of stabilising Europe's neighbourhood.

The third dimension of state failure is linked to international terrorism. It was a latent phenomenon throughout the 1990s. France has been the target of a sustained bombing campaign by Algerian Islamist groups, Moscow was repeatedly hit by attacks from Chechen radicals, the World Trade Center was targeted. These signs of discontent went relatively ignored. The attacks on New York and Washington opened a new chapter in which the old risks of state failure that could at least be contained became a major threat that needed to be addressed. Modern hyper-terrorism is orchestrated by relatively small groups of people using unsophisticated weapons to achieve mass casualties.⁵ In some instances, they are fighting against their hosts, in others, they are benefiting from them; in both cases, boundaries are easily ignored. The GIA in Algeria, Al Qaeda in Afghanistan, Hezbollah in Lebanon, Hamas in Palestine, the JanJanweed in Sudan, all these groups illustrate this phenomenon. All have received a helping hand or gained significant influence domestically; all have international connections and outreach; all profit from state failure by filling a void left by official authorities, willingly or unwillingly. The ESS rightly underlines that

> [i]n an era of globalisation, distant threats may be as much a concern as those that are near at hand. [. . .] Terrorists and criminals are now able to operate world-wide: their activities in central or southeast Asia may be a threat to European countries or their citizens.

Yet, state failure may not be the most significant variable in this phenomenon. The case of Afghanistan did show that weak or collapsed states could be safe havens for terrorist groups. But it is not clear why a failed state is more a threat than a relatively stable authoritarian regime. The record shows that for terrorism, a country like Morocco can be far more 'dangerous' than a country like Somalia. A truly failed state, as Somalia clearly is, is not an ideal environment for a terrorist group. Terrorist networks, like mafias, appear to flourish where states are governed badly, rather than not at all (Menkhaus 2004: 71–75; Rotberg 2002). The lawlessness of a collapsed state increases the terrorists' vulnerability to the most common crimes of chaos, kidnapping, extortion, blackmail and assassination. What is needed is just a portion of territory, from a village to a valley, to train recruits and to plan attacks, while benefiting from the protection given by the outward signs of sovereignty of the failed state. Yet, complete control of the entire territory and its population is more an ambition than a reality for a huge number of states. A stable monarchy like Morocco was a fertile ground for terrorist recruits striking Madrid. The 9/11 attacks were partly planned in Hamburg. A failing state may well constitute a useful environment for the base of a terrorist group, but its networks can prosper and strike at the heart of the modern world. By its very openness, Europe more than any other continent is vulnerable to such threats.

Interdependence thus brings opportunities and challenges on every front. If globalisation is about integrating economies and societies, opening borders, creating interdependence and coordinating policies, Europe is indeed its embodiment. For nearly half a century, the European Union has been perceived by governments and opinion alike as a win–win scenario whereby everyone will benefit from liberalisation and competition. Today, an insidious feeling has emerged according to which economic difficulties are produced by these efforts, as if economic growth was a zero-sum game. The enlargement eastwards is blamed, immigration is drastically reduced, national industries are protected from foreign takeover, and trade liberalisation is postponed. In such a context, EU policies are not always as strategic as they should be. Economic challenges and strategic imperatives often push the Brussels institutions apart. Overall, the European Union is increasingly conscious of and responsive to the complex problems and risks raised by failed states, yet the strategic awakening of Europe to its global environment has been difficult, often inward-looking, generally process-oriented and mostly focused on the status quo; nonetheless developments have been remarkable.[6] Globalisation has also brought strategic challenges nearer and inside the European home. The credibility of the European Union as a security organisation may start at home.

The new threats

The post-9/11 world is thus characterised by an unprecedented combination of non-state actors with easily available capabilities to inflict mass destruction or disruption. This means that what was previously a worst-case scenario is now a possibility; what was once unthinkable has now to be contemplated; and what was once an acceptable level of risk has now become unacceptable. The spectre of a nuclear terrorist attack has left the realm of popular novels to enter into that of strategic planning. What is now called the 1 per cent doctrine is a radical new evaluation of dangers and risks that 9/11 has brought firstly to the United States but also to other global powers (Suskind 2006). Among major reassessments the location and availability of WMD, especially nuclear capabilities, figured prominently. In this endeavour, Europe unexpectedly played a prominent role.

The nuclear challenge

Just a few years ago, the very idea of Europe being involved so heavily in nuclear diplomacy would have seemed a dubious if not an implausible suggestion to most commentators and practitioners. Today, the EU3 process of negotiations with Iran is part of the daily routine of European diplomacy. This is all the more surprising since nuclear issues were left to NATO during the Cold War, they were never part of the ESDP horizon after the fall of the

Berlin Wall, and they were in fact a matter of controversy inside the European Union rather than a point of consensus. How to explain this fundamental change? Several reasons can be advanced.

First, the post-9/11 landscape has changed the perception of WMD and has significantly modified the level of tolerance. If nuclear terrorism remains a highly unlikely scenario, it is well understood that the accessibility of fissile material should be controlled and its proliferation prevented, as demonstrated by the revelations about the extent of the A.Q. Khan network, which provided crucial information to Libya, Iran and North Korea.[7] The most worrisome prospect is of course a terrorist organisation getting access to such weapons. As the 9/11 Commission report stated, 'the greatest danger of another catastrophic attack [. . .] will materialize if the world's most dangerous terrorists acquire the world's most dangerous weapons'. This danger was recognised as such by the ESS. The evidence suggests terrorists have made attempts to acquire and use CRBN materials.[8] Overall, however, few terrorist groups have both the motivation and the capabilities to attempt a nuclear incident. In this respect, the principal risk is theft of highly enriched uranium (HEU), which is extensively used in other applications than nuclear weapons. The technical hurdles in the way of constructing a nuclear bomb are quite high, and diversions of dangerous quantities of nuclear materials are not known to have occurred.[9] Unfortunately, these hurdles are being lowered as more nations work on nuclear technology. In particular, some newer nuclear states may have less security and safeguards on their nuclear arsenals, making theft of a usable bomb an increasing possibility. Despite increased efforts under the Cooperative Threat Reduction programme at the G8 level, former Soviet Union nuclear facilities, storages and transports remain serious security concerns (Clay *et al.* 2004; Ferguson and Potter 2004). Even if the risk of a nuclear terrorist attack was present during the cold war, some pessimistic assessments consider that the possibility of nuclear terrorism is in fact significant in the next decade.[10]

Second, there is an increasing erosion of and opposition to the international nuclear non-proliferation regime. A decade ago, when South Africa gave up its nuclear programme, when Brazil and Argentina renounced theirs, and when Ukraine and Kazakhstan gave back the nuclear weapons they had inherited from the Soviet Union, there was a belief that the non-proliferation norm had prevailed, and that eventually even the great powers would significantly reduce their nuclear weapons. Today, such a prospect seems as remote as ever. With overt attempts by Iran, North Korea, and other states to achieve nuclear status, the non-proliferation regime is severely tested and the world seems to has arrived at 'a nuclear tipping point', at which further proliferation could unleash a domino effect that could double or triple the membership of the nuclear club (Perkovich *et al.* 2004: 11). Such perceptions and fears are by no means new; they date back to 1946 and have regularly made the headlines during the Cold War. For example, in December 1964 a US memo written just after the Chinese test predicted that

> [a]t least eleven nations (India, Japan, Israel, Sweden, West-Germany, Italy, Canada, Czechoslovakia, East-Germany, Rumania and Yugoslavia) have or will soon have the capability of making nuclear weapons, given the requisite national decision. Within the foreseeable future, the number will grow substantially. The Union of South Africa, the United Arab Republic, Spain, Brazil and Mexico may be included.[11]

These grim forecasts have repeatedly been proved wrong. Yet today what makes these renewed fears different is the nature of those regimes that are pursuing nuclear programmes. Even if the qualification of 'rogue states' does not exist in European terminology, a member of the NPT like Iran appears to be a crucial test case of the non-proliferation regime.

Third, the EU focus on Iran is closely related to the experience of Iraq. The very day of the US–UK-led invasion of Iraq, the Political and Security Committee started to discuss WMD proliferation. As early as May 2003, a broad counter-proliferation strategy was agreed. It was based on the strengthening of international institutions, especially the IAEA with more coercive verification mechanisms, on a close partnership with Russia and the United States, on the promotion and enforcement of a more efficient export control regime, and on the application of stricter conditionality with partners.[12] The Union was keen to demonstrate its capacity to present a united position after the divide about Iraq and as soon as October 2003, the EU3 got the agreement of Tehran on an IAEA additional protocol and the suspension of uranium enrichment. The pre-emptive strike and the regime change in Iraq also acted as a foil for the management of the Iranian nuclear issue. What has been done in Iraq should not be repeated with Tehran. By seizing the issue, the EU3 pre-empted any similar attempt by the United States or Israel. Moreover, since the late 1990s the Union has tried to normalise its relations with Iran and has been deeply engaged in a constructive engagement strategy.[13] Since Washington refused to even talk with the Iranian regime, the EU3 were thus at the forefront of nuclear diplomacy. The implicit and initial division of labour was thus a bad cop–good cop combination. Increasingly, however, the worsening situation in Iraq changed that balance: it empowered the status and the influence of Iran in the region and significantly weakened the position and credibility of

Washington. The contradiction between the axis of evil leading to a necessary regime change in the Middle East and the increasing need for a more constructive or at least non-interfering role of Tehran in Iraq drove Washington towards the European position, which was finally endorsed and supported by the White House in spring 2005. In the same period, however, the initial successes of the carrot-and-stick approach favoured by the EU3 were negated by a clear hardening of the Iranian stance, especially since Mahmud Ahmadinejah came to power in June 2005. The initial agreement broke down in August 2005 and again in January 2006 with the resumption of enrichment activities by the Iranians. In September 2005, a European-drafted resolution was approved at the IAEA meeting in Vienna, condemning Iran for non-compliance with the NPT. The case was subsequently referred to the UN Security Council where under Chapter VII sanctions have been imposed.[14]

Without reviewing the details of the already long and surely far from finished nuclear diplomacy with Iran, it is worth emphasising what is at stake.

The diplomatic issue at stake is relatively narrow, yet it encompasses far broader questions that make this specific point of contention difficult to manage. The narrow issue is the right to enrich uranium which is inscribed in Article IV of the IAEA Treaty. From a legalistic point of view, this prerogative is thus officially recognised. Yet, by failing to report its programme for nearly two decades, Iran has lost this right (Spring 2006). An IAEA Resolution has unanimously condemned Iran in this regard. Behind this controversy, fundamental questions are raised regarding Iran's actual capabilities and intentions. As for the first, after the intelligence failure in Iraq, it is crucial that any claim of Iranian WMD be able to point to a 'smoking gun', i.e. concrete evidence of Iranian capabilities and actions linking the nuclear programme to a weapons purpose. So far, there are some indications that the nuclear programme has a military dimension. For example, most of Iran's centrifuge workshops are under the direction of the Defence Industries Organisation and some are on military bases, a factor that has complicated IAEA access. In 1987, Iran received information from the A.Q. Khan network about the reconversion and casting of uranium metal for detonation.[15] The so-called Project 111, brought to the knowledge of the West by a defector, contained plans to redesign the Shahab-3 medium-range ballistic missile to accommodate a nuclear head; scientific notes described sophisticated detonators for explosives and other designs to pursue other means to enrich uranium. All these elements, shared among European and American intelligence services, strongly indicate that Iran may indeed pursue a parallel military nuclear programme.[16] This evidence in turn raises questions about the timing of a possible nuclear bomb and the scope of the current diplomatic window. Studies and assessments converge to estimate that Iran cannot have a bomb before 2010.[17] Iran is thus not an imminent threat. However, intelligence is just an educated guess, and knowledge about Iran remains elusive. As Pollack (2006) has argued, 'we are all reading tea leaves when it comes to trying to predict Iran's behaviour'.

This led to a second broader issue. To what extent does a nuclear Iran represent a threat against Europe? The Union framed this issue in general terms. It considers that WMD proliferation *per se* is a problem, and that the issue is not related to a specific government. At stake is the future of the non-proliferation regime. If a country is able to acquire nuclear military technology inside the NPT, then the regime itself will lose its credibility. A nuclear Iran may trigger a chain reaction throughout the region. Turkey, Iraq and Saudi Arabia could be tempted to achieve the same objective, and a nuclear Middle East would be a quite different type of powder keg. Beyond that, proliferation can reach Asia. The issue of a nuclear Iran is thus fundamentally a question of order and status quo in international relations. How to stop, contain or accommodate a state willing to change the rules? So far, the Union has engaged and enhanced the political dialogue with the regime in Tehran.[18] The carrots have been decidedly more numerous than the sticks. The last EU offer, although not public in its details, has been deemed very generous, yet it was rejected instantly (Weisman 2006). The difficulty is to find incentives to convince the Iranians to give up enrichment, which they consider an inalienable right. It has to be acknowledged, however, that the EU3's best efforts have so far failed to stop Iran. A new period of sticks will thus be opened. For Europeans, there are no military solutions to this issue; any strike could only postpone the programme for a limited number of years, but in parallel any attack will trigger a renewed willingness of the regime to build a bomb. Tehran will make sure that the new facilities will be underground and spread in urban centres. Moreover, the reaction in the Muslim world will likely be more devastating that the attack itself, not even mentioning the capacity of Iran to retaliate in very damaging ways (Betts 2006). In other words, the solution to the problem brings more difficulties than the problem itself. As for sanctions, it is not clear whether European public opinion is ready to endure a three-digit price for a barrel of oil and it remains doubtful whether Russia and China are ready to continue to endorse them.

If the objective is to increase the costs of non-cooperation for Iran, a more united international community is needed. In particular, the United States will have to be more engaged. Washington has addressed the issue of proliferation through a regime change angle. For Bush, the combination of mullahs and nuclear weapons is just plainly unacceptable. The rhetoric about regime change and the 'axis of evil' approach offered a perfect alibi for Tehran to continue its enrichment programme. The fundamental suspicion between Washington and Tehran remains a serious obstacle to a constructive dialogue and it puts the Europeans in a difficult position. The United States has supported the EU3 initiatives, but very late in the process and without strong conviction. Yet, Washington's role is critical, especially to alleviate security concerns expressed by Iran. Washington must make clear that its ultimate objective is a non-nuclear Iran, and not a regime change in Tehran (Kagan 2006; Yglesias 2006; Boureston and Ferguson 2005). This discrepancy between the United States and the EU3 will have to be lifted eventually in order to better engage the international community, especially China, Russia, and the neighbouring States. Weakened by the failure in Iraq, Washington is increasingly forced to talk to Tehran and other regional powers. The Bush revolution in world affairs has come to an end (Gordon 2006; Hoffmann 2006; Kissinger 2006). A renewed 'realism' is emerging in Washington, which should lead to a more effective transatlantic partnership based on a shared belief in effective multilateralism. Iran will be its most difficult yet critical case.

The terrorism threat

As far as Iran is concerned, the proliferation issue is not an immediate danger and *in fine* its intensity will depend on mutually accepted rules of deterrence. By contrast, the threat of terrorism represents a clear, present and enduring danger. Europe has been attacked on several occasions, European casualties are counted in hundreds rather than scores and the probability of future terrorist acts in Europe remains extremely high. Terrorism is not a new phenomenon; Europe has been hit by terrorist attacks well before Al-Qaeda. Throughout the 1970s and 1980s, terrorist groups such as ETA, the Irish Republican Army, Action Directe, the Red Brigades and the Red Army Faction were active. Palestinian and Libyan terrorists also carried out attacks in Europe. Because of their desire to win people over to their cause, most were restrained in their willingness to use unlimited violence. As one expert argued, the terrorists wanted 'many people watching, but not many people dead'.[19] Terrorist campaigns such as those of the IRA and ETA were based mostly on regular but relatively small attacks. Indeed, regularity was part of their strategy. Counter-terrorism experts learned to discern patterns and to profile terrorists. Even with the Islamic terrorist wave that hit France in the 1990s, the objectives of the GIA group were circumscribed to the civil war in Algeria.

The current wave of modern international terrorism has left some of the familiar characteristics behind and exhibits new ones.[20] Among the new elements, the religious factor and the revolutionary ideology, the transnational dimension and the global agenda, the nihilism and the commitment to mass casualties are most often underlined.[21] While some experts highlight the specific organisation and ultimate goals of Al-Qaeda itself, others deny that contemporary international jihadism is particularly new or even lethal (Duyvestein 2004; Mueller 2005). For the United States, the unique character of Al-Qaeda was never in doubt and consequently it demanded an unprecedented 'war on terror'. By and large, Europe has taken a different approach, not because the challenge is not genuine but because it has specific characteristics in Europe.

The US-led Operation *Enduring Freedom* deprived Al-Qaeda of its training camps in Afghanistan and drove its leaders further into hiding. Expert commentators agree its organisation has since become more decentralised and 'virtual'. Al-Qaeda is built on small, adaptable cells. Its strength lies in its non-military nature: its clandestine character, transnational dispersal of personnel, decentralised command and control, organisational flatness, reliance on asymmetric threats, and extensive and successful use of globalisation of information (Stevenson 2004; Stern 2003; Jeesee 2006). After the destruction of their sanctuary in Afghanistan, the group's leaders have largely dispersed, though they are still being sought in the border regions of Pakistan and Afghanistan. Since 9/11 about 3000 members of Al-Qaeda have been arrested in 90 countries. This loss, however, does not appear to have affected Al-Qaeda's ability to mount terrorist attacks to the extent hoped (Hoffmann 2004).[22] Al-Qaeda's objectives have been modified according to circumstances and opportunities. It was first a movement aimed at reversing Saudi acceptance of foreigners on its soil; then it switched to combating other regimes, like Algeria's; then it attacked the West itself. Today, it is more likely to endorse attacks against Western targets than to initiate new ones: it seems more a sponsor or legitimating framework to independent groups than an initiator. Al-Qaeda has demonstrated a capacity to forge broad alliances and to operate in a vast number of countries around the world, including Europe. From an army on a battlefield, Al-Qaeda has transformed itself into a less tangible movement; it has become more an idea, a brand name than an organisation. It is a method, or a precept, as some translations of its name, Al-Qaeda, suggest. This has serious implications for Europe.

A brief overview of the recent arrests of suspected Al-Qaeda terrorists in Europe gives a clear indication of its level of activity. Hundreds of people have been arrested in France, Germany, Italy, the UK, Bosnia, Belgium, the

Netherlands . . . There is barely a week without a major plot being unfolded, on trains, aircraft, metro hubs and cruise ships. Recruitment of extremists in Europe seems to be successful and Al-Qaeda networks are Europe-wide. Some have argued that its most dangerous members are Europeans, who tend to be better educated, more capable, more mobile and better able to blend into Western societies.[23] After the London bombings, commentators were keen to blame the British tolerance symbolised by 'Londonistan'. Yet, similar cells and networks have been dismantled in Milan, Amsterdam, Paris, Madrid and Hamburg. The fundamental challenge is thus to tackle recruitment of extremists in Europe more effectively and to better understand why young people turn against their own countries. Several Islamic groups were active before 9/11. Most were associated with a specific cause linked to their countries of origin. Now it appears that Islamic groups in Europe have ceased to use their country of origin as their point of reference, and have instead turned to an idealised and abstract conception of a universal Islam. From diaspora-based movements aimed at nationalist issues, new Islamic groups have turned to an ideological radicalisation that takes the form of a transnational Islam divorced from its country of origin. This mechanism is notably at play where a second or third generation of young people have lost their connection with the diaspora. From what intelligence services in Europe are gathering, it appears that hubs of recruitment are found around mosques and prisons but also on the internet.[24] The identification process is not built on specific historical and geographical roots, but rather on the sense of belonging to a universal *umma* or Muslim community. This development is facilitated first by the number of Muslims in Europe, estimated at 15–20 million, and second by certain fundamentalist organisations which promote a pure and pristine conception of Islam leading to a total separation from the outside world. Groups like Hizb ut-Tahrir or Tablighi Jamaat are revivalist organisations that aim to create better Muslims through 'spiritual jihad'; they focus on education, integrity, the Islamic way of life and Muslim values (Zeyno 2004; Cohen 2003).[25] The main risk from these movements is that they provide an ideological background and education that could prompt violent action by individuals.

It remains extremely difficult to sketch a precise profile of a would-be European home-grown terrorist. The common stereotype is that terrorism is a product of poor, desperate, naïve, single young men from third-world countries, vulnerable to brainwashing and recruitment into terror. But profiles of arrested suspects reveal that such personal characteristics as age, sex, national origin, religion, education, and socioeconomic background are of very little value in identifying true terrorists. What seems clear is the absence of both top-down recruitment and brainwashing of the plotters (Leiken 2004; Sageman 2004; Taarnby 2005). Instead, what is found is first a network of friendships or family links that solidified and preceded formal induction into the terrorist organisation. Participation in the religious rituals, ideological education and social processes of the mosque is an important step. Without strong attachments outside their circles, adherents progressively adopt a strict interpretation of Islam, their religious faith intensifies and they bond more closely with their social group. Sacrifices and hardships strengthen these communal bonds. However, although a few Salafi mosques are sites of emergent terrorism, most fundamentalist mosques are not. Mosques are as apt to constrain as to facilitate the global jihad. A military training then takes place, either abroad or at home. With the destruction of the Afghan training camps – around which networks were organised all over the world – and the emergence of spontaneous cells reaching out for support, this last step may be quite superficial and elementary.

Yet, the picture of spontaneous cells of terrorists turning against their home countries in the name of a universalist view of Islam must be amended by two new elements: the war in Iraq and the signals given by Madrid and London.

First, if very few Muslims in Europe appear to have been inspired by Middle Eastern conflicts, Iraq seems to be a notable exception. At the international level, some analysts have pointed out that the conflict in Iraq has provided international jihadists with a new sense of purpose and unity. Links between sunni and shi'ite terrorist organisations seem to have flourished after the invasion of Iraq, and a strong convergence in strategy seems to have occurred on how to fight in Iraq (Hegghammer 2006). In Europe, the salience of the war in Iraq has undoubtedly contributed to a further radicalisation of Islamist extremists and has provided them with a cause to fight. Estimates of recruits sent from Europe to Iraq vary greatly, with the upper figure reaching around 3000 (Nesser 2006). If a direct link between Iraq and terrorism in Europe is difficult to find, it is clear, however, that this conflict has reinforced the popular view among European Muslims that 'the West is at war against Islam' (Neumann 2006). A recent Channel 4 documentary has revealed how this worldview receives overwhelming support among British Muslims. This appears to be the case in other European countries as well. Indeed, even in countries that have opposed the war in Iraq, recruiting cells have been dismantled. French and German intelligence services do consider that one of the highest dangers in the forthcoming years will be the flow back effect of Iraq, when Europeans who joined the insurgency will come back to their countries with the status of a fighter and a large expertise in explosive devices. Iraq is becoming the new training ground of radical extremists, and offers new infrastructure that replaces the training camps of Afghanistan. This widely spread assessment indicates that terrorism in Europe is here to stay and that it will likely increase in the coming years. Rather than targeting countries of origin, today the host countries are seen as enemies of universalist Islam. The far away guerrilla in Iraq could be brought back home. In this context, no European country is immune.

The second element is the very obvious fact that Madrid and London have occurred. In the specific framework of suicidal terrorism, a 'successful' precedent plays like a signal to two types of audience. First, violence is used as a means of modifying the behaviour of the state. In the case of the Madrid bombings, one of the objectives of the terrorists was to change the position of Spain regarding the Iraq conflict. And they succeeded. Second, suicide is used to demonstrate the commitment and the ability to strike to sympathisers or identification groups. Suicide is the ultimate signal of communication to demonstrate that the objectives are absolute and non-negotiable. Suicidal attacks capture the headlines, build solidarity inside the group, play as a catalyst for other terrorist sympathisers and enhance widespread recruitment to their cause.[26] Suicidal terrorism has long been associated with an efficient way of resisting foreign occupation (Pape 2003). Weapons of choice of specific organisations, like Hamas in Palestine or the Liberation Tigers of Tamil Eelam in Sri Lanka, suicide is often associated with a specific organisation and structure (Moghadam 2003). Relatively new in the European landscape – the only case so far is London – the suicidal tactic is not an organisational phenomenon but appears to be a spontaneous choice of convenient tactic. Yet, the precedent, because it was 'successful', can nonetheless trigger a wave of such attacks, all the more so because European counter-terrorism has become increasingly more efficient. To deter a potential suicide terrorist willing to blow himself up in a major urban city centre or transport hub is nearly impossible. The willingness of attackers to die blunts the effect of a criminal justice system based on deterrence through punishment and other traditional negotiation methods. A potential suicide bomber may be deterred if the tactic does not appear likely to be successful in achieving the expected effects that would justify martyrdom, but he will not be deterred by the justice system's penalties. To prevent it is equally difficult: there are few differences between a terrorist and a tourist. With home-grown terrorism, it is nearly impossible to monitor people without violating civil liberties and privacy. There is no absolute security in this framework.

The likelihood of attacks on European targets is also a function of Europe's vulnerabilities. This is particularly relevant given the openness of

Europe's economy. Some borders are extremely porous. Border controls are under-equipped, and the Schengen arrangements mean that between many EU members there are no border controls: once inside the European Union, people and goods can move freely. Nearly 5 million commercial vehicles of over 3.5 tons circulate on European roads each day. There are 41,435 landings and take-offs per day at Europe's airports. Numerous inland waterways traverse capitals and cities throughout Europe. Europe's coastline is 89,000 km long with 1,116 container ports. Rotterdam, the largest seaport in the world in terms of volume, moves about 10,000 containers on any given day. An attack on such infrastructure could cause large-scale disruption of European economies.[27] While the majority of bulk shipments carried by the world's fleet of 23,281 bulk/general cargo vessels are relatively inert materials, some cargoes are hazardous, such as ammonium nitrate, a fertiliser but also a powerful explosive. Even if some initiatives have been launched, like the Customs–Trade Partnership Against Terrorism (CTPAT) and the Container Security Initiative, there remain obvious and numerous vulnerabilities throughout Europe.

The threat of terrorism in Europe is thus extremely high and enduring. Since Madrid and London, European efforts in counter-terrorism have dramatically increased. Without reviewing the measures taken so far at the national and European level (Keohane 2005; Bures 2006), it is worth noting that the bulk of counter-terrorism policies remain national. What is needed at the European level, however, is a strategy. As one of the leading intelligence officers acknowledged, 'we still do not have the necessary consensus, beyond the level of rhetoric, on the fundamentals of the strategy to be followed in the long term'. What Europe is lacking is strategic planning, i.e. an agreement on the goal and what is necessary for its solution (Oman 2005). Given the size of Muslim communities in Europe, and since the threat of terrorism is mostly home-grown, the first priority is to agree on a counter-narrative that should help minorities to consolidate their sense of Western belonging and identity. The worst nightmare would be to witness dividing lines between these minorities and European societies flaring up on Europe's streets. Yet, so far, European governments have not sufficiently tackled this battle for hearts and minds. Since terrorism is an ideology, it also demands an ideological response. What is true at the European level is even truer at the transatlantic one.

Conclusion

Taken together, the old risks and the new threats represent significant challenges. Since the end of the Cold War, the security environment of Europe has greatly deteriorated. Yet, public perception of this new landscape remains vague and somewhat detached. External events seem to be imposed on a reluctant and distracted Europe. The malaise triggered by the failure of the Constitutional Treaty is another element in this increasing inward-looking posture of Europe. Austrian chancellor Wolfgang Schüssel when holding the EU Presidency admitted that 2005 was 'catastrophic' for the European Union in public opinion terms, adding that, 'if we don't win over the public to the European project, then Europe has come to an end'. Increased national protectionism and competition among Member States are not conducive to collective action.

Yet, in security, Europe is increasingly the level of analysis that matters. Answers – if they exist – to the old risks and management of the new threats will need to be collective, all the more so because the United States has failed in its global agenda. From this failure, a constructive pragmatism has emerged, but a more radical isolationism could well materialise sooner rather than later. In any case, Washington has lost its capacity and its credibility to play its traditional role of honest broker and pacifier. This role will increasingly fall to Europe. Moreover, US actions in the world have serious consequences inside Europe. The impact of the war in Iraq, and other controversial issues like Guantanamo, are felt on European streets. There is an asymmetry of vulnerabilities between the United States and Europe. Both America's actions and Europe's inaction have mutual and global consequences. This recognition should lead to a more prudent and multilateralist America and to a more coherent and secure Europe in an increasingly dangerous world.

Notes

1 Recently, Lieutenant General Jean-Paul Perruche, Director of the EU Military Staff, added that 'all the threats identified in the Security Strategy have civilian facets'.

2 As Bobbitt (2003: 667–714) puts it, this has blurred the traditional division between the foreign (the realm of strategy) and the domestic (the realm of law). For a more positive view, see Rosecrance (1987).

3 The Responsibility to Protect has now acquired the status of an international norm. It was endorsed at the UN 60th Anniversary Summit in September 2005 and reaffirmed by the UN Security Council in April 2006. As argued by Evans in a speech at the G8 Summit on 15–17 July 2006: 'We have to get to the point where, when the next conscience-shocking mass human rights violation comes along, the reflex response of both governments and publics around the world, is to find reasons to act, not reasons to pretend it is none of our business. Our common humanity demands that the responsibility to protect be a permanent item on the global security agenda as a matter not just of principle but of operational practice'. Gareth Evans, *The responsibility to protect: Unfinished*

Business, G8 Summit, 15–17 July 2006. Available at: www.crisisgroup.org/home/index.cfm?id = 4269

4 On the EU–UN partnership, see *EU-UN co-operation in Military Crisis Management Operations, Elements of Implementation of the EU-UN Joint Declaration*, adopted by the European Council on 17–18 June 2004.

5 The expression is from Heisbourg (2003). By using easily available modern technologies offered by open societies, these groups do not have to rely on substantial structural and logistical support. Their base can be extremely elusive and their financial means pretty modest (Takeyh and Gvosdev 2002).

6 Failures are part of the ongoing learning process. For each failure, a renewed willingness and ambition have usually emerged. This method was at the core of Monnet's philosophy (Duchêne 1994; Everts and Keohane 2003).

7 'Nuclear investigators from the United States and other nations believe that the black market network run by the Pakistani scientist, Abdul Qadeer Khan, was selling not only technology for enriching nuclear fuel and blueprints for nuclear weapons, but also some of the darkest of the bomb-makers' arts: the hard-to-master engineering secrets needed to fabricate nuclear warheads' (Broad and Sanger 2005). Moreover, Coll (2006) has argued that 'A.Q. Khan is one case, but not the only one. It was discovered that two Pakistani nuclear scientists, of lesser experience than Khan but still significant, had become involved with a charity that had worked with the Taliban, and at least one of them had contact with Osama bin Laden. You had Pakistani nuclear scientists delivering lectures at universities in Islamabad, talking about international Islamist ideas and radical philosophies that most people in the West would find rather alarming. So there's been both a physical breakdown in control, as evidenced in the A.Q. Khan case, and ideological breakdowns that, at least from the point of view of the potential targets of jihadis, are cause for concern'.

8 In February 2005, Reuters reported that Al-Qaeda had planned an attack using chemical weapons against the US naval base in Rota, Spain. A foiled attack against the Jordanian intelligence agency and the US Embassy in Amman also involved CRBN materials. Police officers found 'a dossier in Arabic containing detailed steps on manufacturing explosives and bacteriological poisons' at a safe house in Amman. Information on weapons and military tactics were kept on compact discs and computer (Halaby 2005).

9 Some experts argue that building the simplest form of a nuclear device does not require a large technical team. The most basic gun-type device would probably require 40–50 kg of HEU. The other way is an implosion-type device, which requires high-speed electronics and high-explosives lenses, a very complex technology. Enriching uranium is quite a demanding process: one needs 1,500 centrifuges working about one year to gather enough uranium 235 (90 per cent) for a single bomb. The other way is plutonium 239, produced through a nuclear reactor. Both are basically out of reach for terrorists. For a list of nuclear smuggling incidents, see Steinhäusler and Zaitseva (2005) and the IAEA Illicit Trafficking Database. The peak of illicit activities occurred in the early 1990s from Russia.

10 'A nuclear terrorist attack on America in the decade ahead is more likely than not' (Allison 2004).

11 Quoted in Gavin (2006: 55–56). On 8 August 1945, in a message to Harry Truman, Clement Attlee argued: 'The very speed of our joint achievement seems

to indicate that any other country possessing the necessary scientific and indus-trial resources could also produce atomic bombs within a few years if it decided now to make the effort.' Quoted in Goldberg (1964: 411).

12 The strategy on proliferation was adopted at the same time as the ESS in December 2003. Syria was presented with a 'non-proliferation clause' in its trade talks with Brussels.

13 The Comprehensive Dialogue was established in 1998. For a review of EU–Iran relations, see Posh (2006).

14 It is worth noting that the US already has a strong sanctions regime *vis-à-vis* Iran and that this issue was a point of contention with the EU during the Clinton Administration. Whether sanctions would actually work is another issue; the record so far is not encouraging.

15 This has been characterised by Dr El Baradei as 'related to the fabrication of nuclear weapons components'. IAEA, Implementation of the NPT Safeguards Agreement in the Islamic Republic of Iran, GOV/2006/15, 27 February 2006: 5.

16 As former German Foreign Minister Joschka Fischer declared: 'There can no longer be any reasonable doubt that Iran's ambition is to obtain a nuclear weapons capability.' French Foreign Minister Philippe Douste-Blazy has accused Tehran of conducting a 'secret military nuclear programme' (de Barochez 2006). See also Albright and Hinderstein (2006).

17 The most common date is 2010, which is the timeline recognised so far by Washington. For a complete dossier, see International Institute for Strategic Studies, *Iran's Strategic Weapons Programmes*, September 2005. Other scenarios put it at 2008. For example, Bruno Tertrais, *Iran: la Bombe fin 2008?* available at: www.frstrategie.org/barreCompetences/prolifDissuasionDefenses /20060315.pdf

18 In August 2005, the EU3 tried to reassure Iran by explicitly saying that the French and British nuclear arsenal will not be used against Tehran. Tehran has security concerns but these are not related to Europe, they focus on Israel, the US presence in the region and the balance of power of the region. Others, notably Hans Blix, are ready to offer security guarantees to Iran (Ruppe 2006).

19 Brian Jenkins quoted in Müller (2003: 22).

20 It has been argued that contemporary terrorism constitutes a fourth wave of international terrorism after the anarchist movement of the 1890s, the anti-colo-nial terrorism of the 1960s and the leftist terrorism of the 1970s (Rapoport 2004).

21 Since terrorists only answer to a deity and not to any specific constituency, they are uniquely dangerous (Cronin 2002; Sedgwick 2004).

22 For some, however, Al Qaeda is failing: 'The principal goal of terrorism – to seize power in Muslim countries through mobilisation of populations galvanised by jihad's sheer audacity – has not been realised. In fact, bin Laden's followers are losing ground' (Ignatius 2004: A27). See also Kepel (2004).

23 More than 1,000 suspected militants with known connections to Islamic funda-mentalist groups are considered to be operating in Europe (Burke 2004; Phillips 2006; Vidino 2005).

24 'Most radicalized Muslim youth in Europe are western educated, often in tech-nical or scientific fields. Very few come out of traditional madrasas and most experience a period of fully Westernized life, before becoming "born-again Muslims" in European mosques or jails' (Roy 2003).

25 Hizb Ut-Tahrir was often cited when the British government decided to outlaw terrorist-linked organisations after 7/7. Yet, they were not outlawed.

26 'Under these circumstances, terrorist actions are designed to create a self-fulfilling prophecy in which popular beliefs in the group's ability to challenge the state permit to mobilize the level of support it requires to go on to win' (Hoffman and Gordon 2004: 247).

27 The fear that terrorists could exploit the container transport system for their ends was confirmed on 18 October 2001 when port authorities in the southern Italian port of Gioia Tauro discovered a stowaway within a shipping container complete with bed, heater, toilet facilities and water. The man had a satellite phone, a laptop computer, and airport security passes and an airline mechanic's certificate valid for airports in New York, Newark, Los Angeles and Chicago.

3 The European Security Strategy's global objective

Effective multilateralism

Richard Gowan[1]

> The first great commitment is to defend our security and spread freedom by building effective multinational and multilateral institutions and supporting effective multilateral action.
>
> George W. Bush, Halifax, Nova Scotia, December 2004

The European Security Strategy (ESS) often manages to be simultaneously resonant and opaque, but rarely more so than in its call for 'an international order based on effective multilateralism' (European Council 2003a: 10). The formula was in vogue as *A Secure Europe in a Better World* was in preparation in 2003, and it was not the monopoly of any one party in the debates following the Iraq war. In an August communication on the 'choice of multilateralism', the European Commission cautioned that 'an active commitment to an effective multilateralism means more than rhetorical professions of faith' (European Commission 2003c). In October, George Bush and Tony Blair made a joint declaration that their policies were driven by just such a commitment: 'effective multilateralism, and neither unilateralism nor international paralysis, will guide our approach' (Blair and Bush 2003).

Yet this convergence on the phrase only highlighted the extent to which its meaning remained contested, both in terms of values and institutions – and one institution in particular. This was the UN. At the start of 2003, Europe had played out its internal divisions on Iraq in the UN Security Council. Now the European Commission declared that the UN's role as 'the pivot of the multilateral system was necessary not only for peace and security but also for developing a rule-based international trading system'. By contrast, the British and American leaders' 1,266-word October statement found space for the European Union, NATO, the G8, a variety of multilateral initiatives (and even 'US–UK school partnerships', surely an example of *bilateralism*) but yet made no mention of the UN. Nor did they refer to 'rules', appealing instead to a sense of 'common purpose' among free nations and 'our responsibility to work for the common good in the world'.

The drafters of the ESS thus had to navigate between competing definitions of multilateralism. They nonetheless shifted from an ambivalent attitude to the UN to a clear affirmation that 'strengthening the United Nations, equipping it to fulfil its responsibilities and to act effectively must be a European priority'. This has inspired an admittedly small but noticeably growing body of European policy literature arguing that the EU–UN relationship is of long-term strategic importance (Eide 2004, Ortega 2005a, Biscop 2005, Ojanen 2006). Advocates of stronger EU–UN ties have highlighted the extent to which both the European Union and UN are associated with comprehensive long-term approaches to peace and security that involve economic development. And they have also identified a growing political and institutional inter-linkage between the two organisations, as in this interpretation of the ESS and the draft European Constitution:[2]

> The European Union and the United Nations need each other. On the one hand, the EU has presented a multilateral vision of the world [. . .] The United Nations constitutes the centerpiece of this proclaimed multilateral 'faith'. On the other hand, the United Nations needs the active engagement of EU Member States, for the Europeans act as a political catalyst in many issues, and also for more practical reasons, since the Europeans provide the lion's share of the UN budget.
>
> (Ortega 2004: 11)

Such proclamations of partnership have encountered scepticism. Some promoters of Europe's international profile hold that its value lies in its *differences* with the UN, not their similarities. For those who believe that the EU's greatest successes have been to prove the viability of regional integration and to demonstrate the non-viability of traditional sovereignty, it seems likely that the future global order 'will be centered around neither the United States nor the United Nations, but will be a community of interdependent regional clubs' (Leonard 2005: 140). More immediately, Europeans face two dilemmas. Firstly, whatever the significance of the UN to the EU's identity, the UN's own identity remains the subject of an international debate – involving the United States and rising powers such as China – to which Europe is not central. Secondly, fundamental questions remain as to how the EU, as a multilateral entity, can behave effectively within another multilateral system. While the ESS calls for a 'more coherent' EU, this is yet to be fully achieved inside the structures of the UN.

The EU is thus confronted by both external and internal disputes over the UN's role. This chapter describes these disputes and contends that the EU has responded to them by developing a diffuse set of *ad hoc* forms of cooperation with elements of the UN system. This echoes Hanns Maull's suggestion that 'effective multilateralism' cannot be reduced to legal regulation or common values: it is essentially a question of political negotiation and innovation. Arguing that 'only recently [. . .] has the EU given close attention to the difficulties of organizing global multilateralism effectively', Maull has claimed that:

> Effective multilateralism requires not only broad international support and legitimacy, but also the capacity to generate initiatives, and political leadership to set the agenda, define deadlines, mobilize resources and promote effective implementation. A key qualification in this context is the ability to form and sustain broad-based coalitions.
>
> (Maull 2005: 786)

This is the sense in which the EU can act as 'political catalyst' within the UN system – much of this chapter concentrates on European efforts to create momentum within the UN on two areas highlighted by the ESS. These are responding to state failure ('an alarming phenomenon, that undermines global governance, and adds to regional instability') and the proliferation of weapons of mass destruction ('potentially the greatest threat to our security'). This inevitably excludes other important threats identified in the ESS and the holistic approach to security and development associated with both the EU and UN. But state failure and proliferation are two areas in which there has been significant EU–UN collaboration since 2003, with a focus on Africa in the former case, and Iran in the latter.

However, the European approach to innovation within the UN system is not solely a matter of responding to concrete threats – since 2003, European governments have engaged in discussions of more formal institutional reforms of the UN system. From the time that the ESS was being finalised onwards, both the political and operational aspects of the UN have been under unusually intense scrutiny thanks to the reform process launched by Kofi Annan in September 2003. The initial phase of this process centred on the drafting of the widely publicised report by the Secretary-General's High-level Panel on Threats, Challenges and Change – thereafter it moved on to increasingly rancorous inter-governmental negotiations. While the final section of this chapter will describe the European role in this process, it should be noted in advance that the EU's members were widely expected to be important drivers of the reform process. As one of the European members of the Panel argued as debates over reform reached their climax in 2005:

> The good news is that the fit between the Panel's proposals and EU objectives is astonishingly close, a remarkable fact since only two of the 16 panel members came from the EU. This fit suggests potentially widespread support for the EU's aim of effective multilateralism. But it also presents the EU with a fundamental challenge: can its foreign policy move beyond warm words and fine-sounding communiqués to action; and can it deploy its influence to convince less enthusiastic members to move forward?
>
> (Hannay 2005)

2003: After Iraq

Before we consider the strategic relevance of the EU–UN relationship, we must turn to the tactical reasons for its prominence in the ESS. This was by no means assured. The first version of the text, presented by Javier Solana to the European Council in June 2003, appeared to play down the UN's role. Its section on 'strengthening the international order' referred to the importance of the World Trade Organization, NATO and European and non-European regional organisations before turning to the role of the UN:

> The fundamental framework for international relations is the United Nations Charter. Strengthening the United Nations, equipping it to fulfil its responsibilities and to act effectively must be a European priority. If we want international organisations, regimes and treaties to be effective in confronting threats to international peace and security we should be ready to act when their rules are broken.
>
> (Solana 2003c)

The draft contained little indication of what it meant by the UN's responsibilities or the phrase 'act effectively'. It made only one other reference to the UN, and this was simply to note that 'the European Union took over the police mission in Bosnia and Herzegovina from the United Nations' – an oblique reference to past failures rather than future cooperation. It was thus notable that, when the European Council approved a revised version of the ESS in December 2003, the text placed much greater emphasis on the UN.

It was now the first organisation addressed under the 'effective multilateralism' heading, with the additional statement (taken nearly verbatim from the North Atlantic Treaty) that 'the United Nations Security Council has the primary responsibility for the maintenance of international peace and security'. And while the ESS still highlighted the EU's role in Bosnia, the implicit comparison to the UN's operational difficulties had gone. Instead, there was a new statement that 'the EU is committed to reinforcing its cooperation with the UN to assist countries emerging from conflicts, and to enhancing its support for the UN in short-term crisis management situations'. Approving the text, the European Council requested Solana's office to follow up on 'effective multilateralism with the UN at its core', as well as the Middle East and Bosnia (European Council 2003a).

The UN seemed to have moved from an almost peripheral role in the ESS to its centre. The importance of this transition should not be overstated. Many alterations to the ESS probably owe more to the need to polish a rapid first draft rather than major philosophical shifts (Bailes 2005b). However, there was also a recognition that, after the Iraq crisis, the problem of the UN could not be resolved through silence. At one of three expert seminars on the draft strategy organised at the behest of the European Council, participants had argued for an even greater expansion of references to the UN, including 'giving examples of EU contributions' and 'a comprehensive understanding of the UN's importance' (Gnesotto 2003: 6). 'The UN matters not only for the international order but also for the EU identity', they argued, for 'one essential precondition for promoting effective multilateralism is for the EU itself to act as an effective multilateral institution'.

This declaration reflected immediate realities: the task of restoring the UN's credibility in 2003 had an additional function of rebuilding a degree of post-Iraq consensus within the EU. Iraq's own reconstruction was important to this dual process. In August 2003, the Security Council mandated a UN political assistance mission to the country (in the same month, its Baghdad headquarters were bombed and Special Representative Sergio de Mello killed), and in October it also provided a mandate to the US-led force there. Britain and other EU members that had backed Washington now had a belated form of the legitimacy they had tried to win in the Security Council earlier in the year. This did not mean that there was a common European position on the UN's tactical purpose in Iraq. For many of those who urged that it should take on a high degree of responsibility, 'the primary aim of ousting the US was undisguised' (Youngs 2004). Nonetheless, it now seemed possible to argue on a more conceptual plane that Europe's internal clashes in the Security Council had been an 'unplanned good cop/bad cop routine' that had somehow managed to serve a fundamental EU goal of keeping the UN relevant (Leonard 2004).

The EU had also been able to find some consensus through backing the UN elsewhere. In May 2003, the rapid deterioration of the security situation in the Ituri region of the Democratic Republic of Congo led UN Secretary-General Kofi Annan to request that France launch a mission to reinforce the beleaguered UN mission there. At Paris's suggestion, this request was redirected to the European Council, which launched *Operation Artemis* in June – not only the EU's first operation in Africa, but also its first autonomous deployment outside Europe. This was a short-term and casualty-free military success, although arguably its longer-term ramifications are questionable, as Ituri was soon to return to violence (Gowan 2005). But it has justifiably been argued that 'the impact of *Artemis* lay more in its European character than its military merits or even its effect on the situation in the Democratic Republic of Congo' (Loisel 2004: 70). In the months running up to the approval of the ESS, the potential benefits of EU–UN relations had been to the fore, lessening if not erasing memories of earlier Iraq debates.

International attitudes to the UN: from Kosovo to Asia

While the circumstances surrounding the finalisation of the ESS were thus conducive to positive references to the UN, EU–UN relations must be understood in the longer-term context of other international perceptions of the UN's contribution to global order. As we have seen, the final draft of the ESS refers to the legal status of the UN charter, the political primacy of the Security Council and the operational significance of the UN in post-conflict and conflict-prevention scenarios (as we will note later, a separate EU strategy on Weapons of Mass Destruction agreed alongside the ESS also emphasised the UN's role in fighting proliferation). But while the brief text of the ESS thus suggests a continuity between the UN's legal, political and operational identities, the linkage between them is in reality unclear and deeply contested. There is a growing division between the United States and rising powers, most obviously China, as to whether the UN is an operational tool or a serious locus for negotiation.

This division is clearly demonstrated in policy documents and statements published around the time of the ESS. The best known is the 2002 *National Security Strategy of the United States* (NSS), with which the ESS has been compared all too frequently (Bailes 2005a: 12). This notoriously had nothing to say about the UN's political or legal status, other than 'multilateral institutions can multiply the strength of freedom loving nations'. Its sole additional reference to the UN was to observe that it could provide help alongside NGOs in 'providing the humanitarian, political, economic and security assistance necessary to rebuild Afghanistan'. Here is the UN as an operational agency alone.

By contrast, the policy documents of evolving powers highlighted the political role of the UN – and, as Chinese president Hu Jintao remarked in a speech of June 2003, the need 'to actively uphold the authority and dominant status of the United Nations in international affairs' (Foot 2006: 91). As a later Chinese position paper affirmed, efforts to reform the UN should 'enhance the UN's authority and efficiency' in such a way as to 'safeguard the purposes and principles enshrined in the UN Charter, especially those of sovereign equality, non-interference in internal affairs, peaceful resolution of conflicts and strengthening international cooperation, etc.' (Ministry of Foreign Affairs 2005). Here, the operational role of the UN is very much subordinated to its political function. India's attitudes to reforming the UN are also based on the primacy of politics:

> The UN Security Council is not a corporate enterprise: greater efficiency in achieving its objective will not result from limiting its membership to just a few countries but from decisions that are sound, widely acceptable, and that will thereby minimise the need for the use of force over time.
>
> (Sen 2006: 233)

We have seen that the drafters of the ESS were required to balance differing conceptions of 'effective multilateralism' *within* Europe – but this only reflected the ways in which EU governments have been faced with different conceptions of the UN among non-European powers with which the ESS calls for 'partnership'. If the UN is claimed as a framework for the European Union's identity, it simultaneously has parts to play in the international profiles of the United States (for which it may be a useful *operational* tool for addressing failing or failed states) and for the rising powers of the developing world (for which a voice in UN affairs is *political* evidence of sovereignty and prestige). If the European Union is to act as a 'catalyst' in the UN system, it must take the resulting debate into account. The difficulties in doing so have been exacerbated by the fact that, while the powers involved in the debate might be outside Europe, it echoes a crisis within it: Kosovo.

While the immediate circumstances of the ESS were dictated by Iraq, the ramifications of debates over Kosovo can clearly be detected in the text. The 1999 decision to take on Slobodan Milosevic without a UN mandate – supported by both current and future members of the European Union – had laid out the terms for discussing the linkages between the political and operational dimensions of the UN. For many Europeans, the action was justifiable in terms of the UN's norms, even if it lacked formal support from the Security Council. When Russia and China threatened to veto any UN

mandate for action, the Slovene ambassador complained that 'not all permanent members were willing to act in accordance with their special responsibility for the maintenance of international peace and security' (Wheeler
2001: 119). If the Security Council thus arguably failed to fulfil the political
remit of the UN, the distinction between legality, UN decision-making and
operational activities was further confused when the Council mandated a
large civilian and police mission to administer Kosovo in June 1999. As later
in Iraq, the United States and its allies appeared to be able to win the UN's
support and legitimacy after they had acted without the Security Council's
endorsement.[3] This suggested a disconnection between the political and
operational elements of the UN.

The ESS was a response to the Iraq crisis, therefore, it was also a contribution to an older argument over the bases for international action rooted
in events four years before. The text retains considerable ambiguity. While
'equipping the UN' may be a priority, the declaration that 'we should be
ready to act' when 'rules are broken' implies that the European Union
should retain its decision-making and operational autonomy in such crises.
And – coming closer to the US position that multilateral organisations
should multiply the strength of friendly states rather than constrain them –
the ESS avers that 'the quality of international society depends on the quality
of the governments that are its foundation. The best protection for our security is a world of well-governed democratic states'.

This dual emphasis on the necessity of action and the primacy of governments over organisations has been cited as evidence that the purposes of the
ESS included fostering 'cohesion between the EU and the United States'
(Ojanen 2006: 19). Read in this light, it may appear that the ESS is ultimately closer to the conception of 'effective multilateralism' based on the
common values rather than that relying on the UN as a 'pivot'. Nonetheless,
the importance that the ESS places on building 'strategic partnerships' with
powers wedded to more traditional visions of the UN's authority – including
not only China but Russia – suggests its drafters' awareness of the difficulties in balancing alternative conceptions of multilateralism. Since its publication, Javier Solana has made this explicit. In a 2005 address, he sounded a
gloomy note. If the 'intellectual strength and attractiveness of the West'
remained strong, 'our relative political strength is weakening, while our
physical vulnerability is increasing' (Solana 2005). He called for new
'bargains' on key issues such as development cooperation and energy security, but offered a further warning:

> Time is not neutral in this respect. We should realise that in 20 years
> time, it will be harder to convince giants like China, India and others

that a rules-based international system is in their interest too. By 2020, the world's population will have reached close to 8 billion. Some 56 out of every 100 people will be Asian. Only 5 will come from Western Europe and 4 from the United States. The West, if we can still call it that, suddenly will look a very small place.

If European support for the Kosovo campaign once set the terms of debate over the UN's role, therefore, EU leaders are now conscious that both the focus and locus of debate over the future of multilateralism are shifting away from them. While the ESS appeared to adopt a position relatively close to Washington's, the intervening period has seen a growing emphasis on winning rising powers' assent for multilateral initiatives. Thus the reasonably standard text of a 2005 EU–China joint statement affirmed that both 'were committed to efforts to promote world peace, security and sustainable development, with the United Nations at its core. [. . .] The two sides reiterated that any model of reform should be decided upon by consensus through consultations'.

In this context, Maull's argument that effective multilateralism requires the development of 'broad-based coalitions' has been reflected in the European Union's efforts to combine alignment with the United States with outreach to new powers. As we will see, this has had only limited results in terms of UN reform. However, it should also be understood in terms of the complexities of the European Union's own profile within the multilateral system, and its evolving attitude to the relationship between the legal, political and operational aspects of the UN.

Incoherence and interpenetration

The European Union is not a coherent actor in the UN. As we have noted, the aftermath of the Iraq crisis saw the divided European governments reach some consensus on the UN's role in spite of differing motivations *vis-à-vis* the United States. Yet at the same time, the European Commission was ruefully describing the limitations to the European Union's coherence in the UN system. In its previously mentioned communication of August 2003, it complained that while significant progress had been made in coordinating EU members in UN bodies: 'votes in which the EU is unable to agree on a common line continue to occur, mainly on issues in the area of the [Common Foreign and Security Policy]'. If this problem had reached crisis-point over Iraq, it continues to frustrate many advocates of better EU–UN relations.

This frustration is heightened by the fact that a fully coherent European Union could carry immense weight within the UN system. Its members represent one-eighth of the UN's overall membership, hold one-third of the seats on the Security Council (including the permanent seats of France and Britain) and pay roughly two-fifths of its general and peacekeeping budgets (Jørgensen and Laatikainen 2004: 3). Since 1994, the holder of the rotating EU Presidency has been authorised to make statements on its behalf across a spectrum of UN forums, including in the Security Council – a tactic that is in increasingly frequent use.[4] It seems fair to say that 'Europe is clearly over-represented in the UN' (Ojanen 2006: 38).

But this quantitative over-representation has often failed to translate into an equal level of influence. Within the UN's General Assembly, there is typically a high degree of cohesion, but at the level of the Security Council EU common positions 'are often too general in nature' or conversely 'too detailed and too rigid' to be useful in complex diplomatic interplay (Biscop and Drieskens 2006: 124). The European members of the Council – and especially Britain and France – prefer to maintain the flexibility and prestige that acting in their own right allows. In the most significant debates on peace and security, therefore, the European Union often appears to lose coherence in the face of a crisis. And even where it can find consensus, questions remain over its readiness to leverage its relationships with other countries on non-UN issues to gain advantage in UN debates.

Advocates of a stronger EU presence have offered a number of potential solutions, of which the most eye-catching and idealistic is that of a single EU seat on the Security Council. But this continues to encounter opposition from not only Britain and France, but also Germany, which has sunk considerable political capital into gaining a permanent seat of its own. An alternative potential mechanism for creating a more coherent European Union is that of an 'EU Security Council' that might search for consensus on threats and crises outside the formal structures of other international institutions (Everts and Missiroli 2004).

Such options would arguably permit the European Union to act more coherently within the UN system. Yet to focus on coherence as the only measure of the European Union's standing within the UN system is to overlook the alternative forms of influence it has come to exercise. As the European Commission noted in 2003, the European Union's interaction with the UN is not confined to the political level of the General Assembly and Security Council, but involves a variety of operational dialogues ranging from direct European financing of UN initiatives to the development of common strategies with UN agencies such as the World Health Organization and everyday desk-to-desk contacts between EU and UN officials.

These forms of cooperation are symptoms of an increasing *interpenetration* between the European Union and UN. As we have seen, the debate between the United States and countries such as China is (in simple terms) an argument over the political and operational dimensions of the UN. By contrast, the EU's relationship with the UN has resulted in a blurring of political authority and operational responsibility that reflects the ambiguity of the ESS.

Peace operations

We will now consider this phenomenon in the context of handling the threats of state failure and proliferation. It is easier to quantify in the former. As we have seen, the ESS treats state failure a key threat to the European Union, and argues that the UN's capacity for crisis-management and post-conflict reconstruction should be bolstered. It also notes that Europe must enhance its military assets and, as 'in almost every major intervention, military efficiency has been followed by civilian chaos', the European Union needs 'greater capacity to bring all necessary civilian resources to bear in crisis and post-crisis situations'.

Both the EU and UN have deployed an increasing number of peace operations in recent years: at the end of 2005, the UN was deploying nearly 63,000 military personnel, 7,000 police and 5,000 civilians in seventeen operations (Wiharta 2006). While the European Union's own deployments were much smaller in numerical terms (including 6,000 troops, 500 police and a similar number of civilians), they were spread across eleven missions.

This discrepancy reflects the fact that, while the UN has been mandated to command a number of large-scale military operations (with over 15,000 in the Democratic Republic of Congo, and almost as many in Liberia), the European Union has tended to more specialised police and civilian operations. Yet, in spite of the fact that the European Union accounted for only a twentieth of UN forces in late 2005, the two organisations' deployments demonstrated a potential to complement one another where they were co-deployed. To demonstrate what interpenetration between the UN and European Union means in the field, we will turn to two concrete cases in which the two organisations' operational and decision-making structures have become connected: the Democratic Republic of Congo (DRC) and the Lebanon.

We have already noted the role of *Operation Artemis* in supporting the UN mission in the DRC in 2003. The European Union had deployed two non-military missions alongside the UN force (MONUC) there by late 2005: a police mission (EUPOL Kinshasa) and a security sector reform team (EUSEC DR Congo). These were not large, with a combined manpower of little more than thirty, but in December 2005 the UN requested the European

Union to provide a robust rapid reaction force to back up MONUC during the Congolese elections of July 2006. The European Union also provided 300 observers to cover the polls, while it and the UN jointly presented humanitarian and development plans for the Congo in early 2006.

The decision-making structures for these missions have proved particularly complex. If *Artemis* demonstrated that the European Union was ready to deploy its resources to reinforce the UN, it also highlighted the status of the European Council as a separate locus of decision-making to the UN Security Council. The mission was mandated by UN Security Council Resolution 1484, which called for a multinational force but did not specify its institutional origin. The mission was authorised by a Joint Action of the European Council that located responsibility for launching the mission and 'the powers of decision with respect to the objectives and termination of the operation' firmly in Brussels, while operational control of the largely French intervention force was routed through Paris (Council of the European Union 2003b). Authorised in 2004, EUPOL Kinshasa did not receive a specific mandate from the UN, although it referred to Security Council Resolution 1493 of the previous year, which encouraged support for the Congolese police – EUSEC RD Congo was launched on a similar basis (Council of the European Union 2004a, 2005a). Both were made answerable to an EU Special Representative (EUSR) in Kinshasa, reporting to Brussels.

In the case of EUFOR RD Congo, the authorisation of the mission proved particularly protracted: while the operation was first requested in a letter from the UN Department of Peacekeeping Operations in December 2005, the European Union was only ready to confirm the principles of the mission in late March 2006. It finally received a mandate in Security Council Resolution 1671 in April, and a Council Joint Action authorised the operation shortly thereafter. As in the case of *Artemis*, the European Council retained the 'powers of decision' over the mission's goals and conclusion, but it also recognised the level of organisational complexity that had now been reached on the ground, instructing that:

> The EU Force Commander in coordination with the EUSR and the Heads of Mission for EUPOL Kinshasa and EUSEC RD Congo respectively shall, on issues relevant to his mission, maintain close contacts with MONUC and local authorities, as well as with other international actors, as appropriate.
>
> (Council of the European Union 2006a)

In practical terms, the overlapping operational and political responsibilities of the missions in the Congo reflect both the scale and risks of their environment. But politically, the variety of means by which the missions were initiated – including UN mandates, Council Joint Actions and *ad hoc* informal requests – suggested that the decision-making structures of the European Union and UN were increasingly intertwined. The EU missions drew their legitimacy from both New York and Brussels, while on the ground EU and UN heads of mission and commanders have had to collaborate across institutional lines. Even more complex forms of interpenetration emerged over Lebanon.

During the confrontation between Hezbollah and Israel in the summer of 2006, the UN and EU structures entered into complex discussions around peacekeeping options there. While it became clear that an EU or NATO mission would not be politically acceptable to the Lebanese government, European governments conferred on possible contributions to the UN force there, UNIFIL. Although their negotiations were sometimes confused, they culminated in a meeting of the European Council on 25 August 2006 at which Italy, France and Germany confirmed significant pledges. Attending the meeting, Kofi Annan declared that 'Europe had lived up to its responsibility and provided the backbone of the force', while a European Council press release stated that further contributions were likely and 'this gives a leadership role for the Union in UNIFIL' (Council of the European Union 2006b). This led to an innovation within the UN: the creation of a 'strategic military cell' within its New York Headquarters to liaise with UNIFIL, under the command of a European general.

Neither UNIFIL nor the New York cell has any formal affiliation to the European Union. But while the deployment of troops remained on a state-by-state basis, the role of the European Council as a political clearing-house to generate UN forces was an important precedent. UNIFIL's expansion was the result of overlapping multilateral dialogues in the UN and EU frameworks, with the locus of decision-making shifting between New York and Brussels. Whereas the case of the DRC highlights how the European Union and UN can work together in formal terms, therefore, Lebanon points to a more fluid type of cooperation.

It should be emphasised that the structures developed for both DRC and the Lebanon were not the products of intelligent design but evolutionary responses to events. But the degree of interpenetration achieved has not only been a matter of operational circumstances. Developing UN-compatible yet autonomous resources for peace operations was a source of interest within the European Union even prior to the drafting of the ESS. As early as 2001, it was reported that the question 'could the EU give the UN the Rapid Reaction Capability it needs?' was on the minds of Kofi Annan and 'senior figures in Rome, Paris and London' (Grant 2001). For Javier Solana, elaborating on the ESS in early 2004, distinguishing between direct and indirect aid to the UN seemed fallacious:

> Ultimately, I believe that the best way that Europe can contribute to building a stronger UN is by building a strong and capable Europe; a Europe firmly committed to effective multilateralism. These are not alternatives. These are complementary. Last year, the European Union was able to respond quickly and decisively to the UN's call for peace-keepers in the Great Lakes region. This is EU rapid reaction in practice. Without [the European Security and Defense Policy], the deployment of military capabilities, and the ability to take the necessary decisions, we could not have responded to this call.
>
> (Solana 2004)

In operational terms, this concept has in part been advanced through the development of the battlegroup concept, put forward in February 2004 by Britain, France and Germany. This envisaged the development of rapid reaction forces 'to undertake autonomous operations at short notice, principally in response to requests from the UN' (United Kingdom *et al.* 2004). While the realisation of this concept has encountered obstacles – such as scepticism on the part of countries like the Czech Republic and Slovakia on the need for EU deployments in Africa – it is nonetheless emblematic of the fact that intensifying EU–UN relations is a matter of political strategy, not circumstance.

Proliferation and the case of Iran

Is a similar process of EU–UN interpenetration observable in policy towards weapons of mass destruction (WMD)? The distinction between the political and operational dimensions of the UN is more complex, as the processes of verification and diplomacy involved are harder to map than the deployment of peace missions. Nonetheless, just as the ESS underlined the significance of EU–UN cooperation in conflict management, the European Union set out a framework for inter-institutional cooperation on proliferation in the wake of Iraq in December 2003. Alongside the ESS, the European Council adopted a stand-alone strategy to counter WMD that was far more specific in its recommendations, not only arguing for 'appropriate cooperation with the UN' but also setting out tools that might assist the UN's International Atomic Energy Agency (IAEA) and the Security Council. These included 'a pool of readily available competence in order to carry out the verification of proliferating activities that are a potential threat to international peace and security' (Council of the European Union 2003b). Meanwhile, the European Union committed itself to the UN's political importance. 'The role of the UN Security Council', it underlined, 'as the final arbiter on the consequence of non-compliance [. . .] needs to be effectively strengthened'.

If the WMD strategy was overshadowed by the public debate over the search for Iraq's supposed capabilities, it was also developed at a time of increasing concern for key elements of the anti-proliferation architecture within the UN system, and most obviously the Non-Proliferation Treaty (NPT). In structural terms, the European Council has undertaken a series of Joint Actions to assist the operational agencies of the UN system – in May 2004, for example, it designated some €3,329,000 to the IAEA's programmes to assist states identifying and safeguarding nuclear materials (Council of the European Union 2004b). Nonetheless, the European Union also looked outside immediate UN structures to find new ways of promoting non-proliferation. One of these, pioneered in negotiations with Syria in 2003, was to introduce a non-proliferation clause into a proposed Association Agreement aimed at promoting free trade (Bailes 2005b). While recognising the primacy of the Security Council in the last resort, therefore, the European Union aimed to widen the proliferation debate beyond simple support for the UN's mechanisms. In this sense, it was trying to co-opt the UN into a strategy that relied on its 'soft power' economic assets. It was in this context that it approached the problem of Iran's uranium enrichment, a case made all the more problematic by broad disagreements between Russia, China and the United States.

As the ESS and EU WMD strategy were being negotiated in 2003, the governments of Britain, France and Germany (the 'EU3') were already engaged in talks with Tehran on nuclear ambitions. During these talks, separate discussions on trade were effectively suspended – but while the European Union might hope to gain leverage by this means, its goal was to strengthen the IAEA's hand by prompting Iran to sign the Additional Protocol of the NPT, which allows for intrusive inspections of civilian nuclear facilities. In October 2003, Tehran indicated that it would sign the Protocol – but while it appeared to continue with enrichment activities, Javier Solana and other European leaders continued to emphasise that any progress on a Trade and Cooperation Agreement with the European Union would still be predicated on proliferation issues (Bailes 2005b). In November 2004, Solana declared that economic talks would resume in December, and the EU3 (on behalf of the European Union) linked Iran's suspension of enrichment to the negotiation of an agreement that would 'provide objective guarantees that Iran's nuclear program is exclusively for peaceful purposes. It will equally provide firm guarantees on nuclear, technological and economic cooperation and firm commitments on security issues' (the 'Paris Agreement').

Here, as with Syria (if with considerably higher stakes), the European Union appeared to be providing an incentive structure to validate the role of the IAEA. The level of interpenetration between the two appeared high, and the EU3/EU was explicit in offering its support to the IAEA's Director-General Mohamed El Baradei's approach to implementing Iran's obligations. In so far as El Baradei reported to the IAEA Board, on which all the EU3 and a number of other EU members sat, the Europeans were able to deal with Iran from across a range of multilateral platforms. While talks with Iran faltered badly in early 2005, both sides were now accustomed to negotiating across these platforms, and in May Iran set out a framework for dealing with the IAEA that included 'greater access to the EU market for Iranian goods' (Kile 2006: 621). The European Union's response included a variety of economic sweeteners, including cooperation on issues ranging from railway and maritime transport to 'ecological agriculture, including herbicides and pesticides' and 'developing [Iran's] reputation as tourist destination and support [for] cooperation in development of new tourist resorts' (International Atomic Energy Authority 2005).

After this offer was rejected by Iran, a new round of negotiations began that would – after a series of setbacks and moments of hope – lead to the European members of the IAEA taking a symbolic lead (backed by the United States, China and Russia) in referring Iran to the Security Council. At the time of writing, the eventual outcome of this process is highly uncertain, but it remains striking that the EU3 and Javier Solana have continued to play a leading role in direct negotiations with Tehran. The EU capacity to offer incentives to Iran has established it as a *de facto* political actor in this drawn-out crisis, alongside the formal political role of the Security Council and the operational IAEA.

This is evidently specific to the case in hand – the European Union has not played a major role in dealing with North Korea's far more advanced nuclear threat – but we can compare this case to that of the Congo. There, we noted significant interpenetration between the European Union and the UN in the field, reflecting intersecting decision-making processes – in the Iranian case, the European Union does not have an operational role, but has tried to give the IAEA additional legitimacy while maintaining the political relevance of the Security Council. Again, the precise locus of decision-making, at least until February 2005, thus becomes obscured.

UN reform: a return to incoherence?

We have sketched out a European approach to the UN that reflects the complexity of two multilateral entities with overlapping membership attempting to relate to one another. It is undeniably an approach more easily explained in terms of process than intentions or outcomes. It has often been argued that one of the EU's strengths in relating to individual countries lies in its ability to entangle them in complex legal, political and economic processes (precisely as it hoped to do with Iran). On reflection, it may appear that its strength in dealing with the UN follows a similar pattern: the European Union exerts itself not through a single and coherent political voice in the Security Council, but a capacity to co-opt, reinforce and shape the operational and political processes of the UN system. Again, this harks back to the ambiguity of the ESS in blurring the line between autonomous EU action and support for the UN, but it also relates to a far wider shift in the multilateral environment by which 'a reliance on diversity' is increasingly a hallmark of multilateralism (Forman and Segaar 2006). In Maull's terms, the European Union appears to be responding to this diversity by developing alliances not only of states but of elements of the UN system – to which we might all follow the ESS and add other regional and international organisations – to sustain complex security processes. In the context of interpenetration between the European Union and UN, incoherence may sometimes be a virtue.

Yet this inherently fails to resolve the problem of the debate between the United States and rising powers as to the political role of the UN – a problem demonstrated by the European Union's role in the UN reform process initiated through the High-level Panel on Threats, Challenges and Change. As we have seen, there were high hopes that the European Union might be able to take a lead role in that process. But by mid-2005, there was a growing chorus of complaints that 'the appropriate *synergy* between the European Union and the UN regarding UN reform has not been arrived at during the last two years' or, to put it more bluntly, that the Europeans had 'punched below their weight' (Ortega 2005b). This was underlined when final negotiations on the reform package came close to failure in September 2005.

It can be argued that this was because the reform process attempted to address both the political and operational problems of the UN at once – in political terms through proposing possible reforms to the Security Council; and in operational ones by setting out a series of significant alterations to the workings of the UN system and secretariat. It also made a number of proposals that had both political and operational implications. One example that enjoyed widespread European support was the Peacebuilding Commission to help coordinate policy towards states emerging from conflict.

The practical utility of such a body was easy enough to define in operational terms, but its composition and relationship to existing bodies including the Security Council proved politically divisive.

Meanwhile, the legacy of the Iraq debates lingered in other proposals emerging from the High-level Panel's report. On the use of force, for example, it suggested a set of 'basic criteria for legitimacy' that the Security Council should always refer to when considering military action – this was politically unacceptable to the United States. Yet it also endorsed the 'responsibility to protect' civilians from genocide, disliked by many states as a potential mechanism to overturn the principles of sovereignty and non-interference. While the report as a whole firmly favoured the enduring political primacy of the Security Council, it thus fed into the broader debate about the UN's identity without resolving it.

This was bound to create divisions within the European Union. Germany joined Brazil, India and Japan in demanding a permanent seat on the Security Council, splitting European governments: while Britain and France indicated somewhat half-hearted backing for Berlin's claim, Italy declared outright opposition. The result was a surprisingly bitter dispute within New York, during which the idea of a single EU seat was largely left to idealists and think-tankers to chew over. Ultimately, Security Council reform faced insurmountable obstacles in the form of Chinese, American and Russian opposition, but the energy expended by the European Union in this debate reduced its ability to build effective alliances to pursue progress on lower-profile but significant operational reform issues.

Yet, more broadly, the lack of EU leadership also reflected the lack of clear European vision of the UN's future. During the deliberations of the High-level Panel, the European Council had submitted a paper linking the ESS to the Panel's report. It began by reasserting that, through the ESS, the 'EU has established as its objective the development of a stronger international society, well-functioning international institutions and a rules-based international order, within the fundamental framework of the UN Charter' (Council of the European Union 2004c). But whereas the ESS had been able to condense the European Union's relations to the UN into a few resonant sentences, the Council now attempted more detail. The resulting explanation of the UN's role was an almost unreadable mélange:

[The threats defined in the ESS] demand economic, political and legal instruments, as well as military instruments, and close co-operation between states as well as international organisations across a range of sectors. The UN is uniquely placed to provide the framework for such co-operation. A wide-ranging collective response is the best way to deal with complex, inter-connected threats. But multilateralism alone is no guarantee of an effective response: collective tools and collective will to use them must be built together. For its part, the EU, under the ESS, is determined to make effective use of the instruments available to it and to continue to pursue an active, coherent and capable approach to present-day threats and challenges. The UN Charter remains the basis for any legitimate response to threats to international peace and security. The EU will work closely with its international partners with a view, as a priority, to strengthening the UN and equipping it to fulfill its responsibilities and to act effectively.

If this presentation of the ESS is very far from inspirational, it is nonetheless a strikingly accurate depiction of the EU–UN relationship we have described. The overarching theme is complexity. The European Union searches for coordination and partnership across governments and organisations, responding to complex challenges with equally complex international alliances. As we have suggested this means blurring political and operational elements: 'collective tools and collective will to use them must be built together'. This is a functionalist, evolutionary multilateralism – one that, as we have seen, does give the European Union international influence.

Nonetheless, the European Union's failure to lead within the reform process still raises questions about how far the European Union can translate its influence into a response to larger political questions about the future of the UN. In September 2005, a number of reforms advocated by the European Union were approved, including the formation of the Peacebuilding Commission and the responsibility to protect. But as even Javier Solana had admitted, the reform package had a 'limited scope' (Solana 2005). The European Union has yet to shift from gaining influence through its interpenetration with the UN to setting out a coherent vision of its future. 'Time is not neutral in this respect', but the question for the European Union remains not *when* it will be able to lead effectively at the UN, but *if*.

Notes

1 This chapter was completed at a time of great uncertainty for both the European Union and the UN in the Middle East, and dramatic events may have intervened before its publication. It should be read as an argument of mid-2006. I would like to thank Shepard Forman, Sara Batmanglich and Benjamin Cary Tortolani for their advice on earlier drafts.

2 Article III-292 of the draft Constitution notes that the 'Union's action on the international scene shall be guided by the principles which have inspired its own creation, development and enlargement, and which it seeks to advance in the

wider world', including 'respect for the principles of the United Nations Charter and international law'. It adds that the European Union 'shall promote multilateral solutions to common problems, in particular in the framework of the United Nations'.

3 The foregoing paragraph should be read as a *political* rather than *legal* interpretation of the events involved, and one from a European perspective.

4 Biscop and Drieskens (2006: 122) note: 'In 2004, 39 Presidency Statements were issued, of which 25 on specific states and regions and 14 on horizontal issues. In comparison, in 2001, 2002 and 2003, the Presidency delivered respectively 45, 38 and 32 statements. The items covered in 2004 included: the Balkans (8), West and Central Africa (5), the Middle East (4), Timor (4), Afghanistan (2), Sudan (1) and Haiti (1), as well as terrorism (5) and non-proliferation (2), and issues in the field of conflict prevention, crisis management and post-conflict reconstruction (7)'.

4   The European Security Strategy's regional objective

The neighbourhood policy

Roland Dannreuther

The drive towards the enlargement of the European Union to include ten new members in 2004 dominated the agenda and policy-making energies of the European Union's regional engagement over the last decade. The resulting accessions have undoubtedly represented a key success story of the European Union's adaptation to the challenges of the end of the Cold War and to the vocation of East Central Europe (ECE) to integrate into European political and economic structures (Smith 2004; Dunay 2004). As such, it is hardly surprising that the European Security Strategy (ESS) places particular emphasis on the European Union's regional ambitions and outreach. The aim of 'building security in our neighbourhood' is explicitly set out in the document as one of the two core pillars of the European Union's strategic priorities, along with the ambition of contributing to an international order based on 'effective multilateralism'. The ESS recognises that the European Union has a special responsibility towards its neighbourhood and that its strategic aim and vision is to 'promote a ring of well-governed countries to the East of the European Union and on the borders of the Mediterranean with whom we can enjoy close and cooperative relations' (European Council 2003a: 9). The urgency of this task is underlined by the definition of the European Union's neighbourhood, including an area where there is 'violent conflict, weak states where organised crime flourishes, dysfunctional societies [and] exploding population growth' (European Council 2003a: 8).

The objective of this chapter is to assess the extent to which the ESS has contributed to giving greater strategic coherence and policy capacity to the European Union in dealing with its neighbouring regions. This is particularly important for the strategic role of the European Union in two ways. First, as the ESS implicitly recognises, the European Union is only partially a 'global actor' and cannot hope to have the same global strategic reach as the United States. But, the European Union's ambitions to be a global actor do have meaning in the context of its engagement with neighbouring regions, where the European Union can potentially project itself with the full complement of economic, political, diplomatic and military instruments and can most effectively promote its distinctive comprehensive conception of security. The European Union's neighbourhood is, thus, a testing ground for the European Union's strategic ambitions to be taken seriously as an autonomous and powerful actor in international politics. Second, and closely related, the importance of the immediate neighbourhood for the European Union is that it is also the principal testing ground for the European Union's claim to have developed a unique capacity to promote the internal transformations of states, which is driven less by a realist calculus of military power than by the civilian tools of economic integration and moral persuasion (Schimmelfennig 2001; Keohane 2002; Sjursen 2002; Manners 2002). It is this capacity for 'transformational diplomacy', through imitation rather than imposition, which is again central to the European Union's claim for its distinctive role in international affairs and which differentiates its power projection so strikingly from the United States. This is expressed in the ESS in the ways the European Union's 'progressive spread of the rule of law and democracy has seen authoritarian regimes change into secure, stable and dynamic democracies' (European Council 2003a: 2).

The issue of the European Union's neighbourhood policies is also significant as it is here that the ESS can be seen to have had specific and concrete policy outcomes. The development and promotion of the European Neighbourhood Policy (ENP) might not have emerged solely from the strategic impulse of the ESS but it was certainly influenced by it. The ESS was itself partly driven by the enlargement of the European Union to include ten new Member States in 2004 and the realisation that a territorially enlarged European Union could no longer be a disinterested actor in relation to the countries on its periphery. The ESS reflected a common resolve for the European Union to be recognised as having too many interests of its own to accept an uncritical devolution of its responsibilities to other external actors, such as Russia and the United States. This need for a more defined and cohesive strategic capacity was only confirmed by the fall-out of the 2003 Iraq war where European divisions undermined any prospect for a unified EU stance over a crisis which took place closer to Europe's than the United States's strategic neighbourhood. The ENP was, thus, at least in part, an attempt to give substance to the ambition of the ESS for the European Union to develop a greater degree of coherence and capacity for dealing with the multiple security challenges – such as terrorism, the proliferation of weapons of mass destruction, regional conflicts, state failure and organised crime – which find their source in many of the countries in the European Union's immediate neighbourhood.

The ENP does, therefore, provide an excellent prism through which to examine the relative success and failure, and the challenges and difficulties, of the European Union as it seeks to implement the ESS. The broader context also necessarily includes a number of the travails and difficulties that the European Union has faced since the publication of the ESS in 2003, such as the French and Dutch rejections of the European Union's draft constitution, the concerns that the European Union has moved too quickly in offering the prospect of membership to countries such as Turkey, and the limits of EU solidarity seen in the protracted negotiations over the European Union's budget. The ENP is interesting as it seeks both to accommodate these internal tensions and obstacles, while also promoting the strategic objectives set out in the ESS. Thus, on the one hand, the ENP does seek to give substance to the ESS claim that 'successive enlargements are making a reality of the vision of a united and peaceful continent' (European Council 2003a: 2) and that the current enlargement of the European Union should not create 'new dividing lines in Europe' (European Council 2003a: 9). But, on the other hand, the ENP also reflects the feeling within Europe that there are limits to enlargement. This was clearly confirmed by Chris Patten, the former external relations commissioner, when he stated in 2003 that 'over the past decade, the Union's most successful foreign policy instrument has undeniably been the promise of EU membership. This is not sustainable. For the coming decade, we need to find new ways to export the stability, security and prosperity we have created within the enlarged Union'.[1] It is for this reason that the 'neighbouring' countries, which are the object of the ENP, only include the countries of the western NIS, the Caucasus and those southern Mediterranean countries which have no explicitly recognised perspective for membership.[2]

It is this question of how the European Union can define a regional foreign policy which aims to promote the goals of transformation, as set out in the ESS, but without offering the perspective of membership which is the main focus of this chapter, which has four sections. The first section provides the immediate background, where it is argued that the ENP is attempting to overcome the legacy of the failure of earlier European Union policies to promote transformation in the absence of some offer of future membership. Indeed, it is argued that these failures have meant that the European Union has consistently followed a 'logic of generosity', whereby it has proliferated offers of membership to promote its broader transformational diplomacy. The second section argues that the ENP does reflect a significant advance on, and has 'added value' to, existing policies which have in turn contributed to furthering the aims of the ESS. The third section identifies nevertheless the continuing internal tensions within the ENP, which reflect competing sets of interests within the European Union and which significantly limit the potential for the ENP's transformational agenda. The argument here is that the European Union's clear ambitions for regional transformation are counter-balanced and often negated by more narrow security-driven strategic interests, such as immigration, energy and counter-terrorism. The ESS is, at least in part, a significant contribution to this more security-driven agenda. It is argued, though, that for the European Union to unleash the full transformative potential of the ENP, and thereby to fulfil the comprehensive security ambitions of the ESS, a significant reconceptualisation of the European Union's interests needs to take place. The final section also notes that, as the European Union defines its policies towards its neighbours in ECE and in the Middle East, the interests and policies of other external actors need to be taken into account, most notably those of Russia and the United States. The ESS is, again, a reflection that the enlarged European Union now has a regional foreign policy which is in the realm of 'high politics' and which therefore needs to take into account, and more importantly seek decisively to influence, the policies of other key external actors.

The context and background to the ENP

The Orange Revolution in Ukraine at the end of 2004 provides a good illustration of some of the key challenges and tensions in the European Union's regional engagement. At one level, the revolution in Ukraine appeared strongly to confirm the European Union's normative claims and international status. The European Union played a central and pro-active role in supporting the claims of electoral malpractice by the pro-Western Presidential candidate, Viktor Yushchenko, and thereby ensured his eventual election. It was particularly noticeable how many EU flags were flown by the thousands of protestors in Kyiv. These events appeared to be a striking demonstration of how the enlarged Union had emerged as a more powerful and activist power in international politics. However, the crisis also exposed the limitations of the European Union's policies. Despite the radical shift in Ukraine's policies, and the explicit demands from its new leaders for Ukraine to be given a concrete perspective on eventual EU membership, the European Union refused to consider any such change in policy.[3] The subsequent difficulties within Ukraine during 2005, and the failure of the new government to advance and implement its policies and objectives, can at least partially be linked to this lack of strategic commitment from the European Union.

The events and developments in Ukraine do highlight one of the underlying realities of the European Union's transformative capacities. This is that these have been very much dependent on the offer of the 'prize' of future membership and, when this is absent, the European Union's power of attraction diminishes substantially. Indeed, it can be argued that the whole history of the European Union is a history of the success of promoting a 'logic of generosity', whereby the essentially altruistic offer of European Union membership provides the necessary incentive for radical domestic economic and political transformation. In the 1980s, this led to the democratisation and stabilisation of the Northern Mediterranean countries of Greece, Spain and Portugal (Preston 1977). As with these formerly authoritarian Mediterranean countries, the candidate countries of East and Central Europe clearly understood that accession to the European Union required a fundamental internal transformation in their economic and political systems. For a set of countries which had just regained their sovereignty from the Soviet imperial embrace, the radically surprising aspect of their European vocation was the willingness to accept a regime of continual erosion of sovereign autonomy through constant EU intervention into their domestic affairs. The strategic prize of eventual EU membership made this sovereignty-eroding and, at times, humiliating experience politically acceptable.

The regional and international power and influence conferred by offering the perspective of EU membership has not been lost on the European Union or EU Member States. Despite the frequent concerns that enlargement threatens the dynamic of integration, and perhaps more critically threatens the interests of key domestic constituencies within the Union, the clear pattern has been for the European Union to opt, at critical junctures, for embracing the influence-enhancing 'logic of generosity'. For example, when a decision had finally to be made in 2001 about the timetable for the accession of the candidate countries, the agreement on an inclusive 'big bang' entry in 2004 was clearly highly favourable to the candidate countries. Only the accessions of Romania and Bulgaria were temporarily suspended but it was also made clear that their accession was pretty much set in stone for 2007. In a similar, but more surprising, vein was the consensus reached in 2000 for offering the perspective of membership to the countries of the west Balkans, something unthinkable even a few months earlier but, in the aftermath of the Kosovo crisis, was seen to be a necessary strategic investment for future conflict prevention and political reconciliation. The European Union's success in suppressing tensions in Macedonia in 2001, between Serbia and Montenegro in 2002, and in encouraging greater regional cooperation towards the International Criminal Tribunal for the former Yugoslavia can, at least partly, be connected to the additional diplomatic muscle provided by this advancing of a perspective for membership (Pippan

2004: 240–41). Given this pattern of generosity, it was fairly predictable that the European Union would bite the bullet and agree in December 2004 to start accession negotiations with Turkey in 2004. The European Union Member States felt that they simply could not ignore the unprecedented internal reforms that the prospect of accession had already been instrumental in encouraging within Turkey.

Failure of alternatives to enlargement

The growing attraction of the 'logic of generosity' is not just linked to the much acclaimed 'success' of offers of EU membership. It is also driven by the rather less acclaimed 'failure' of other EU policies and instruments for encouraging regional economic and political reforms. Overall, the European Union has been much less successful in developing 'silver' or 'bronze' carrots, which fall short of offering the 'golden' carrot of prospective membership but still provide sufficient incentives for economic and political reforms. Indeed, it is the failure in developing such alternative tools which has often driven the European Union to offer its 'golden' carrot with a greater degree of generosity than it would ideally wish.

This experience of failure is particularly relevant to the principal targets of the ENP – the countries of the Southern Mediterranean and the western Newly Independent States (NIS). For the countries of both these regions, which have never been offered the perspective of membership, the European Union developed ambitious regional strategies which sought to encourage regional stabilisation and integration through partnership with the European Union. For the NIS countries, the initial EU ambition in the mid-1990s focused on encouraging cooperation between Russia and the other states through the Commonwealth of Independent States. Partnership and Cooperation Agreements (PCAs) were agreed with each of the western NIS, along with financial support from Tacis, but the most that was offered was the vague promise of a free trade area once substantive progress on economic and political transition had been made. In the late 1990s, the new Scandinavian members of the European Union added a Northern Dimension to European Union policy-making to the region, which was intended to integrate Russia, the Baltic States and the Scandinavian countries (Haukkala 2004). But, the desired regional cooperation and integration failed to materialise, with developments in the CIS moving in precisely the other direction and with the Northern Dimension being undercut by the EU accession of the Baltic states. The PCAs also signally failed to provide the European Union with the degree of influence over regional developments which it had expected. The European Union found itself impotent as Russia continued to wage war in Chechnya; as Belarus has remained stagnant under the authoritarian regime of President Lukashenka; and as Ukraine consistently failed to initiate substantive economic and political reforms.

A very similar pattern can be seen in the Southern Mediterranean, where the unveiling of the Euro-Mediterranean Partnership (EMP) or Barcelona Process in 1995 promoted an ambitious vision of an integrated Mediterranean entity, including both Arab countries and Israel, to act as a partner to the European Union (Joffe 1999; Phillipart 2003). Much as the CIS failed to develop any momentum, so the promotion of pan-Mediterranean integration was undermined by renewed hostilities in the Arab–Israeli conflict. Towards the end of the 1990s, the eruption of the second Intifada completely derailed the strategic ambitions of the EMP, undermined the painstaking and expensive investments made by the European Union to the development of self-sustaining Palestinian institutions and statehood, and exposed the European Union as impotent to Israeli actions and US strategic hegemony. In addition, even if some countries made some genuine economic progress, such as Tunisia and Morocco, this was also generally matched by a deterioration rather than an improvement in domestic political freedom (Gillespie and Youngs 2002). The European Union's expectation that socio-economic development would necessarily lead to political democratisation was undermined by the absence of strong economic actors in the region who were committed to the policies of economic liberalisation and economic integration. The failure of European countries and of the European Union to respond more decisively against such economic and political backsliding only added to the perception of European weakness and vacillation.

The ENP and its innovations

The ENP is, in an important sense, an attempt at reforming these failed strategies towards Russia, the NIS and the Southern Mediterranean, and the European Union has demonstrated a considerable seriousness of intent in this regard. This reflects the fact that, as the ESS states, 'the integration of acceding states increases our security but also brings the European Union closer to troubled areas' (European Council 2003a: 9). But, at the same time, it needs to be recognised that the ENP maintains the principal foundation of these earlier policies which is to exclude the perspective of future membership. The ENP is not, therefore, designed as a radically new policy and does not seek to replace but rather to reinforce the *acquis* of earlier policies and the institutions and policies set up by the PCAs and the Association Agreements. Nevertheless, the ENP seeks to provide a new urgency and concentration so as to accelerate the progress within these policy frameworks and to provide new incentives and paths for economic and political reform. There are four main aspects or innovations within the ENP which can be said to provide 'added value' to existing policies and, it is hoped, convert the legacy of failure into success.

The first is the claim that the ENP offers a bigger prize (a better 'silver carrot') to its Partner countries which, while falling short of membership, is nevertheless attractive and substantial. The offer of a 'stake in the European Union's internal market' and 'further integration and liberalisation to promote the free movement of persons, goods, services and capital (four freedoms)' represents the most concrete expression of this improved offer or prize.[4] In practice, though, this is a more evolutionary than revolutionary offer and the ENP has been notably reticent towards making promises on issues which primarily concern the peoples of these neighbouring countries, such as greater freedom of movement and reduced agricultural protection. As such, the main innovation and progress is more on the procedural than the substantive level in that the ENP offers greater support, particularly of a technical nature, in ensuring that neighbouring countries come closer to approximating international and EU regulatory standards so that they are less vulnerable to EU non-tariff barriers, such as anti-dumping measures. This means that, certainly at the popular level, the offer of a bigger prize short of membership appears ill-defined and without clear concrete expression.

The second innovation or reform within the ENP is the shift towards a more selective and differentiated approach. The ENP demonstrates a clear resolve to lower some of the unfulfilled rhetoric and ambition of earlier policies with their expansive plans for regional integration and to cement 'strategic' partnerships. The emphasis in the ENP is on the need for a more differentiated approach which takes into account the 'existing state of relations within each country, its needs and capacities, as well as common interests' (European Commission 2004: 3). This reflects a recognition of the great diversity of countries included in the ENP and that a 'one size fits all' policy is counter-productive and frustrates the ambitions of those genuinely seeking to engage substantively with the European Union. For example, this inclusive regional approach, where progress is dependent on poorer performers catching up, is one significant factor behind the delays in the establishment of a Mediterranean Free Trade area. The European Union also now has a considerable experience, drawn from the ECE accession process, of setting up country-specific priorities, action plans, annual reviews and other benchmarks and targets for economic, social and political reforms. This is reflected in the ENP Action Plans unveiled in December 2004 which cover a considerable range of topics and issues and where, for example, the Action Plan for Ukraine includes over 300 bullet points for proposed targets and objectives.

There is a problem of a distinct vagueness, similar to that of the eventual 'prize' to be offered, of how the multiple targets are to be prioritised, the time-scale for their completion, and the exact benefits gained by their fulfilment. As Smith (2005: 765) argues, 'clear benchmarks these are not'. In addition, there is something normatively counter-intuitive for the European Union, as a body dedicated to regionalism, to be promoting a 'hub-and-spoke' model rather than encouraging sub-regional integration. But, there are distinct advantages of this more targeted approach in that it does provide a degree of 'local ownership' and greater transparency to the eventual action plans, since the governments of these countries have to agree and sign up to the relevant plans and goals. This fits in with the increasing recognition that economic reform and democracy cannot be imposed from outside but have to be nurtured from within. Although this more *laissez-faire* approach does not guarantee compliance, there is greater embarrassment for those governments whose agreement is merely rhetorical and whose fundamental interests are precisely in resisting economic and political reforms which might undermine their narrow base of legitimacy.

A third reform that the ENP seeks to promote is a greater coherence and consistency in its neighbourhood policy. During the 1990s, the regional policies to the NIS, the Balkans, and the Mediterranean all developed independently of one another and each had their specific financial instruments, bureaucracies and rationales. The internal complexity of the European Union as a policy actor only added to this confusion, most notably with the three different pillars of the European Union all having their distinctive contributions to make to these policies.[5] The resulting Byzantine bureaucratic structure weakened the prospect of a genuine partnership between the European Union and its partner countries, limited the effectiveness of the instruments available to the European Union, and contributed to the failures in policy implementation. Symptomatic of this is, for example, the failure of Meda, the aid and financial assistance programme to the Southern Mediterranean, to disburse more than 21 per cent of its funds in the period 1996–99 (Patten 2001). In a similar vein, one commentator has not unfairly described the financial assistance provided by the Tacis programme as being 'very hard to get, takes a long time to disburse, and is largely consumed by the salaries of those EU citizens doing the implementing' (MacFarlane 2004: 130).

The ENP seeks to improve on this poor legacy by setting up a new European Neighbourhood Policy Instrument (ENPI) which will cover all the new neighbours in the NIS and Mediterranean, replacing both Tacis and

Meda. The ENPI will also be especially designed to provide more effective and coordinated support for transborder and sub-regional cooperation across the external border of the European Union, which was notoriously difficult to promote with the earlier proliferation of financial instruments (INTERREG, PHARE, CARDS and Tacis and Meda). It is also hoped that the aid and finance provided by the ENPI will be more effectively disbursed than previously, given that it can be more clearly targeted to achieving the objectives of the country-specific Action Plans. It should also be noted that, with the eastward enlargement process completed, more attention and energy will be dedicated to utilising aid and support to the ENP countries in a more effective and efficient manner.

The fourth and final reform that the ENP proposes is that it will be better resourced than the pre-ENP neighbourhood policies. In December 2004, it was announced that the Commission would seek a budget of €14.9 billion for the ENPI for the period 2007–13 which would represent a significant increase from the €8.5 billion allocated to Tacis and Meda from 2000–2006. This sum of €14.9 billion is not, though, assured as the negotiations over the size of new EU budget, which was eventually agreed in December 2005, fell considerably short of what the Commission was requesting. Nevertheless, it is reasonable to assume that more resources will be allocated towards the western NIS and the Southern Mediterranean than before.

Overall, the reforms, proposals and new procedures in the ENP might not represent a radical departure from earlier policies but do nevertheless reflect a new strategic urgency, a greater policy coherence and a genuine opportunity for the European Union to influence positively future developments in its neighbouring regions. In this way, the ENP does add substantial weight to the ambitions and objectives of the ESS to promote a more cohesive and capable strategic capacity for the European Union. The key question, though, is whether this strategic ambition can be translated into effective action. The policy framework is in place; the key issue is political will.

Internal challenges and the ENP

The issue of political will relates very much to the underlying priorities and objectives that the European Union accords to its policies towards neighbouring regions. Certainly, the European Union, as a unwieldy non-state and quasi-supranational body, is a less proactive and more reactive policy-maker than classical nation-states, and thus more deeply affected by the unpredictable turn of events, such as the Orange and Rose Revolutions in Ukraine and Georgia. Some of the likely external challenges are addressed in the next

section. But, the importance of external stimuli does not reduce the significance of the critical internal challenges to the future prospects of the ENP.

The main problem or internal challenge that the European Union faces is
that its clear interest in promoting economic and political transformation
in its neighbourhood is counter-balanced by a number of strategic and
security-driven interests which support a much more conservative and status
quo-oriented approach. In many ways, the ESS can be seen to exacerbate
these tensions, as the document arguably concentrates more on the security
threats posed by the European Union's neighbours than on their prospects
for change and transformation. The challenge, though, is to undermine this
strategic orientation and shift the balance of interests from the more conservative security-driven set of concerns to the transformational agenda.

Interests in transformation

The importance accorded to the transformative side of the agenda is perhaps
most evident in the European Union's frequent assertion of the need to overcome the 'welfare divide' between the enlarged European Union and its new
neighbours. The nature and extent of the problem is striking. On the
economic side, the 450 million population of the European Union enjoys a
GDP per capita of €21,300, while the ENP countries with a combined population of 400 million (or a population of 500 million if Turkey and the
western Balkans are included) have a nominal GDP per capita which is
generally less than €2,000 per capita. The only major exception to this is
Israel which comes close to the EU average (€19,578). Lebanon comes
second with (€5,284), Russia some way behind at third (€2,382) and there is
then a long tail until Moldova, which is the poorest neighbouring country
(€417) (European Commission 2003a: 19). The causes of the poor economic
record of Russia, the Balkans and the western NIS are well-known but the
countries of the Middle East have also had a dismal growth record, where
GDP per capita actually fell at an average rate of 0.3 per cent per year from
1985 to 1995, but with admittedly a return to growth in the late 1990s
(Richards 2003: 59–60; for a more general analysis, see Henry and
Springborg 2001). On the political side, this 'welfare divide' is matched with
just as visible a democratic or governance gap, where the majority of the
countries in the region are either authoritarian or have weakly institutionalised democracies, or what Zakaria (2003) aptly describes as 'illiberal
democracies'.

Clearly, for a Union which so closely identifies itself with 'European
values' of economic freedom, human rights and democracy, the proximity
of countries with a high degree of relative poverty and the presence of

authoritarian governments represents both a developmental and moral challenge. The normative agenda that this presents is clearly identified in both the ESS and the ENP with their assertions that the aim of the policy is to ensure that there should not emerge new 'dividing lines' – a 'welfare curtain' or a 'fortress Europe' – between the enlarged union and its neighbours. The offers of a 'greater stake in the internal market', the proposed increased financial resources to the neighbours, and the more active hands-on support from the European Union as provided by the Action Plans and annual reviews, are all aimed at helping to bridge this divide.

A second but connected dimension of the European Union's transformative agenda is its growing capacity for political reconciliation and conflict resolution. One significant outcome of an enlarged European Union is its increased proximity to a number of long-standing ethno-nationalist, religious or communal conflicts, most notably those in the former Soviet Union as well as the Middle East. The causes of these conflicts are certainly linked to the conditions of economic deprivation and political repression identified above. But, they are more deeply rooted in the unresolved legacies of the dissolution of former multinational states or empires in the neighbouring regions. During the 1990s, it was the legacy of the dissolution of Yugoslavia, and the multiple wars of secession that followed from this, which dominated the European Union's conflict resolution agenda. The Union found that its economic power and influence was an insufficient instrument for ensuring its interests, resulting in a tortuous process of acquiring the necessary political and military capabilities for effective intervention. By the end of the 1990s, the European Union had become the most powerful and influential actor seeking conflict resolution and political and economic reforms in the west Balkan region (Greco 2004). The ESS reflects this growing EU role in the Balkans, asserting that 'the credibility of our foreign policy depends on the consolidation of our achievements there. The European perspective offers both a strategic objective and an incentive for reform' (European Council 2003a: 9).

With the enlargement in 2004, the European Union finds itself again being increasingly drawn into seeking a resolution of some of the most difficult ethno-nationalist conflicts in the former Soviet space, most notably in Transnistria and in the Caucasus. In the Middle East, the European Union has similarly had a long-standing concern and interest over the unresolved legacy of British imperial rule in Palestine. As the ESS states, 'resolution of the Arab/Israeli conflict is a strategic priority for Europe' (European Council 2003a: 9). However, this has now been supplemented by an interest, if not as yet direct involvement in the overturning of the post-Ottoman legacy of Sunni-dominated rule in Iraq and the resulting internal civil conflict that this has generated. If Iraq were to represent a precedent for a further unravelling of the post-Ottoman order in the region, the European Union will certainly be drawn into the subsequent political crisis.

Status quo interests

However, these interests, which provide a clear rationale for an activist European Union agenda to pursue substantive economic and political reforms among its neighbours are counter-balanced by other interests with potentially more conservative policy implications. It is only if these interests, which impede such a transformative agenda, are redefined and reconceptualised that the European Union's ambitions of playing a more dynamic international role are likely to be realised.

In terms of such obstacles, the most prominent of these, at least from the perspective of the ordinary Arab or East European citizen, are the issues of agricultural trade and freedom of movement. The issue of immigration illustrates the dilemmas and challenges in a particularly stark way (Geddes 2000; Huysmans 2000; Boswell 2003). If control of migratory flows is already perceived to be a major problem amongst EU Member States, this is likely only to intensify in the future with the diverging demographic trends between the European Union and its neighbours, particularly in the South. While at the present time, the populations of the European Union and the Middle East and North Africa (MENA) are roughly similar at 450 million, by 2050 it is estimated that the MENA population will double while the European Union's will remain static or decline. Ensuring the economic integration and development of the Southern Mediterranean countries, so that there is sufficient economic activity to support their growing populations, provides the long-term solution to this problem.[6] But, as the experience of United States with Mexico in the NAFTA context shows, the short-to medium-term prospect is an intensification of migratory flows, as relative improvements in economic prosperity create more incentives for outward migration.[7] A European failure to provide more generous prospects for out-migration would only intensify the internal insecurity for the North African states, which in turn only magnifies the security challenges for Europe. The key reconceptualisation of migration that is required is for the European Union to understand migration as a joint security concern for both European and neighbouring countries, and not as a problem whose solution is dictated solely from the European side.

A further area of policy which promotes a more cautious approach to 'transformational diplomacy' relates to the one key interest where the European Union is the economically vulnerable party in its relations with its neighbours – its energy needs. The ESS notes that energy dependence is one of the critical global challenges facing Europe and that 'most energy imports come from the Gulf, Russia and North Africa' (European Council 2003a: 4). Indeed, the energy resources of the Gulf, Russia, the Caspian region and North Africa are appropriately described as the economic 'umbilical cords' which connect and make the European Union dependent on its periphery. If there is one thing which connects these diverse regions together with the European Union it is the energy connection. The European Union's energy dependence with its neighbours is also set to grow substantially over the coming decades. Europe's oil import dependence is set to grow from a current 52 per cent to 85 per cent in 2030, and for gas from 36 per cent to about 63 per cent as a consequence of increased projected demand and a decline in European oil and gas production, primarily in the North Sea.[8] While about 40 per cent of the oil currently imported into Europe comes from the Persian Gulf, an even larger proportion of about 48 per cent comes from Russia and North Africa. For natural gas imports, the concentration is much higher with 96 per cent of Europe's imports coming from either Russia or North Africa.

Europe's energy dependence on its ENP partners is, therefore, already very high. In the future, this will only intensify as Gulf oil will increasingly find itself directed towards meeting Asian demand and the needs of the rapidly developing markets of India and China (Wu 2002: 20–23). As a consequence, the reserves found in the former Soviet Union, the Caspian Sea and North Africa will only grow in importance for Europe. It is also salutary to note that the investment required to meet Europe's future energy requirements is massive. For example, it is estimated that up to $150 billion will be required to meet Europe's natural gas imports by 2020 (Gault 2004: 176). These sums dwarf the few billion euros available to the European Union's financial instruments to its neighbouring regions. It is in this context of substantial and increasing energy dependence that the bargaining power of the authoritarian governments of the petroleum-rich countries in the former Soviet Union and the Middle East is significantly enhanced. In this context, the European Union's resolve in promoting its agenda of political and economic reforms also tends to falter when such activism is seen potentially to threaten energy supplies. Such reticence is already seen in the European Union's relations with Russia where the European Union is relying on Russia doubling its gas exports to European markets.[9] The relative quiescence of the European Union and some of its principal Member States to authoritarian practices in North Africa is similarly attributable to energy security concerns.

Such quiescence and passivity is not, though, inevitable. The problem with conceiving of energy security in this traditional geopolitical manner is that it ignores the even greater dependence of the energy-exporting countries on the importing states. The nature of this dependence can be seen in the fact that the Soviet Union, even in the heat of the Cold War, never considered cutting off the gas supplies to Europe, which in turn provided the essential foreign currency for maintaining Soviet imperial power. Furthermore, energy security is now generally understood to be more effectively enhanced through the liberalisation of markets rather than by more traditional geostrategic manoeuvring (Andrews-Speed *et al.* 2002). There is, therefore, no necessary reason why the European Union, and its Member States, cannot take a braver and more resolute stance towards their energy-rich neighbours or, at the very least, not to be too ready to sacrifice European transformational values on the altar of energy security.

A similar internal logic which tends to promote a more conservative acceptance of the prevailing status quo is also evident in strategies to deal with the transnational threats identified in the ESS, such as international terrorism, the proliferation of WMD, and transnational organised crime. The ESS does admittedly recognise that such transnational threats prosper and proliferate in weak or failed states and that, to the extent that such states exist in the European Union's immediate neighbourhood, there is a strategic interest for EU Member States to promote the economic and political reforms which can strengthen the capacity of these states. But, given the immediacy and directness of these threats, the more short-term policy implications often appear to be needing to work with existing governments, rather than awaiting a longer-term internal transformation within these states. This has meant, in particular, the European tendency to accept the argument of many Arab regimes that the only alternative to their authoritarianism is anti-Western Islamist radicalism. The security-driven fall-back for the European Union has been to view the ENP countries as a strategic buffer from threats emanating from other parts of the world, such as drugs from Afghanistan, WMD proliferation in Central Asia or terrorism from the Gulf region. Preserving and strengthening this strategic buffer tends to require making stronger, rather than weakening, customs and border controls and acquiescing in, rather than challenging, authoritarian practices. If this security-driven focus is predominant, then the prospects for the European Union to follow through with its more transformational agenda are greatly reduced.

External challenges and the ENP

The argument so far is that the most important constraints and limitations to the implicit transformative agenda of the ENP, reflecting and seeking to implement the ambitions of the ESS, are found in the European Union's articulation of its internal interests which promote, in certain security-related issue areas, a conservative and status quo orientation. The ESS does, to a certain extent, contribute to this risk-averse strategy by focusing attention on the security threats posed by the European Union's neighbours rather than identifying the potential for change and transformation. The task is, therefore, to promote a significant reconceptualisation and reprioritisation of these interests so as to unleash the full transformative potential of the ENP. However, these internal dynamics also need to take into account external stimuli and dynamics which will also undoubtedly influence the evolution of the European Union's neighbourhood policy.

One such external challenge has already been exposed by the crisis in Ukraine. A major tension in the ENP is that, while the Arab countries and Israel are currently willing to accept that they are not potential candidates of the European Union, this is not the case for the western NIS, in particular Ukraine, Belarus and Moldova. A policy which does not explicitly recognise the European vocation of these countries is likely to breed a sense of disillusionment and continual pressure for that policy to be revised. Such pressure is not only likely to come from the western NIS countries but also from the new members of the European Union, in particular Poland and the Baltic states, who have already spearheaded the European Union's eastward engagement. Their argument for extending the 'logic of generosity' will in particular focus on the dangers of the European Union losing Ukraine and the other states to an increasingly authoritarian Russia. However, it is far from clear that these new EU members have the necessary weight to convince other EU members, particularly those in the South, who have considerable scepticism of a Ukrainian candidacy and who would tend to privilege their relations with Russia over the other NIS. The danger for the ENP is that, as in the past, policy paralysis might emerge in relations with Ukraine, as Kiev demands its perceived rightful recognition of its European vocation *before* it engages in reforms while the European Union demands implementation of those reforms *before* it would be willing to consider Ukraine's application. The Ukrainian example could potentially be extended to Belarus, if there were to be a change to a pro-EU government, or even to some of the Mediterranean countries, such as Morocco, where hopes of eventual EU membership are certainly present, if currently dormant. The European Union's acceptance of Turkey as a candidate country has only emboldened the ambitions of Ukraine and other ENP countries of a future perspective of membership.

A second major challenge has also been evident in the Ukraine crisis and that is the inevitable interaction with other powerful external actors, most notably Russia and the United States. This reflects the reality that, unlike the western Balkans where the European Union operates essentially within a *domaine exclusif*, the western NIS and the Mediterranean engage the interests of other powerful independent actors who do not feel constrained by the need to fulfil the principles and policies of the ESS and ENP. The ENP is, as a consequence, part of the European Union's 'high politics', a critical component of Europe's broader security strategy as set out in the ESS and a key element in its projection as an influential regional and international actor. As regards the EU–Russian dimension of the ENP, the most immediate problem is that the current Russian government tends to view the European Union's engagement in geopolitical terms and as zero-sum competition for regional influence. In this context, the challenge for the European Union is to ensure that its strategic interest with Russia does not undermine its support for internally driven Western-oriented economic and political reforms among the western NIS. But, Russian opposition is not an inevitable constant and, were Russian political developments to lead to a more cooperative and constructive relationship, the challenge would be for the European Union to develop a more overarching pan-European framework through which EU–Russian cooperation could be effectively institutionalised.

A similar more expansive regional framework can be seen to be particularly urgent in the Middle East. In the aftermath of the Iraq war and the enlargement of the European Union, the Barcelona Process appears anachronistic, limited in membership to just Israel and Arab states as in the older 'Euro-Arab dialogue', and artificially disconnected from the wider Middle East, particularly Iraq, Iran and the Gulf states. Although the ENP emphasises the need for differentiation and selectivity, the geostrategic interests of the European Union articulate the need for a more overarching regional framework to replace the Barcelona Process. The ESS hints at this when it states that 'a broader engagement with the Arab World should also be considered' (European Council 2003a: 9). This, in turn, directly confronts the European Union with the dominant external actor in the region: the United States and its close ally Israel. Clearly, as with Russia, the main objective of the European Union should be to ensure that the ESS, the ENP and any broader Middle Eastern policy complements and converges with the interests and policies of the United States. However, the real test will come with policies adopted by the United States or Israel which are perceived in Europe to be undermining the objectives of the ESS or ENP, such as an Israeli failure to negotiate with the Palestinians in good faith (which derailed the Barcelona Process) or a further Iraq-style demonstration of the US preference for imposed 'regime change'. For Europe to be able better to respond to such challenges will also require overcoming some of the most significant weaknesses in its current policies, most notably its extremely poor political relations with Israel and its ambivalence over political reform in Arab states. There are encouraging signs that the European Union is already moving in this direction. The EU–Israel Action Plan offers greater access for Israeli firms to EU policies and programmes in exchange for Israeli recognition of the European Union as a negotiating partner in the Middle East Peace Process and for accepting a EU–Israeli dialogue over WMD proliferation. The Action Plans with the Arab states are similarly considerably more explicit about such issues as democracy, the rule of law, human rights and other fundamental freedoms.

Conclusion

These external challenges illustrate most clearly the need for the European Union to engage in the art of 'grand strategy' as it seeks to adapt to an enlarged Union of 27 states with borders on what Zbigniew Brzezinski once called the 'arc of crisis', stretching from Soviet Eurasia through the Middle East to North Africa. It is the striking contribution of the ESS that the European Union now does have some form of clearly identifiable 'grand strategy'. Like all grand strategies, though, the ESS is necessarily shorter on detail and discrete policies than on broad objectives and principles. The ENP fills this policy gap and seeks, within its particular but very critical remit, to reaffirm the central European conviction, as clearly set out in the ESS, that democracy and economic reform are essential if the deeper roots of insecurity are to be resolved. However, the challenge for implementing the ENP in the future requires the European Union to be considerably braver in integrating this transformative agenda with its multiple security-driven interests, most notably immigration, energy and counter-terrorism. Without such a reconceptualisation, the ENP's transformative potential, and the European Union's ambitions to be a serious global actor as set out in the ESS, will be greatly reduced.

Nevertheless, it would be a mistake to dismiss the ENP purely as an exercise in empty rhetoric. There are potential analogies with other EU policies which initially faced considerable scepticism and even outward rejection, such as eastward enlargement, but which then developed an internal dynamic and momentum, transforming the very nature and self-identity of the Union in the process. The ENP is certainly an adaptive and incremental policy and it is far from radical or revolutionary in its current form, but it does potentially articulate a new vision and policy framework, where the European Union's interests in its neighbouring countries become more heavily invested in seeing their political and economic transformation and their convergence with European values. Developments in Ukraine, and similar indications of political change in the Middle East, could act as potential catalysts for encouraging and sustaining such a normative shift within the European Union. It is this possibility which makes the ENP a significant and potentially even a radically innovative policy. If the ENP does develop in this positive and radically challenging way, then the ESS can be said to have contributed to a policy outcome which fulfils the ambition expressed in the ESS of a Europe 'ready to share in the responsibility for global security and in building a better world' (European Council 2003a: 2).

Notes

1 'Wider Europe-Neighbourhood: Proposed New Framework for Relations with the EU's Eastern and Southern Neighbours', IP/03/358, 11 March 2003.
2 The geographical coverage of the ENP was originally conceived for Russia, Ukraine, Belarus and Moldova; and, in the Mediterranean, for Algeria, Egypt, Israel, Jordan, Lebanon, Libya, Morocco, Syria, Tunisia and the Palestinian Authority. In 2004, it was extended to include the countries of the South Caucasus – Georgia, Armenia and Azerbaijan. Russia has so far refused to be part of the ENP and has sought to preserve its bilateral relationship with the European Union. In addition, the ENP does not cover Romania, Bulgaria, Turkey and the Western Balkans.
3 The details of the revised EU–Ukraine Action plan can be found in 'Prospects of Ukraine's EU's Membership "Realistic"', *EurActiv*, 25 January 2005.
4 It is notable that the references to the opening of the four freedoms found in the European Commission (2003a) 'Wider Europe-Neighbourhood' paper are not repeated in the European Commission (2004) 'European Neighbourhood Policy' paper.
5 As one commentator on the Northern Dimension noted as regards the three pillars, 'its instruments derive from the first, its objectives from the second, and its problems from the third' (Ojanen 2000).
6 An example of the challenges that this presents to Middle Eastern countries can be seen in Iran, where the government must generate 800,000 jobs annually to meet demographic trends but is only producing 400,000 (Vakil 2004: 47).
7 The linkage between migration and development, and the evidence that migration increases with development, is set out clearly in Skeldon (1997).
8 These are IEA projections as set out in International Energy Agency (2002). The EU is also aware of this growing import dependence, as set out in European Commission (2000).
9 It is notable, for instance, how reticent some European leaders, for example Gerhard Schroeder of Germany, have been in criticising Russian policies under Putin and this is generally seen to be connected to concerns over energy security.

5 The European Security Strategy and military capacity

The first significant steps

Jolyon Howorth[1]

If anybody had predicted, as 1998 drew to a close, that within five years the European Union would be engaging in autonomous military and policing missions in 'non-permissive' theatres, under a European command chain and the European flag, they would have been regarded by most serious analysts as wildly optimistic dreamers. The years 1997 and 1998 probably represented a low-point in European hopes of establishing a military capacity allowing the Union to engage in peacekeeping and crisis management missions independently of the United States (Gnesotto 1998; Gordon 1997). In 1999, the brief campaign in Kosovo demonstrated to all and sundry that, compared with the US military, European forces could hope to do little more than play a facilitating or back-up role (Brawley and Martin 2000; Bozo 2003). The Franco-British summit in Saint Malo in December 1998, which effectively kick-started the drive towards a serious European security and defence project, was immediately followed by the chaotic and ineffectual conference at Rambouillet, co-chaired by France and the United Kingdom, which signally failed to avert the Kosovo war, for which the Europeans were so manifestly unprepared. Yet in late 2001, the European Council declared its objective of being able to field operational combat-ready troops by 2003. The reaction from strategic experts around the world was one of serious scepticism (Centre for Defence Studies 2001; International Institute for Strategic Studies 2001: 283–91). Yet the 2003 deadline was met and by 2006 the European Union had launched sixteen missions in as many countries on three continents. Six of those missions were primarily military. This massive transformation of the European Union's intervention capacity was achieved in a context in which, on both sides of the Atlantic, critics tended to view the European Union as woefully unprepared to face the test of military engagement, let alone the harsh strategic reality of the post-9/11 world.[2]

The impact of the end of the Cold War

After the Cold War, all European nations had no option but to transform their militaries. The type of forces required for the territorial defence objectives of the Cold War was quite inappropriate for the new crisis management and peacekeeping missions of the post-Cold War world. In 1988, as the Cold War was ending, the NATO alliance had almost 5.4 million active-duty service personnel, backed up by over 7 million reservists. Of these, the European members of NATO contributed the vast bulk, with 3.1 million active-duty service members and 5.5 million reservists. Against these forces were ranged over 5 million active-duty troops from the Warsaw Pact, backed by 6.2 million reservists (International Institute for Strategic Studies 1989).[3] However, within three years, both the Warsaw Pact and the Soviet Union had disappeared and a dozen years later, the numbers of armed forces in the NATO alliance had been radically reduced. By 2003, total European forces numbered only 4.9 million, a 43 per cent decrease. The paradoxical reality about these forces, however, was that substantial numbers of the 12 million men and women under arms at the height of Cold War tensions virtually never saw action, whereas by 2005 their counterparts – from both the United States and the European Union – were seriously overstretched, large numbers of them being at one stage or another of the three-stage cycle of deploying, resting, or preparing to deploy. Moreover, whereas in 1989 the 'peace' was kept essentially by massed conscript-based line-defences backed by a nuclear deterrent, in 2003, crisis management operations were carried out by professional soldiers using sophisticated conventional equipment demanding high levels of technical skills and ongoing training.

The basic shift was from quantity to quality. As the United Kingdom's 1998 Strategic Defence Review stated: 'defence is a highly professional, increasingly high technology, vocation'. The challenge was to recruit highly motivated people, to train them appropriately and to a very high standard, to equip them properly, and to retain both their motivation and their services (Ministry of Defence of the UK 1998). This chapter will examine the process whereby the EU Member States, both individually and collectively, shifted their military thinking away from the fixed 'legacy' weapons and systems of the Cold War years and towards the power-projection and crisis-management enablers of the present. The professional soldier of 2006 and beyond will require a range of skills – not just military skills, but also political, social, and even cultural and linguistic skills – undreamed of only two decades earlier. We have witnessed a wholesale transformation of the European Union's plans, structures, weapons systems and equipment: in short, its entire military mindset. This translates into a massive shift in the demand side of the European military personnel equation.

The challenge of transformation was especially acute for Europe. During the Cold War, European forces were rarely deployed far from home (indeed almost never, if 'home' is taken to mean Europe); they spent most of their time on exercises and virtually none of it on active combat duty. General de Gaulle, justifying France's decision to spend around 40 per cent of its defence budget on nuclear weapons, had coined the formula 'nuclear weapons mean the absence of battle'.[4] As a result, when the Gulf War overtook them in 1991, French forces, although among the most robustly trained and experienced in Europe, were shocked to discover that very few were deployable: just 15,000 out of a total land army force of 300,000. Their vaunted AMX-300 combat tanks were badly in need of servicing; only forty were combat-ready out of a notional 1,300 in service. When the lightly armed *Daguet* division finally arrived in Saudi Arabia, it found that its AMX-10RC light armoured vehicles were quite literally blind to the topography of the desert theatre until equipped with American global positioning (GPS) guidance systems. When, less than six months later, the Europeans were again caught off guard with the outbreak of the Balkan wars, it came as an even harsher revelation to many – even within the security community – that the Europeans were far from able, as Luxembourg's Foreign Minister Jacques Poos had imprudently implied, to take over from the Americans responsibility for European security.[5] They were unable even to project any forces to a region which lay, technically, within the geographical bounds of the European Union itself.[6]

The basic explanation is simple. Whereas US forces, throughout the twentieth century, had devoted massive effort – financial, technological, and logistical – to a capacity for 'force projection' across both the world's great oceans, European forces since 1945 had been configured for line-defence across the great European plain. The West German armed forces in 1989, for instance, boasted almost 500,000 active troops, with a further 850,000 reservists. Their main equipment featured 5,000 main battle tanks, 2,136 armoured infantry fighting vehicles, 3,500 armoured personnel carriers, 2,500 artillery pieces, 2,700 anti-tank guided weapons, almost 5,000 air-defence guns, and 800 surface-to-air missiles. Little of this would prove useful in the new tasks of distant crisis management facing the European Union in the 1990s.

Although NATO, in its new Strategic Concept of November 1991, drew attention to the need to shift focus away from massed tank and artillery battles in Central Europe to the new and more diverse crisis management challenges of the post-Cold War world, the emphasis initially was doctrinal rather than programmatic (NATO 1991). New procurement projects have lead-times of around fifteen years, but few European governments were able to imagine, let alone to anticipate, the new force-projection challenges that would be facing them in the twenty-first century. All were keen to cash in on the post-1989 'peace dividend'. On average, European defence budgets fell by more than 20 per cent during the period between 1989 and 1998. The United Kingdom immediately embarked on a series of defence reviews culminating in the 1998 Strategic Defence Review (Ministry of Defence of the UK 1994, 1995 and 1998). France moved rapidly from a defence policy of rigorous national autonomy towards one geared towards integrated European operations (Howorth 1998). The majority of European militaries, however (with the notable exceptions of Belgium and the Netherlands), remained unreformed and unchanged for the greater part of the decade. Europe, in short, revealed a dual 'capabilities gap': there was a growing gap between the advanced weapons systems available to the US military and the increasingly antiquated systems of the EU Member States, and there was also a gap between those existing EU systems and the real military requirements of the European Union in the post-Cold War world. This capabilities gap was initially identified by Hill (1993).

The quest for a European Security and Defence Identity (ESDI)

In the early 1990s, defence planners began to address the problem of developing a serious EU military capacity that would allow the Union to assume responsibility for the new crisis management tasks of the post-Cold War world. At a meeting at Petersberg (near Bonn) in June 1992, the Western European Union (WEU) had defined three such tasks, corresponding to three levels of combat intensity: 'humanitarian and rescue tasks; peacekeeping tasks; [and] tasks of combat forces in crisis management, including peacemaking'.[7] This implied radical transformation of the European Union's existing capacity to provide deployable, professional intervention forces geared to 'out of area' crisis management. But where were these forces to be found? The first task was to end conscription and to move towards all-volunteer forces (AVFs) (Table 5.1). Conscripts, it was generally recognised, tended to have limited training and skills and, largely for political and juridical reasons, were undeployable outside of their home countries. Belgium and the Netherlands moved swiftly: Belgium announced the abolition of conscription in 1992 and ended it in 1994; the Netherlands did the same in 1993 and 1996. France and Spain followed suit in 1996 after agonising debates about the connection between conscription and democracy. In both France and Spain, the last conscripts left the armed forces in 2001. The motivations for abolishing conscription varied from country to country. Most, such as Belgium, Spain, and many Central and Eastern European states, sought to focus on downsizing and reduction of the military budget; others such as the Netherlands, France, and Italy, were intent on transforming their militaries into deployable forces for overseas crisis management (Williams 2005). However, by 2005, sixteen years after the end of the Cold War, only thirteen of the twenty-five EU states had moved fully to AVFs, although several others had plans to phase out conscription, as shown in the overview presented in Table 5.1.

The next step was to arrange for these new professional forces to be equipped to tackle crisis management missions. Such a transformational process would clearly take time, but crises – in the Balkans and elsewhere – would not wait. As a stop-gap measure, the procedures known as 'Berlin Plus' were devised to allow the European Union to bridge the capabilities gap by borrowing necessary assets such as strategic lift, C4I (command, control, communications, computers, and intelligence), and logistics from the United States.[8] EU-only units could be put together from inside NATO by generating European Combined Joint Task Forces (CJTFs) (Terriff 2003: 39–60). A European Security and Defence Identity (ESDI) was thus to be forged, 'separable but not separate' from NATO and overseen politically by the WEU.

In the event, these rather awkward procedures proved unsatisfactory. First, the US military proved far less enthusiastic than the politicians to 'lend' their hard-won high-tech assets to ill-prepared and ill-trained Europeans with little experience in the field. Second, the proposals that EU forces be 'double-hatted' – available either to a NATO/US commander or to a hypothetical EU commander – caused disquiet within the officer corps. Third, the Berlin Plus proposals were, to some extent, predicated on a parallel reform of NATO's overall command structure, with a view to giving more command posts to European officers. The US government's reluctance to confer on a European officer the command of NATO's southern HQ (AFSouth) in Naples effectively sank that agreement (Brenner and Parmentier 2002). It also became clear to most actors that the WEU was too inconsequential a body to assume responsibility for political supervision of EU military missions. Thus, the challenge of improving military capacity in Europe remained essentially unaddressed throughout the 1990s. The project of generating a European security and defence identity from inside NATO proved to be a false start.

From identity to policy: ESDI to ESDP

The decision taken in 1998 by incoming UK Prime Minister Tony Blair, to move resolutely towards improved European capacity, broke the log-jam

Table 5.1 European armed forces 2004

	Professional or conscript[a]	Number of personnel			Total in 2004[b]	Total in 1988	% Red'n 88–04
		Army	Navy	Air Force			
Austria	Conscript	33,200	–[c]	6,700	39,900	54,700	–27
Belgium	Professional since 1994	24,800	2,450	10,250	39,200	88,300	–56
Cyprus	Conscript	10,000	–	–	10,000	13,000	–23
Czech Rep.	Professional since 2005	16,663	–	5,609	22,272	197,000	–89
Denmark	Conscript	12,500	3,800	4,200	21,180	29,300	–28
Estonia	Conscript	3,429	331	193	4,934	n/a	n/a
Finland	Conscript	20,500	5,000	2,800	28,300	35,200	–20
France	Professional since 2001	133,500	43,995	63,600	254,895	457,000	–44
Germany	Conscript	191,350	25,650	67,500	284,500	489,000	–42
Greece	Conscript	110,000	19,250	23,000	163,850	214,000	–23
Hungary	Ended 2004	23,950	7,500	32,300	99,000		–67
Ireland	Professional	8,500	1,100	860	10,460	13,200	–21
Italy	Professional since 2005	112,000	34,000	45,875	191,875	386,000	–50
Latvia	Plans to end 2006	1,817	685	255	5,238	n/a	n/a
Lithuania	Conscript	11,600	710	1,200	13,510	n/a	n/a
Luxembourg	Professional since 1967	900	–	–	900	800	+12
Malta	Professional	2,237[d]	(joint)	(joint)	2,237	1,200	+86
Netherlands	Professional since 1996	23,150	12,130	11,050	53,130	102,200	–48

Poland	Conscript	89,000	14,300	30,000	141,500	406,000	-65
Portugal	Conscription ended 2003	26,700	10,950	7,250	44,900	73,900	-39
Slovakia	Conscript ended 2006	12,860	–	5,160	20,195	n/a	n/a
Slovenia	Professional since 2004	6,550	–	(530)	6,550	n/a	n/a
Spain	Professional since 2001	95,600	19,455	22,750	147,255	309,500	-52
Sweden	Conscript	13,800	7,900	5,900	27,600	67,000	-59
UK	Professional since 1963	116,760	40,630	48,500	205,890	316,700	-35
Norway[e]	*Conscript*	*14,700*	*6,180*	*5,000*	*25,800*	*35,800*	*-28*
Turkey[e]	*Conscript*	*402,000*	*52,750*	*60,100*	*514,850*	*635,300*	*-19*

Source: IISS, *The Military Balance 2005–2006*, pp. 45–150
Bold = Original 15 EU member states prior to 2004

Notes:

a Six of the EU-15 (members prior to 2004 enlargement) still field conscript armies. Half of the EU Accession states (those who became members in 2004) retain conscript armed forces, but one of these (Latvia) plans to end conscription in 2006.

b In some cases, overall numbers are in excess of the sums for the three armed forces because paramilitaries and other forces are included in the official tallies.

c Austria and Luxembourg have no navy and Luxembourg has no air force. Of the newest ten members, joining in 2004, the Czech Republic, Cyprus, Hungary, Slovakia, and Slovenia have no navy, and Cyprus also has no air force.

d Maltese armed forces include all three services.

e Norway and Turkey are included here although they are not EU members, because Norway participates in the ESDP through NATO and the Berlin Plus arrangements, participates in EU joint actions, and has pledged personnel and equipment to the ESDP Rapid Reaction Force. Turkey is included because it has a complex agreement with the EU through the EU–NATO Partnership and, if it joined the EU, would become by far the largest armed force in the Union.

that ESDI had been unable to shift. At a historic meeting with President Jacques Chirac in the French town of Saint-Malo, Blair moved the European defence project to a new level. The Saint-Malo Declaration of 4 December 1998 represented a triple crossing of the Rubicon which has had major consequences for European military capacity.[9] First, it conferred on the European Union directly the political decision-making capacity for crisis-management missions that the WEU had manifestly been ill-equipped to assume.[10] Second, it insisted that 'the Union must have the capacity for autonomous action, backed up by credible military forces, the means to decide to use them, and a readiness to do so, in order to respond to international crises'. The quest for autonomous EU military capacity has proceeded ever since. Third, the Declaration posited a new relationship between the European Union and NATO, contributing to the 'vitality of a modernized Atlantic Alliance', the precise definition of which has preoccupied planners to this day. There is little doubt that Blair's gamble was primarily motivated by a sense that, unless the European members of NATO made a concerted effort to improve their military capacity, the Alliance itself would begin to unravel.[11] The shift from a relatively fruitless quest for a European military identity towards the delivery of a European security and defence policy (ESDP) was a major leap forward.[12] It was not insignificant that the initiative came from the only two EU countries with power-projection capacity. The other European countries were summoned to follow the Franco-British lead.

The British Ministry of Defence took a major role in driving forward the debate on European military transformation. The decisions taken at the EU Council in Helsinki in December 1999, leading to the establishment of a Helsinki Headline Goal (HHG), were inspired by a series of papers drafted in Whitehall, as were most subsequent ESDP initiatives.[13] The HHG was conceived as a rough 'Force Catalogue' from which would be drawn appropriate resources for a range of hypothetical European missions, including the three main Petersberg Tasks. The main elements of the Force Catalogue were to be 60,000 troops, 100 ships, and 400 aircraft, deployable within sixty days and sustainable for one year. The emphasis, however, remained focused on quantities. Via a series of Capabilities Pledging Conferences in November 2000, November 2001, May 2003, and November 2004, this pool of resources was constantly refined and gradually brought into shape. Following the second Capabilities Commitment Conference of November 2001, EU defence officials and military planners in the Headline Goal Task Force (HGTF) sought to ensure at least minimal compliance with the stated objective of operationality by December 2003.

However, there were several major problems with the HHG. The first problem was the way forces were to be built up. Voluntary, bottom-up contributions might secure the raw numbers, but they could not guarantee the delivery, still less the mobilisation, of a coherent fighting force. Instead, the key concept had to be usability. In 2005, there were still almost 1.7 million troops in uniform in Europe. Of that number, only about 10 per cent were adequately trained even for serious peacekeeping operations, let alone for peace-making, still less for war-fighting. Of those 170,000, probably at most 50,000 could carry out the type of military operation needed in circumstances such as those in Iraq since 2003. Rotation requirements drop the number still more, leaving just 15,000 to 20,000 troops genuinely usable at any given time in serious military missions (Venusberg Group 2004). Yet simply increasing quantities was soon perceived as not only insufficient but inappropriate; what was required was far greater quality.

The second problem with the HHG had to do with the procurement of a new generation of strategic systems. If the European Union were to engage seriously in potentially distant crisis management operations, it needed the tools of modern force projection. The Union had identified the main areas of strategic deficiency.[14] But in order to generate an effective EU capacity in the areas of unmanned aerial vehicles, strategic transport, and air-to-air refueling, it was not enough to rely on voluntary efforts, or even to appoint a lead nation to chair a working group. There had to be collective political agreement to drive the process forward towards agreed targets. That implied top-down leadership, pooling, and specialisation. Such processes touched on sensitive issues of national sovereignty.

The third – and potentially biggest – problem with the HHG process was the absence of clear debate about the nature of the military operations the European Union might aim to mount. The original thinking behind the HHG derived from experiences in Kosovo. What the European Union had in mind – especially in the context of the reference in the Saint-Malo Declaration to the notion of autonomous forces – was the ability to carry out a Kosovo-type operation with minimal reliance on US inputs. This could be done in two ways. A Kosovo operation could have been mounted in 1999 with the European Union's existing military assets, but unlike the US-led operation, which depended largely on air power, it would have involved substantial numbers of ground troops and resulted in many casualties. Alternatively, the European Union could aim to develop a US-style capacity to fight high-level network-centric warfare (Arquilla and Ronfeldt 2001). This would require even greater defence spending and a more significant human resources challenge. Would the price be politically acceptable? If not, would something less than a fully integrated system – what has been called a 'network-enabled' capacity – be affordable? A European Network Enabling Capability (ENEC) would enable linkages between European forces rather than provide a single advanced network. Consequently, the ENEC would need to be developed in parallel with *a specifically European interoperability concept* to ensure European interoperability dominance over all operations likely to be generated by the European Security Strategy (Venusberg Group 2004: 12). Would such a system work? Answers were and remain elusive.[15] To confuse capabilities planning even further, the European Union decided in 2004 that it would engage in a more extensive range of missions. Article III-309 of the European Union's proposed Constitutional Treaty extended the Petersberg tasks to include '*joint disarmament operations*, humanitarian and rescue tasks, *military advice and assistance tasks, conflict prevention* and peacekeeping tasks, [and] tasks of combat forces undertaken for crisis management, including peacemaking *and post-conflict stabilization*'.[16] The emphasis was firmly on those missions with both a military and a political component. The 2004 Constitutional Treaty added the need to 'contribute to the fight against terrorism'. Yet that fight would require very different instruments from those needed to drive the Serbian army out of Kosovo (De Wijk 2002). How could Europe afford both when at the time it seemed unable to afford either? These internal contradictions at the heart of the HHG process required urgent attention.

The third EU Capabilities Conference, held in Brussels in May 2003, registered both progress and caution. On the one hand, it noted that the first phase of the European Capability Action Plan (ECAP), launched in 2001 to identify shortcomings in the HHG, had been successfully concluded, with nineteen panels activated to cover the majority of the shortfalls, and all Member States participating. On the other hand, it recognised that, 'at the upper end of the spectrum of scale and intensity', significant deficiencies still existed. The conference adopted ten priority areas in which improvements needed to be ensured, either through additional contributions, or through Member States' existing procurement programmes.[17] The ECAP process began to shift, in summer 2003, away from sheer quantities towards more qualitative approaches and criteria. Project groups were established to focus on solutions such as leasing, multi-nationalisation, and role specialisation. The European Union moved towards the recognition of 'coordination responsibility' for key procurement projects: Germany took the lead on strategic air lift; Spain on air-to-air refueling; the United Kingdom on headquarters; and the Netherlands on PGMs (precision-guided munitions) for delivery by EU F-16s.

From HHG to *Headline Goal 2010*: a qualitative breakthrough?

The most urgent need was soon recognised to be that of assembling a highly trained, deployable, and sustainable force to meet the challenging missions of the revised Petersberg tasks. This process was facilitated by a series of informal meetings of an EU Council of Defence Ministers. The very fact that Member States recognised the desirability of such top-down meetings constituted a major step forward. Defence ministers had previously been kept strictly subordinate to foreign ministers. Now, they were gradually becoming significant security policy-shapers. They were instrumental in helping move the debate on capacity away from the raw numbers of the HHG and towards a clear set of qualitative criteria. In addition, after the start of the Iraq War in 2003, the European Union devised its first ever 'Security Strategy' document, which included the broad outlines of its military objectives.

In 2004, the European Union entered a new and qualitatively different stage in the process of strengthening military capabilities, with the announcement of the new Headline Goal 2010, which was formally adopted at the European Council meeting on 17 June 2004. Building on the Helsinki Headline Goal, HG 2010 commits the Union 'to be able by 2010 to respond to a crisis with rapid and decisive action applying a fully coherent approach to the whole spectrum of crisis management operations covered by the Treaty on the European Union' (Council of the European Union 2004). Interoperability, deployability, and sustainability were at the heart of the project. The Member States identified a list of specific milestones within the 2010 horizon, including the establishment of both the European Defence Agency and the Civilian-Military Planning Cell by the end of 2004; the implementation of an EU strategic lift command by 2005; the ability by 2007 to deploy force packages at high readiness broadly based on EU battle-groups; the availability of an EU aircraft carrier and associated air wing and escort by 2008; and 'appropriate compatibility and network linkage of all communications equipment and assets' by 2010.

HG 2010, by focusing on small, rapidly deployable units capable of high-intensity warfare, successfully shifted the objective from quantity to quality. It also resolved, at least partially, the contradiction between a Kosovo-style capability and the requirements of the 'war on terrorism'. The newly created battlegroups, of which up to fifteen are projected for 2007 (listed in Table 5.2), can be used for both types of operation. Battlegroups (BG) are units of 1,500 troops prepared for combat in jungle, desert, or mountain conditions, deployable within fifteen days and sustainable in the field for up to thirty days. They are defined as 'the minimum military effective, credible, rapidly deployable, coherent force package capable of stand-alone operations or for the initial phase of larger operations'. The BG is based on a combined-arms battalion-size force and reinforced with combat support (CS) and combat service support (CSS) elements. It is associated with a force headquarters and with designated operational and strategic enablers such as strategic lift

Table 5.2 EU Nation-state participation in fifteen new battlegroups

Participating countries	Target date for deployability
France	2005
UK	2005
Italy	2005
Spain	2006
Germany, France, Belgium, Spain	2006
France, Belgium, Luxembourg	2006
Italy, Spain, Greece, Portugal	2006
Germany, Netherlands, Finland	2007
Germany, Czech Republic, Austria	2007
Italy, Hungary, Slovenia	2007
Poland, Germany, Slovakia, Latvia, Lithuania	2007
Sweden, Finland, Norway, Estonia, Ireland?	2007
UK, Netherlands	2007
Greece, Bulgaria, Romania, Cyprus	2007
Czech Republic, Slovakia	2007

and logistics. At a meeting of the Council of Defence Ministers on 21 November 2004, it was announced that thirteen BGs would be established, all to be operational by 2007 or sooner. Two more groups were announced in November 2005.

Member states can also offer niche capabilities, of which the following have been agreed: Cyprus, medical group; Lithuania, water purification unit; Greece, Athens Sealift Coordination Centre; France, structure of a headquarters for a multinational and deployable force. Cyprus has agreed to provide infrastructure. In February 2006 Ireland finally agreed to become a member of the BG structure (Power 2006). The European Union now has the capacity to undertake two concurrent operations, even almost simultaneously if necessary.

A European Defence Agency (EDA) subject to the authority of the European Council was called for in the draft Constitutional Treaty of August 2004. Armaments cooperation had hitherto taken place outside the EU framework. Two main reasons lay behind the change. The first was the relative failure of previous attempts to coordinate procurement and armaments cooperation. The second was the accelerating reality of ESDP and the associated need to link capabilities to armaments production. The urgency of these drivers was reflected in the fact that, in June 2003, the European Union agreed not to await ratification of the Treaty in order to launch the EDA but to create it immediately.

The stated objectives of the EDA were (Article III-311) (Schmitt 2004):

- contribute to identifying the Member States' military capability objectives and evaluating observance of the capability commitments given by the Member States;
- promote harmonisation of operational needs and adoption of effective, compatible procurement methods;
- propose multilateral projects to fulfil the objectives in terms of military capabilities, ensure coordination of the programmes implemented by the Member States and management of specific cooperation programmes;
- support defence technology research, and coordinate and plan joint research activities and the study of technical solutions meeting future operational needs;
- contribute to identifying and, if necessary, implementing any useful measure for strengthening the industrial and technological base of the defence sector and for improving the effectiveness of military expenditure.

The EDA is guided by a Steering Board meeting at the level of Defence Ministers, nominally headed by the High Representative for the Common Foreign and Security Policy (later to be called the Union Minister for Foreign Affairs) and managed by a Chief Executive.[18] It offers the first real opportunity for the European Union to bring its defence planning, military capability objectives, and armaments coordination in line with the urgent tasks it faces on the ground. The EU governments are thus poised to move towards more rational armaments and defence planning. The dynamics of ESDP suggest that they will progressively situate their national plans within a European framework. This will be the first step on a potentially very long road.

Another breakthrough came in 2003 in the field of operational planning. This was a contentious issue which had, for several years, pitted the United Kingdom against France. Paris had always been keen to develop autonomous EU operational planning capabilities, but London had resisted, arguing that this was an expensive duplication of an existing NATO capability. The United Kingdom insisted that, in the event of an 'EU-only' operation (i.e. without reference to NATO and without the support of NATO planning via Berlin Plus), such missions should have recourse to the national operational planning facilities of the United Kingdom (Northwood), of France (Creil) and, to a lesser extent, those of Germany, Italy, and Greece. However, at a contentious defence summit among France, Germany, Belgium, and Luxembourg on 29 April 2003, at the height of the Iraq crisis, the summiteers decided to forge ahead and create an 'EU' operational planning cell at a Belgian army site in Tervuren, a suburb of Brussels. This provoked outrage in Washington and London and, for a moment, seemed destined to derail the entire ESDP project (International Institute for Strategic Studies 2003). However, later that summer, Tony Blair sought to mend fences with his European partners, and a compromise was reached involving three distinct operational planning facilities. For EU operations under Berlin Plus, a dedicated EU unit has been attached to NATO at SHAPE Headquarters in Mons, Belgium. For most 'EU-only' operations, including most BG missions, an appropriate national headquarters will be adapted to planning for multinational operations. For certain 'EU-only' operations, particularly those involving combined civil and military dimensions, a dedicated and autonomous EU Civilian–Military Cell is being developed at ESDP headquarters in Brussels. This facility grew in 2005 to around 120 EU military personnel; it began its substantive work and now has the capacity to generate an operations centre.

By the end of 2004, the European Union was beginning to look like an increasingly credible potential military actor. In May 2005, the European Union published its third Capability Improvement Chart, listing no fewer than sixty-four 'capabilities' and their progress toward meeting qualitative readiness targets (or, in some cases, their shortcomings).[19] Significantly, some major improvements were found in areas with heavy 'legacy' inputs, including composite army aviation battalions and mechanised infantry battalions. Some qualitatively significant areas, such as Headquarters, Strategic Transport, NBC, and Medical Units, were recording better progress than expected. But other areas requiring substantial investment, such as intelligence, surveillance and target acquisition (ISTAR), space assets, SEAD, and PGMs, were still facing serious shortfalls or needing longer timelines for delivery. The Council of Defence Ministers introduced a 'Global Approach on Deployability' in 2003 to accelerate coordination of air-lift and sea-lift centers with a view to developing an EU Movement Coordination Cell (EUMCC). Success at reaching the ECAP targets remained dependent on meaningful political commitments by Member States to invest in shortfall areas and to continue the quest for multinational solutions. The EDA was intended to act both as a catalyst and as a benchmark.

Evaluating the first EU military missions

The process of defining priority areas for quality and capacity has been assisted by the lessons drawn from the first experiences of the European

Union in armed combat. Since January 2003, the European Union has launched (to May 2006) no fewer than fifteen international missions under the aegis of ESDP. With the exception of operation Althea, in Bosnia (which has involved some 7,000 troops), most of these missions involved between a few dozen and several hundred individuals (for a grand total of some 1,200). There have been three military missions and two military assistance missions, five police missions, two border control missions, two rule of law missions and a peace monitoring mission. These have taken place in fifteen different countries on three continents.

On 31 March 2003, the European Union launched its first ever military operation, a peacekeeping mission in the Former Yugoslav Republic of Macedonia (FYROM), taking over from a NATO force. Operation Concordia used NATO planning under the 'Berlin Plus' procedures. It deployed 357 troops, from all European Union states except Ireland and Denmark and from fourteen additional nations, an average of thirteen troops per participating state. In a small mountainous country, it succeeded in keeping the peace between bands of lightly armed irregulars and the Macedonian 'army', which boasts a defence budget less than half that of Luxembourg. This was an operation high in political symbolism and extremely modest in terms of military footprint. Concordia's primary value was that it allowed the European Union to test its recently agreed procedures covering every aspect of the mounting of a military operation, albeit a modest one, such as command and control, use-of-force policy, logistics, financing, and legal arrangements and memoranda of understanding with host nations (Messervy-Whiting 2003).

Then, from June to September 2003, the European Union launched its first ever autonomous operation outside of the NATO framework. Operation Artemis in the Democratic Republic of Congo offered even richer lessons about European Union capabilities (Cornish 2004). The mission involved rapid force projection to a distance of 6,500 km into unknown and hostile terrain. The initial assessment suggests that it was a success. France was the 'framework nation', supplying 1,785 of the 2,200 troops deployed. Sixteen other 'troop contributing nations' were involved, offering strategic air lift (Germany, Greece, United Kingdom, Brazil, and Canada), engineers (United Kingdom), helicopters (South Africa), and special forces (Sweden). Operational planning was conducted from the French Centre de Planification et de Conduite des Opérations (CPCO) at Creil, to which were seconded officers from thirteen other countries, thus demonstrating the potential for multi-nationalisation of a national HQ. The operation exemplified rapid deployment (seven days after UN Security Council Resolution 1484 on 30 May 2003), a single command structure, appropriately trained forces, clear rules of engagement, good incorporation of multinational elements, excellent inter-service cooperation, and adequate communications. NATO procedures were used throughout. Artemis demonstrated that the European Union can undertake a peacekeeping operation on a significant scale, even at some distance from Europe.

The transfer from NATO to the European Union of responsibility for the Stabilisation Force (SFOR) in Bosnia-Herzegovina, in December 2004 (*Operation Althea*), represented an even greater test of the European Union's military muscle. The initial NATO force deployed in Bosnia-Herzegovina (IFOR, December 1995) involved some 60,000 troops. This was scaled down repeatedly, reaching a total of 12,000 in the follow-up SFOR in January 2003. Projections for 2004 foresaw a further reduction to about 7,000 troops organised in ten battlegroups of around 750 soldiers each. *Operation Althea* has been the European Union's most ambitious military mission to date. In addition to stabilising Bosnia-Herzegovina, Althea allowed the European Union to experiment with large-scale helicopter manoeuvres, combating drug-running, organising the voluntary surrender of small arms, and undertaking liaison and observation team (LOT) activities, peace support training schemes, and psychological operations. The operation exemplified the increasing demands on European soldiers for a broad range of skills and training. These military operations were complemented in November–December 2005 and April 2006 by two significant EU-only military exercises (Milex 05 and EVAC 06) which focused, respectively, on the activation of a fully fledged EU Operation Headquarters and on that of an ambitious evacuation mission. A further exercise, scheduled for September–October 2006, focused on the development of procedures for a Comprehensive EU Crisis Management capability.

The most distant mission has been the EU Monitoring Mission in Aceh whose remit has been to oversee the peace agreement between the government of Indonesia and the *Free Aceh Movement* (GAM) which in 2005 put an end to thirty years of civil war. This purely civilian mission has supervised the decommissioning and destruction of weapons, the demobilisation of the GAM and the reintegration of its soldiers into civil society and the return of a civil rights regime in the troubled province. Initially mandated for a six-month stay, the mission was renewed in April 2006 at the request of the two parties. Although all the details of a final settlement – above all political – remain elusive, the European Union has demonstrated its potential to push forward a peace process already in train. The same cannot be said of the situation in Darfur where, after much hesitation and many false rumours, the European Union decided against sending in a major military force. The military challenge and the strategic instability in the area were considered to beyond the scope of ESDP – and indeed of NATO. Both organisations elected for a more supportive role, providing military assistance to the African Union forces engaged in the effort to enforce a peace settlement. It has been a similar story in the DR Congo, where the EU mission has sought essentially to reintegrate into civil society elements of the Congolese army and to help foster good governance. These various missions, minor in scope, suggest that the European Union's capacity to do other than provide band-aid to the deeply torn African continent is limited. While the stakes for the whole of Africa in the outcome to this regional crisis remain exceptionally high, the European Union has failed to contribute in a manner consistent with its future ambitions and historical responsibilities for Africa.

Elsewhere, the European Union has contributed in less martial ways. Two missions for the training of judges, jurists and penitentiary officers – in Georgia and in Iraq – have successfully delivered, respectively, 300 and 800 trained officials capable of contributing to the establishment of the rule of law in societies emerging from totalitarianism. Two border control missions have also been mounted in areas where the shift to stability and good governance is critical for regional security: at Rafah, the main frontier crossing between Gaza and Egypt; and on the Moldova–Ukrainian border. The objective of these missions is to tackle international smuggling and criminality, to inculcate best practice and to stabilise critical choke-points for the passage of human cargoes.

But the European Union's greatest specialism has emerged as that of the police mission. This reflects the enormous energy and input into Civilian Capabilities in the context of the Civilian Headline Goal 2008. In post-conflict situations, the most urgent need is often for local security forces and above all for a highly professional police force. The European Union has made a substantial commitment in this regard both through deployment of police officers and through local training schemes in Macedonia, Bosnia, Congo (Kinshasa) and Palestine. This is a new departure for the international community and one which is proving as necessary and pragmatic on the ground as it is politically symbolic of an entirely new approach to security and stability.

It cannot be argued that, as a result of these fifteen missions, the European Union has emerged as a major new strategic actor in world politics. For the most part, the missions are small in scale and limited in scope. However, they do represent significant progress in a number of important respects. First, they are the first overseas missions undertaken by the European Union and belie the sceptics who have long insisted that the European Union, being incapable of coordinating grand strategy, should stick to what it does best in the area of foreign and security policy: trade and aid. Second, the missions, covering three continents, and addressing some of the most sensitive challenges of regional stability, suggest that the European Union both can and does conceptualize its 'intervention role' in a global context. Third, the missions have covered a great variety of functions, ranging from juridical training to policing, to border controls and robust military peacekeeping operations. That spread reflects the range and complexity of the civil–military culture which underlies the ESDP in general and the ESS in particular.

At the heart of these projects lies the problem of training. Standardisation and the quest for interoperability across the continent is a growing feature of military training. Most future EU missions are likely to be multinational, as part of a UN, NATO, or EU force. Significant standardisation of equipment will have to await the effects of the European Defence Agency and the rationalisation of procurement. It is through NATO's Partnership for Peace programmes, somewhat ironically, that the majority of the EU Member States are currently improving their capacity for interoperability. These programmes affect formerly neutral countries such as Austria and Sweden as well as new-accession countries such as Hungary and Romania. Language skills are highly prized, but English is increasingly becoming the *de facto* language for multinational force communication. (Even Operation Artemis, which was overwhelmingly French in composition and command, was officially conducted in English.) France and a number of other countries have been pressing the European Union to inaugurate a joint EU military training academy, but the resistance of other countries (notably the United Kingdom) has to date prevented this. In 2002, the first of a series of international conferences for cadets from the military academies of all EU Member States (as well as for a number of observers from the US military academy at West Point) was organised at Saint-Cyr; a second such conference was held in 2003 at the Belgian Royal Military Academy.

Notwithstanding these developments, the fact remains that Europe's twenty-five separate militaries are trained to very different levels of combat intensity. Whereas most US troops are trained to be able to cope with the requirements of full-scale warfare involving elements of C4ISTAR, satellite intelligence, sensor-to-shooter networks, and nuclear deterrence, only the United Kingdom and, to some extent, France, have forces trained to this level. A few EU militaries – Germany, Italy, the Netherlands, and Spain – can approach the challenge of advanced expeditionary warfare. As for the rest, force training gives them a capability for medium-level 'Petersberg' peace-support tasks. A sizeable number of countries – Finland, Ireland, Cyprus, Estonia, Latvia, Lithuania, Malta, Slovakia, and Slovenia – are unable to deal with more than the lowest-level Petersberg missions.

Conclusion

European military capacity, after almost a decade of stagnation from 1989 to 1999, has come a long way in a few short years. Progress in procurement, planning, rationalisation, force transformation, and general 'usability' has been impressive since the turn of the millennium. But the European Union still has a long way to go before it can overcome all its shortcomings and emerge as a fully credible coordinated military actor able to carry out the full range of Petersberg tasks. The European Union does not aspire to become a military actor on a par with the United States, nor does it think in classical terms of territorial defence. The crisis management tasks it aims to carry out represent a new, professional 'security fire-fighting' service adapted to the modern world. But the unprecedented nature of its objectives also poses one of its most difficult dilemmas. In order to embark on the type of low-casualty operations implicit in network-centric warfare, the European Union would need to invest far more than is currently available in new R&D projects and in personnel management. That may be justifiable in the United States because the US military, in addition to policing the world, is also configured to guarantee the defence of the United States. However, the more limited ambitions of ESDP rule out such spending levels in Europe. The European Union is likely, therefore, to limit its interoperability aspirations to the challenges of 'network-enabled' capabilities.

At the level of recruitment and training, the European Union faces an enormous task of matching ends and means on the field of operations. A start has been made and progress is visible, but the challenge has only just been taken up. Above all, the European Union needs to address its wasteful spending patterns. The EU-25, in 2004, spent almost US$230 billion on defence – approximately half the US defence budget for that year (see Table 5.3). That is almost four times the defence budget of the second biggest military spender on earth (China, at $62.5 billion) and more than that of the six next biggest spenders put together (China, Russia, Japan, Saudi Arabia, India and South Korea together total $226.5 billion). The European Union collectively gets very little bang for this enormous amount of money. Out of that $230 billion, the European Union still attempts to fund twenty-five armies, twenty-one air forces, and eighteen navies, for no reason that is any longer obvious or clear. Just three countries in the European Union – France, the United Kingdom, and Germany – together spend 61 per cent of the combined EU-25 expenditure. If Italy, as the fourth largest spender, is added to the trio, these countries account for almost 75 per cent of the EU-25 defence expenditure. By contrast, the average expenditure of the other twenty-one EU states comes to just $2,869 million, less the defence

Table 5.3 EU Member States' defence expenditure for 2004, with comparison to the United States

	US$	US$ per capita	Percentage of GDP	Active-duty (000s)
France	51,698 m	855 (1)	2.5 (2)	254.0
UK	49,618 m	823 (2)	2.3 (3)	205.0
Germany	37,790 m	458 (10)	1.4 (14=)	284.0
Italy	30,537 m	525 (7=)	1.8 (5=)	191.0
Spain	12,588 m	312 (12)	1.2 (20=)	147.0
Netherlands	9,607 m	588 (5)	1.6 (8=)	53.0
Greece	5,866 m	550 (6)	2.8 (1)	163.0
Sweden	5,307 m	590 (4)	1.5 (11=)	27.0
Poland	4,605 m	119 (22)	1.9 (4)	141.0
Belgium	4,361 m	421 (11)	1.2 (20=)	36.0
Denmark	3,558 m	657 (3)	1.4 (14=)	21.0
Portugal	2,830 m	268 (15)	1.6 (8=)	44.0
Finland	2,483 m	476 (9)	1.3 (18=)	28.0
Austria	222 m	271 (14)	0.8 (23=)	39.0
Czech Rep.	976 m	192 (18)	1.8 (5=)	22.0
Hungary	530 m	152 (19)	1.5 (11=)	32.0
Ireland	907 m	228 (17)	0.5 (25)	10.0
Slovakia	729 m	134 (20)	1.7 (7)	20.0
Slovenia	511 m	254 (16)	1.6 (8=)	6.0
Lithuania	311 m	86 (24)	1.4 (14=)	13.0
Cyprus	227 m	293 (13)	1.4 (14=)	10.0
Luxembourg	243 m	525 (7=)	0.8 (23=)	0.9
Latvia	179 m	77 (25)	1.3 (18=)	5.0
Estonia	172 m	128 (22)	1.5 (11=)	4.0
Malta	52 m	131 (21)	1.0 (22)	2.0
EU-15 Totals	219,615 m			1,502.6
CEE-10 Totals	10,292 m			255.0
EU-25 Totals	229,907 m			1,757.6
EU-15 Average	14,641 m	503	1.51	
CEE-10 Average	1,029 m	157	1.51	
EU-25 Average	9,196 m	364	1.51	
Norway	*4,431 m*	*968*	*1.8 25*	
Turkey	*10,115 m*	*146*	*3.3 514*	
United States (for comparison)	455,908 m	1,555	3.8 1,473	

Source: IISS, *The Military Balance 2005–2006*
Bold = members of NATO. *Italic* = accession to the EU in 2004.
Ranking shown in parentheses. Again, Turkey and Norway have been added for comparison. Norway would rank as the *biggest defence spender per capita* in Europe, and Turkey would rank as the *largest army* with the *highest percentage of GDP*.

budget of, for example, Vietnam ($3,177 million). As long as this duplication exists, return on investment will be sub-optimal.

A major rationalisation of the European Union's defence spending is overdue. The duplication of infrastructure and support services for these separate armed forces amounts to a huge waste of resources. Alone, most EU member States would be in no position even to defend their own territory. It is not necessarily greater spending that is required, as is so often asserted. Wiser spending would certainly help. But only once the European Union has clearly established what it hopes to achieve, with what force levels and with what state of equipment, can it have any clear idea about how much money is needed. Until then, its force transformation programmes will remain incomplete.

Notes

1 This chapter is a modified version of a chapter originally published as: (2006) 'The Transformation of European Military Capability 1989–2005', in C.L. Gilroy and C. Williams (eds), *Service to Country: Personnel Policy and the Transformation of Western Militaries*, Cambridge MA: MIT Press. The author is grateful to Curtis Gilroy, Cindy Williams and the MIT Press for permission to reproduce large extracts of it here.

2 Gordon (2000), one of ESDP's strongest US supporters, worried that European military capacity could prove to be an 'empty institutional distraction' leading to 'impotence and recrimination'.

3 Other military statistics cited in this chapter are taken from the appropriate annual volume of *The Military Balance* (published by OUP from 1995).

4 'Le nucléaire, c'est la non-bataille'.

5 Jacques Poos uttered the optimistic words: 'It is the hour of Europe, not of the USA'.

6 It is often forgotten, when referring to the Balkans as 'out-of-area', that the region lies inside an EU space bounded by Greece in the south, Italy in the west and Austria in the north. In 2007, the accession of Romania and Bulgaria completed the EU 'encirclement' of the former Yugoslavia.

7 The WEU, dating back to 1948, was reorganised in 1955 as the only European body with responsibility for intra-European defence liaison. Moribund for thirty years, it was reactivated in the late 1980s (Deighton 1997).

8 The 'Berlin Plus' arrangements allowed the European Union to enjoy 'assured access to NATO planning', 'presumed access to NATO [i.e. US] assets and capabilities', and a pre-designated Europeans-only chain of command. The arrangements were agreed in principle at a NATO summit in Berlin in June 1996. The devil proved to be in the detail and it took six years of hard bargaining (the 'Berlin Plus negotiations') to nail down the details. This was finally achieved in December 2002 (Haine 2003: 178–80).

9 The Saint-Malo Declaration is accessible via the *ESDP Core Documents* series published by the European Union's Institute for Security Studies: www.iss-eu.org/chaillot/chai47e.pdf

10 Space does not permit any analysis of the European Union's new security and defence institutions; for such an analysis, see Howorth and Keeler (2003).

11 The author was informed by a senior UK Foreign Office official, in spring 2000, that the United Kingdom 'would never have touched Saint-Malo with a barge-

pole' had London not been convinced that this was the price of keeping the Alliance in business.

12 The acronym ESDP was coined by the European Council in June 1999 to distinguish this relatively ambitious – and autonomous – EU project from the NATO-dependent mechanisms of ESDI.

13 For the Helsinki Headline Goal, see *ESDP Core Documents* series published by the European Union's Institute for Security Studies: www.iss-eu.org/chaillot/chai47e.pdf

14 The ten areas of deficiency identified were: air-to-air refueling; combat search and rescue; headquarters; nuclear, biological and chemical defences; special operations forces; theatre ballistic missile defence; strategic air mobility; space; unmanned aerial vehicle/surveillance, and target acquisition (UAV/STA) units; and interoperability (Missiroli 2003).

15 It should be noted that, in the 2003 war in Iraq, the United States and the United Kingdom fought in different geographic zones partly because their battlefield communications technologies could not be properly networked.

16 Italics indicate new items added to the original (1992) Petersberg tasks.

17 See the list of ten areas of deficiency in note 14.

18 After a fierce turf battle between France and the United Kingdom, Nick Witney, the former head of the UK MOD's International Security Policy Division, was named as the first Chief Executive.

19 It is notable that a further draft of this Capabilities Improvement Chart was published at the time of the Defence Ministers meeting in Brussels on 21 November 2005. Absolutely no changes were recorded between May and November.

6 The European Security Strategy and the partners

Roberto Menotti and Maria Francesca Vencato

In search of partners to secure Europe

The genesis and direction of the ESS cannot be viewed in a vacuum: the policy context – both international and internal to the European Union – is essential to assess its full potential and ongoing evolution as a framework for action. At least two international developments were crucial to the rather swift adoption of the document: the 9/11 attacks and the transatlantic/intra-European rift over Iraq. Simultaneously, two issues internal to the Union affected the European debate that eventually produced the ESS: the first is enlargement, as a process which is reconfiguring the European Union's interface with the outside world to its East and South as well as its membership. The second, more technical issue is the growing recognition among the primary contributors to CFSP and ESDP that a limit had been reached: the bottom-up approach to strengthening ESDP (which can be summed up as policy convergence through joint or integrated capabilities) was insufficient to generate consensus on too many post-9/11 priorities, particularly the 'Wider Middle East'. This is how the key actors became convinced that a basic common vision had to be solemnly reaffirmed in very broad terms, but also formulated (for the first time ever) in the specific form of a threat assessment, a set of strategic objectives and the related policy implications.

Due to the interplay of these factors, the ESS needed to reconcile partly conflicting tendencies, by setting the foundation for a solid but reformed transatlantic relationship while beginning to define areas (both geographical and functional) of EU specialisation and increased autonomy. Simultaneously, it had to open up the Union's external action to new and growing partnerships while reaffirming the central value of established links and commitments (from the EU–NATO arrangement to the Euro-Med framework). Lastly, the macro-regional role of an enlarging Union had to be connected to its responsibilities in the much broader context of the UN as the prime multilateral institution.

Even looking at the ESS as a self-contained document, the specific section on 'working with partners' – which comes last – should be understood as part of a broader argument rather than as a stand-alone statement. First, a key element of Europe's post-WWII history is recalled early on: 'The United States has played a critical role in European integration and European security, in particular through NATO'. It is a recognition of the fact that the transatlantic legacy is still relevant. This is immediately followed by a concise lesson learned from the post-Cold War experience: 'The end of the Cold War has left the United States in a dominant position as a military actor. However, no single country is able to tackle today's complex problems on its own' – in other words, reminding even the United States of its own limitations. The second individual country to be singled out is Russia as 'a major factor in our security and prosperity', pointing to an important but incomplete process: 'Respect for common values will reinforce progress towards a strategic partnership'. Then follows what we may label the European Union's 'global outreach': 'Our history, geography and cultural ties give us links with every part of the world: our neighbours in the Middle East, our partners in Africa, in Latin America, and in Asia. These relationships are an important asset to build on'.

Beside this rather diverse list of neighbours and actual or potential partners, to which we will return in the conclusion of our analysis, the concept of partnerships is presented as a general modus operandi for the Union: 'There are few if any problems we can deal with on our own. The threats described above are common threats, shared with all our closest partners. International cooperation is a necessity'. The multilateral mode is of course naturally suited to the European Union's own founding principle of multilateral cooperation – and this assumption (which most Europeans take for granted) has been reinforced by the explicit adoption of 'effective multilateralism' as the hallmark of Europe's external action. Leaving aside the UN framework as the main expression of effective multilateralism – which is the subject of a separate chapter in this study – we will focus on the more selective groupings. The general notion of partnerships cuts across various areas of EU external action. The ESS explicitly envisages two options in pursuit of the Union's objectives: 'multilateral cooperation in international organisations' and 'partnerships with key actors'. For the purposes of the present analysis, we will identify three main formats and a large question mark: in the first, the Union leads a policy effort by offering a framework for potential partners but acting in full autonomy; in the second format, the European Union plays a supporting role by virtue of its expertise or particular value added; in the third format, it 'inter-operates' in the context of efforts led by the United States. The last type of relationship, which we pose as a question mark, is a sort of great power concert. In reality, these scenarios will sometimes overlap, but the ESS seems to point to different contingencies in which features of one of the four will be predominant. We will return in our conclusions to the question of how clear this distinction actually is and whether it should be better articulated. A central argument we will make is that, if and when the European Union will find itself having to team up with 'key actors' – mostly on an *ad hoc* basis – sharing costs and responsibilities, the ESS has been and will remain insufficient to provide much guidance.

A broad perspective is justified, in our view, by the fact that the ESS is a fairly recent policy document, and one which has to blend with other established policy areas, institutional channels and instruments. Therefore, we will take into consideration a range of issues, including the ongoing definition of the European Union's neighbourhood, since this is the practical starting point for the wider projection of the European vision of the world. The Union's own identity, like that of any other world-class power of the past and the present, is shaped, first and foremost, by its immediate environment. In the context of conflict prevention and threat prevention, the European Union redefines its role in building security in its proximity, or neighbourhood. One of the goals set in the ESS is indeed to shape the quality of governments and improve the democratic quality of international society, starting with 'a ring of well governed countries' to the east and along the Mediterranean shores. While the irreplaceable transatlantic link and the much broader (but looser) UN framework are essential requirements for the implementation of the ESS to the South of Europe, particularly the Mediterranean basin and the African continent, to the East the European Union seems more willing to play a direct role in increasing regional security and stability. The enlargement to the new Member States of Central and Eastern Europe has firmly established a leading position of the Union in the region, ensuring significant leverage through bilateral channels (in a sort of hub-and-spokes configuration). Even more importantly, the European Union is laying here the foundation for its global role: to be taken seriously as a world security actor, it will first have to develop and nurture a working model for stability and prosperity in its own region. This is why the development of the Neighbourhood policy and the engagement with 'partners' cannot be wholly separated, politically and conceptually.

The European Union has several peace-building, crisis-management and resolution instruments at its disposal: development co-operation, trade, human rights/democratisation, environmental protection, electoral observation, arms control, political dialogue, support for peace initiatives, post-conflict relief and humanitarian aid, confidence-building measures, rebuilding of government structures, police reform, peacekeeping, etc. All these forms of external action require, to varying degrees, close cooperation with local groups (governmental and non-governmental) as well as other outside actors – thus, forms of partnership.

Approach and mechanisms

The European Union's policy statements are replete with references to what we can loosely define as a partnership approach to security. Conflict prevention has long received attention from the Commission and the (former) Development Council.[1] In the 2001 Commission Communication (European Commission 2001) and in the Development Council meeting reports, the element of conflict prevention is understood as inherently related to all external assistance policies of the Union, particularly those supporting regional integration and trade links. Poverty is seen as a threat to stability and a source of insecurity. The growing gap between haves and haves-not (especially in key areas such as the Mediterranean basin) is aggravated by the fact that state policies often reflect the lack of government accountability. Development presupposes a fair and efficient provision of public goods.

The concept of 'structural stability'[2] (put forward already in a 1996 Commission Communication) is also consistent with this overall approach, as well as the notion of human security. The promotion of sustainable economic development, of democracy and respect for human rights, of viable political structures, healthy environmental and social conditions represent the core elements of structural stability. A crucial condition is to manage change without resorting to conflict. A sound macro-economic environment is considered by the Union as a critical factor to both structural stability and human security. To this end, in the framework of the new financial perspectives 2007–13, the macro-economic assistance instrument of the Union aims precisely at making a substantial contribution to economic stabilisation while supporting economic reforms in partner countries.

A similar approach is applied to the evolution of the European Union's defence capabilities. The Petersberg tasks and the Headline Goal 2010 specify that the European Union envisions its engagement in crisis management primarily in coordination with other international actors – chiefly NATO, the UN and regional actors.

Within three months of the adoption of the ESS, Western Europe suffered its worst terrorist attack, the Madrid bombings. This led to the acceleration of measures already under way for improved EU coordination on homeland security and a Council declaration on combating terrorism (Robinson 2005). This contains numerous references to the use of policy dialogue and aid instruments with third countries in countering the terrorist threat:

> Target actions under EU external relations towards priority third countries where counter-terrorist capacity or commitment to combating terrorism needs to be enhanced. [. . .] Include effective counter-terrorism clauses in all agreements with third countries. [. . .] Make more efficient use of external assistance programmes to address factors which can contribute to the support for terrorism, including in particular support for good governance and the rule of law. [. . .] Analyse and evaluate the commitment of countries to combat terrorism on an ongoing basis.
>
> (European Council 2004)

In sum, as this wording indicates, even the European Union's reaction to one of the most shocking – if not unpredicted – events in several years was not to shift dramatically the centre of gravity of its external policies, but instead to adjust existing approaches and initiate some new mechanisms.

Although we will not get into the details of the Neighbourhood Policy, a brief overview of some of its elements is relevant to clarifying the challenges of implementing the 'partnership approach', particularly with regard to the crucial regions of the former Soviet space and the Mediterranean/Middle East area.

Europe as regional leader

The new instruments for the European Union's external assistance redefine the role of the Union as a global actor. The geographic instruments redefine the role of the Union according to the logic of interlocking circles: the Western Balkans with the new Pre-Accession Instrument; the Eastern European and the South-Mediterranean countries with the European Neighbourhood and Partnership Instrument; some of the developing countries with the Development Cooperation Instrument and the 'developed' countries with a separate instrument for Cooperation with Industrialized Countries. Each instrument comprises a 'policy mix' encompassing the components of structural stability and human security. The most innovative is the ENPI, whereby the allocation of the Union's assistance is made truly *conditional* on the implementation of *ad hoc* political reforms for each security dimension as outlined in the ENPI's Action Plans. Through these contractual arrangements, embracing cooperation and de facto avoiding negative conditionality, the European Union relies on a system of 'passive enforcement' of its own rules.

Beside the Partnership and Cooperation Agreements and the Association Agreements, another important channel the European Union can activate is the regional programmes, designed to extend the Neighbourhood framework to specific regions where inherent political instability could provoke destabilising effects on the Union's neighbours. The European Union has recently developed a regional ENPI programme, which includes Central Asia even though the region is not a mainstreamed recipient under the instrument. The programme is heavily influenced by continuing commitments from the Tacis regional programme (transport networks, energy, trade, education, border management).

It is worth noting that knowledge of local situations becomes increasingly critical in the context of the 'negotiable' approach of the ENPI: unlike the enlargement process, which was mainly unilateral (with the Union dictating specific conditions to the partner country), here the Union has to agree with the partner country (mainly the national government) about the priority areas where reforms and assistance are needed.

Just as the ENPI Central Asia programme can be considered as an extension of the Neighbourhood policy to the East, the formulation of the EU Strategic Partnership with the Mediterranean can as well be considered as an extension of the Neighbourhood Policy to the Mediterranean basin. The EU Strategic Partnership with the Mediterranean and the Middle East was adopted in June 2004[3] and should be seen as complementary to the Euro-Mediterranean Partnership (EMP)[4] launched in 1995. In the framework of the EMP, the Southern partners do not act as a group and have shown very little enthusiasm for multilateral programmes and activities. This lack of political integration reflects the limited nature of economic links among the Southern States themselves. The June 2004 Strategy has reaffirmed the EMP's approach, adding a politico-military dimension to the traditional economic focus of the European Union's Mediterranean policies.

Since at least 2003, there has been an interest in extending the coverage of the EMP (and of what would become ENPI) to countries outside the Barcelona process.[5] Reinforcing the 'pull effect' of the EMP and the ENPI on countries such as Iran, Iraq, and the whole Gulf region, has probably become essential in order to tackle some of the most delicate and controversial issues mentioned in the ESS, particularly WMD proliferation and the fight against terrorism. A policy framework already exists to incorporate the entire 'Wider Middle East': the strategy document carrying precisely that title that was adopted in June 2005 by the European Council. This would clearly require transatlantic coordination as well, and such an exercise would, in turn, facilitate more synergy with the NATO Mediterranean Dialogue (MD).[6]

An interesting case of an EU-led regional framework is the Northern Dimension, which embraces those countries situated in the region extending from Iceland in the west across to Northwest Russia, from the Norwegian, Barents and Kara Seas in the north to the southern coast of the Baltic Sea. The initiative was launched at the Luxembourg European Council in December 1997 and aims at the promotion of policy dialogue and concrete cooperation. It interacts with other regional bodies, such as the Council of the Baltic Sea States (CBSS) and the Barents Euro Arctic Council (BEAC), the Arctic Council (AC) and the Nordic Council of Ministers.

The Action Plan for the Northern Dimension will be increasingly related to the PCA between the European Union and Russia and the ENPI Neighbourhood Programmes. Through enhanced cooperation in particular areas such as cross-border management, justice and home affairs, transport routes and energy supplies, the European Union Northern Dimension could become a model of the EU capability to integrate with sub-regional fora.[7]

Supporting others

The European Union can serve as a useful counterpart to other regional organisations in their effort to strengthen regional cooperation, reduce political tensions and increase economic interdependence. Growing links with the African Union and ASEAN represent indeed two instances in which the ESS can be implemented by supporting a regional set-up with an *ad hoc* European Union instrument (Africa) and promoting security dialogues in a multilateral framework (ASEAN).

Africa

The Union has recently formulated a new Strategy for Africa in an effort to coordinate bilateral and multilateral efforts for the region to address the challenges of sustainable development while achieving the Millennium Development Goals. It proposes to launch a number of new initiatives, including an ambitious Governance Initiative and a Partnership for Infrastructure. Under the former, the European Union will, for instance, provide support for reforms triggered by the African Peer Review Mechanism (APRM), a tool for peer review and peer learning in good democratic governance by and for Africans. There is a clear understanding of the key requirements without which sustainable development in Africa will not be possible: peace, security and good governance.

For the purpose of strengthening the political and economic integration of Africa, the Union mainly relies on the African Union and the NEPAD contributions to African sustainable development. Cooperation with the African Union has consisted mainly of support for capacity building and logistical transfer rather than active European Union involvement. The new Strategy attempts to provide a coordinated response to the problems of poverty, insecurity and instability within a multilateral framework.

The creation of the Peace and Security Council of the African Union (at the 2002 Durban Summit) for the prevention, management and resolution of conflicts, modelled on EU structures, was warmly welcomed in Europe. This has given impetus to the launching of the African Peace Facility, as the first EU attempt to contribute directly to a common security goal within the framework of the UN system. Under the Peace Facility, no funds can be transferred to support direct military expenses. The long-term sustainability of the Facility will mainly depend on the development of the Peace and Security Council, which is expected to manage it. An EU grant of €250 million to the African Peace Facility came in 2004, in response to an African Union request for help in strengthening its regional peacekeeping capability. The modality was controversial because Member States funded the initiative by shaving 1.5 per cent off the development allocation of each African country in the European Development Fund. This was meant to be a one-off decision, but the framing of the new Stability instrument will provide the opportunity to replicate this type of support from the European Community budget.

The proposed EU instrument is rather similar to the stability funds set up by the Danish and Dutch governments, as well as in the two 'pools' (global and African) whereby the Foreign, Defence and Development ministries in the UK have agreed to make coordinated responses to peacekeeping needs. Like these national models, the Stability instrument would combine ODA-eligible and ODA-ineligible funding. Its aims are to respond to crises in order to re-establish the conditions for regular aid, and confronting global and regional transborder challenges, technological threats and weapons proliferation. There is still no policy document setting out criteria for the instrument's use, but the draft articles specify that the 'development of peacekeeping and peace support capacity in partnership with international, regional and sub-regional organisations' is envisaged along with 'military monitoring and peacekeeping' and the provision that 'peace enforcement operations shall require a UN mandate'. But, 'with the current exception of some elements of peace support operations, most assistance delivered will qualify as DAC-eligible', meaning that arms, ammunition, recurrent military expenditure, military training for combat, and any direct financing of

EU military activity would not be permitted. Given its nature, this form of support seems particularly suited for EU initiatives in the African continent, to the extent that there will be sufficient determination to tackle potential conflict situations early on, in close cooperation with local partners and possibly with the involvement of international institutions such as the World Bank.

The European Union has expressed its readiness to undertake peace-support operations as a 'subcontractor' to the UN, making use of the 'battle-group concept' providing for the creation of 1,500-strong rapidly deployable force packages. The European Union and the UN already closely cooperate in the field of conflict prevention and early warning – a necessary tool for the implementation of the approach outlined above – and in September 2003 a joint declaration on cooperation on crisis management was signed. Such a format is widely expected (and partly designed) to be used first and foremost in Africa.

ASEAN

The whole of the Asian continent is becoming increasingly important for the European Union. Interestingly, the Association of Southeast Asian Nations (ASEAN) is by far the European Union's oldest regional partner. In recent years, the Association has rather successfully promoted the integration of its members by redefining its role through the creation of three main 'sub-communities': the ASEAN Security Community (AEC), the ASEAN Economic Community (AEC) and the ASEAN Socio-Cultural Community (ASCC).

ASEAN has opened up its founding Treaty of Amity and Cooperation to other partners (most notably India and China), and has established links with the Asia–Pacific Economic Cooperation (APEC, which includes the United States), thus further raising its relevance from a European standpoint – beside the existing commercial ties and growing energy interests. In fact, the Asia–Europe Meeting (ASEM), launched in 1996, was in part a response to the establishment of APEC. ASEAN has become an increasingly attractive partner for the European Union insofar as its logic of interlocking circles (ASEAN members; ASEAN sub-communities; APEC; and ASEM itself) resembles the European approach, linking security, economic and political concerns at a macro-regional level.

Throughout the years, the Union has increasingly supported the Association's efforts to promote regional dialogue on security, particularly through the European Union membership in the ASEAN Regional Forum (ARF) and in the Council for Security Cooperation in Asia–Pacific (CSAP).

Given the growing focus on the fight against terrorism, regional security in Asia has been increasingly perceived as potentially affecting Europe's security much more directly than in the past. The 14th ASEM meeting and the adoption of the Joint Declaration on Cooperation to Combat Terrorism represent an attempt to make the European Union's external action more complementary with existing regional efforts. The deployment in September 2005 of a monitoring mission to Aceh, with the contribution of some ASEAN countries, as well as Norway and Switzerland, marked a direct commitment by the Union to support the implementation of the peace agreement between the Indonesian government and the Free Aceh Movement. This is an ESDP civilian operation (the first of its kind in Asia) which dovetails reconstruction and institution-building objectives in the context of a new political process.

Interoperating with the indispensable ally: the EU–US link

The United States is indisputably the dominant actor in the field of 'hard security', not only by virtue of its unmatched capabilities, but also in terms of Washington's established practice of claiming the key positions in the chain of command of any large scale multinational military operation. From a European perspective, the NATO experience contributes to this state of affairs, since the integrated military structures of the Alliance have long been relying on key US assets and procedures. This is why so much of the security cooperation with the United States can be placed under the rubric of 'interoperability'. In abstract terms, interoperability is a neutral concept: as explained in the European Union's Headline Goal 2010, it can be broadly defined as

> the ability of [EU] armed forces to work together and to interact with other civilian tools. It is an instrument to enhance the effective use of military capabilities as a key enabler in achieving EU's ambitions in Crisis Management Operations' (Council of the European Union 2004).

In the context of the transatlantic debate, it has acquired a narrower connotation, often becoming equivalent to 'plugging' into American systems and networks. However, a wider political premise is needed to make sense of the current predicament in this area from the European Union's perspective.

The starting point for any analysis of the prospects of a functioning EU–US partnership must be the existence of the NATO alliance. This obvious fact is, in itself, part of the problem and part of the solution. Of course, the transatlantic relationship, enshrined in the 1949 Atlantic Pact, precedes the creation of the European Communities. With the watershed event of the Cold War's demise, both NATO and the EC/EU quickly evolved in response to a new international setting, but did so along distinct and independent paths. The nature of the two organisations has remained profoundly different: NATO is a political–military alliance between a (growing) group of fully sovereign states – although it has developed elements of a 'security community'; the European Union is a unique experiment in mixed supranational and intergovernmental cooperation, constantly transforming itself while shifting the boundaries of sovereignty in key areas. Without retracing the complex trajectory of transatlantic relations, suffice it to say that these constitute the historical and political foundation of current efforts to work in partnership but also, simultaneously, a barrier to a fully functional and rational Euro-American deal. In other words, we are not in the business of 'inventing' a Euro-American relationship from scratch, if only because a whole network of rules of behaviour, exchange of information and personal ties has crystallised over the years. After all, the ESS recognises just as much by stating explicitly – as we have seen at the outset – that the United States is an irreplaceable ally with a unique position *vis-à-vis* Europe.

Given this background, progress has been slow and uncertain in strengthening the direct EU–US link in the security field. Washington (under three administrations) has systematically reiterated that no arrangement should be changed to the detriment of NATO, which remains the primary forum for consultation among the allies. On their part, the Europeans have painfully reached agreement on at least two basic points: certain autonomous military (and civil–military) capabilities are indispensable to Europe's own security; the goal of developing these capabilities can realistically be pursued only in cooperation with the United States, thus preserving NATO. Virtually every twist and turn in the complicated story of the European Security and Defence Identity (ESDI), CFSP, and ESDP can be understood in light of those two imperatives. It is thus paradoxical that NATO (i.e. the transatlantic link we inherited from the Cold War) and the fledgling EU–US partnership have come to be viewed by some policymakers and observers alike as almost antithetical formulas or alternative arrangements.[8] They are not, but it is nonetheless true that many issues will have to be carefully managed and finessed through calculated ambiguity, lest the prophecy may fulfil itself. The predicament has been worsened by differing reflexes across the Atlantic. Between September 2001 and George W. Bush's re-election in November 2004, American behaviour – in combination with the lack of consensus among the Europeans themselves over the Iraqi war – has done a lot to reduce the vitality of NATO, but most Europeans have come to realise that this does nothing to enhance the international role of the European

Union. In sum, the Western allies have discovered the worst of all possible worlds: the 'coercive-diplomatic' effectiveness of the United States has been reduced by the fragility of the *ad hoc* anti-Iraqi coalition, while the European Union's avowed support for effective multilateralism has been everything but effective – also damaging the UN in the process.

It is against this backdrop that the message of the ESS should be understood. The ESS casts the Euro-American link as an 'ordering' principle, notably stating (under the heading of 'effective multilateralism') that 'one of the core elements of the international system is the transatlantic relationship'. Thus, the somewhat abstract promotion of multilateralism is grounded in the well-established practical reality of a uniquely successful alliance. This is further clarified by stating that 'NATO is an important expression of this relationship' – an obvious attempt to reassure the NATO-first advocates. A concept that is reinforced in one of the paragraphs on improved capabilities: 'The EU–NATO permanent arrangements, in particular Berlin Plus, enhance the operational capability of the EU and provide the framework for the strategic partnership between the two organizations in crisis management'. Besides reflecting the agreed transatlantic formula, such a statement alludes to the notion that cooperation (especially interoperability) is a sort of capability-multiplier. The careful wording is also a deliberate effort at confidence (re-)building across the Atlantic. Three years since the adoption of the ESS, it is still too early to assess whether it can be successfully 'implemented' in this respect. The Strategy may be seen as just one of a series of steps designed to manage the tricky transition from a NATO-only arrangement, through a NATO-first deal, to a genuine EU–NATO relationship. As long as the operational requirements continue to make the European Union dependent on indispensable US assets, the uneasy coexistence of a 'Transatlantic' track (i.e. NATO, plus the hub-and-spokes network with Washington at the core) and an EU–US track will not be overcome.

Of course, there is a vast array of policy initiatives and areas where the European Union can already play an autonomous role, to the extent that security – as we have seen – is understood and pursued in a comprehensive and multi-faceted manner. However, the reality of US preponderance in the military sphere has consequences well beyond the conduct of military operations, providing mighty incentives for national governments (especially NATO members) to bypass the EU institutions and engage Washington bilaterally on specific issues. As things stand, the reasoning put forth by the ESS looks more like good analysis than a recipe for action: 'Our aim should be an effective and balanced partnership with the USA. This is an additional reason for the European Union to build up further its capabilities and increase its coherence'. Coherence (i.e. full commitment to an EU-first approach) is indeed a precondition for pooling the existing and future capabilities in an effective manner and achieving a more balanced relationship with the United States. At the same time, the NATO-first approach that several members adhere to in practice (and as codified for all in the Berlin-Plus arrangement) puts a premium on *incoherence* at the European Union level. We are thus left with a sort of circular reasoning.

Who is a partner? The other great powers and the missing criteria

In the very last paragraph of the ESS's section on 'working with partners', a pretty odd grouping is mentioned with which the Union intends in particular to develop 'strategic partnerships': Japan, China, Canada and India. There is no easily identifiable order here, nor a specific feature common to all, except that all four countries are *not* located in the European Union's neighbourhood. The list is not linked to the existence of consultative fora, and not even the diplomatically prudent alphabetical order. More importantly, the wording chosen in the final sentence of the paragraph (teaming up with those who 'share our goals and values, and are prepared to act in their support') may suggest a mixture of community of democracies (China being the obvious exception) and large economic powers (Canada being the weak link, in absolute terms). But such logic can only be inferred from the thrust of the whole document. In fact, the criteria to evaluate who qualifies as a potential partner are left virtually unspecified.

As a result, the somewhat casual usage of the term 'partnership' casts doubts over the whole concept – strategic or otherwise. This observation brings us back to the difficulty of precisely qualifying the relationship with Russia (which we mentioned earlier): a major problem, given the obvious overlap of European and Russian interests in North-Eastern and Southern Europe. The strange list is revealing of an unwillingness to rank traditional, actual, or future partners according to a precise criterion. Close or growing economic interdependence is, rightly, a key consideration, but the European Union will have to find ways to differentiate explicitly between global relationships at various levels of maturity and intensity. To illustrate the point, a quick review of the state of relations with two key countries, Russia and China, seems warranted – also in consideration of their status as permanent members of the UN Security Council.

Russia

As we have seen, Russia is described as a major factor for EU security and prosperity, although more progress is called for on the way to a full 'strategic partnership'. The incentives for cooperation are evident to both sides, at least in the economic field and in the fight against terrorist and criminal activities. However, issues of contention abound, as we have noted in analysing some areas of common (not necessarily shared) concern in or along the neighbourhood.

The 1997 PCA has been potentially strengthened with the conclusion of negotiations on the 'four common spaces' in May 2005. Yet, the Russian reaction to the ENPI has been sceptical at best: predictably, many in Russia view it as a form of interference. The significant political obstacles have been de facto recognised on both sides by deciding to focus mostly on practical cooperation in the economic (particularly energy) field – i.e. only one of the four 'spaces'. While this may be a wise and realistic course to take in order to lock in certain mutual economic gains, one could question whether it is truly compatible with a 'comprehensive' approach to security. If one needed any confirmation, the interaction of economics and security proved very problematic in early 2006, as Moscow decided to apply the 'energy weapon' with increased vigour not just toward Ukraine but also toward Russia's European customers.

A similar concern can be raised with regard to the ongoing attempt to encourage Russian 'ownership' of the PCA process, which is likely to further constrain the European Union's leverage on issues such as democracy standards and human rights in conflict situations. In this perspective, Europe's desire to play a leading role in crisis prevention/management clashes directly with Moscow's determination to preserve its influence in places such as Transnistria and Kaliningrad, while of course exercising its sovereign prerogatives in Chechnya.

Overall, it seems fair to say that the European Union has little alternative but to proceed on the path of managing the (growing) level of economic interdependence with Russia through various forms of engagement, while striking a delicate balance with the commitments it has already made to most of its Russia-weary neighbours.

China

No one can treat China as an ordinary country – or partner. Its sheer size and rapidly growing global impact in virtually all dimensions of power and influence make China a core question for the future of the whole international system. It is thus surprising and worrisome that, until at least early 2005, the European Union has tended to adopt a sort of simple economics-first approach toward Beijing. The main documents on the EU–China relationship are remarkable for their lack of a wider strategic perspective beyond the strictly bilateral channel (European Commission 2003b).

The economics-first orientation had major repercussions in the case of the tentative decision, made in 2004, to lift the arms embargo that Brussels had declared in response to the 1989 Tiananmen repression. To be true, the embargo is not binding for Member States, nor particularly effective in preventing the significant growth of military-related sales. Yet, it was odd to watch top-level officials from countries such as Germany and France, as well as the European Union institutions, announce the imminent lifting of the embargo as a low-profile step. In sum, the underlying rationale on the European side seemed to be commercial, but the Chinese counterpart saw it mostly as a political and symbolic move. It should have been obvious, at that point, that the embargo issue had potential strategic repercussions, which in fact were vociferously emphasised by the Bush administration as it launched a diplomatic offensive to stop the European Union from proceeding. Eventually, by the summer of 2005 the decision was made to postpone the question indefinitely.[9]

The discussions on the embargo offer an almost perfect case study in the ambiguity of the 'partnership' concept as a policy tool. What we witnessed in the span of just few months was a kind of accelerated learning process, in which wider considerations were hastily added to the European strategic calculus, and the conclusion was reached that the arms embargo deserved more reflection and more consultation. The European Union's official policy currently qualifies the relationship with China as a 'maturing partnership' but indicates a commitment to a 'fully fledged strategic partnership'. Of course, engagement across the board is a legitimate European approach (just as the mixture of containment and engagement that Washington is testing) to the rise of China. Nonetheless, effective multilateralism should imply careful consideration of the opinion and interests of the closest allies, as well as the regional consequences (however unintended they may be) of European decisions. In these respects, we might say that the European Union's skill in managing multiple partnerships is painfully maturing, but still has some way to go.

Conclusion: the limits of partnership

The most striking feature of the various partnerships described or envisaged in the ESS is their diversity. The expression 'closest partners' might have been a good way to differentiate among different types of partners, especially if it had been taken further along the lines of an explicit 'democratic clause'. Instead, it appears to have fallen victim to the desire to reassure every potential reader of the ESS by avoiding any sense of exclusion.

But even beyond this troublesome lack of precision, there is an unresolved tension between two visions: on the one hand, an explicitly discriminatory concert of great powers (with the two variants, capability based and democratically oriented); on the other, the horizontal, non-discriminatory multilateral philosophy of 'one government, one vote'. Such tension is certainly not unique to the European Union's Security Strategy, but rather quintessential to our post-Westphalian global system in which states, non-governmental organisations and individuals uneasily coexist. But it is a particularly acute dilemma for the European Union, as an unprecedented 'confederal' unit which claims a role on the world stage as – according to the ESS – 'inevitably a global player', but does so while rejecting pure power politics in favour of multilateralism.

This need not be an either–or proposition, in fact: a partial way out of the dilemma could be for the European Union to act responsibly not just toward the multilateral ideal or its institutionalised manifestations, but also toward the existing balances of power, influence and interests in the main regions of the world. These mostly informal structures often underpin stability and are essential to any prospect for progress, as is the case with the US network of alliances in various parts of the world. Improving (or at least not damaging) such structures requires a heightened awareness of the interplay of economic, diplomatic and security/military factors.

Given the recent obstacles encountered in the attempt to 'politicise' relations with key countries (Russia and the MEPs), there may be a strong temptation to revert to a pragmatic pursuit of economic ties (witness the initial attitude toward the China arms embargo). After all, in light of the European Union's own experience, close economic interdependence is in itself a form of security policy, potentially engendering fruitful contacts at all levels of government and civil society. However, a single-minded approach is not viable, especially when two or more economic giants are dealing with each other. In the absence of firm political guidance, the pursuit of business interests may quickly backfire: the Union's capacity to be open to international market forces but also internally cohesive (as its citizens seem to demand through forms of protection) is becoming doubtful under the highly competitive conditions of today's global economy. European citizens will not easily tolerate the short-term costs of globalisation unless their leaders put those costs in the larger context of long-term political and security objectives. It is no accident that protectionist impulses have made a vigorous comeback precisely in reaction to China's commercial offensive in the past few years. Partly as a consequence, the European Union's counterparts do not see it as the champion of cooperative multilateralism, as reflected for instance in the strong pressure that both traditional allies and emerging countries have brought on Brussels in the WTO Doha Round. The competitive challenge had come mainly from the United States and Japan until the rise of new trading powers, especially in East Asia, in the 1970s and 1980s; now it is the turn of the demographic giants, beginning with China, followed by India and possibly Brazil and others.

In such a fast-changing setting, the European Union would be well advised to play to its strengths, but some of the very ingredients of its success are beginning to erode: first and foremost, partnerships will be of limited value for others unless Europe promptly regains economic vitality, and the self-confidence needed to carefully embrace opportunities instead of inordinately fearing new competitors. At the same time, European Union officials need to develop a truly global strategic outlook (in parallel to the more operational strategic culture they are constructing) based on a clearer assessment of the security setup of non-neighbouring regions. In so doing, they must openly confront some hard strategic realities – such as Europe's economic and political force of attraction but also its still marginal role in the security arrangements of parts of the Greater Middle East, East Asia and Latin America (all areas where its stakes are high).

The dilemma is that economic weight and security leverage affect and often reinforce each other – which is exactly what sets the United States apart from any other power in the world.

Given the limited resources available to the European Union's common foreign policy in the foreseeable future, the most urgent step is to further clarify the security priorities of the Union in implementing and refining the ESS. Hard choices are required, particularly in translating the embryonic regional assessments of the Strategy into actions. Sometimes this will occur silently and through indirect routes: it might be turn out to be the case, for instance, with the 2005 Barcelona conference, which at least had the merit of signalling to the Mediterranean partners a sense of urgency on the terrorist issue – at the cost of discouraging any substantive concession and even a top-level attendance on their part. In the longer run, Europe's choice may be vindicated, especially if the European Union makes good on its promise to regard resolution of the Arab–Israeli conflict as 'a strategic priority' (again, borrowing from the ESS), which would eliminate a permanent alibi for the Arab/Muslim countries. This is an open-ended prospect at the present stage, but we should not rule out a gradual improvement of cooperation between the two shores of the Mediterranean, despite the gloomy outcome of Barcelona. Ultimately, constructive engagement cannot become an end in itself, and it is more effective when it is conditional to a practical commitment to shared values, interests and goals. Similarly, the tortuous decision-making process on the China arms embargo could mark the beginning of a more comprehensive strategic assessment of East Asia as a whole, which must incorporate security and military considerations. In the presence of worrisome signs of commercial tensions with Beijing, it is of crucial importance that the European Union formulates a China policy by design, not by default due to the interplay of business lobbies[10] and American pressures.

On any major international issue, the European Union has a web of relations and interests to reconcile, often pitting established partners in competition with potential new partners. Of course, we should not expect to find all the solutions to these dilemmas in a general policy document like the ESS, but more can and must be done to apply the principles of the Strategy to specific regional settings in all their complexity. Men are created equal; international partners are not – and should not.

Notes

1 The Development Council was part of the configurations of the Council of the European Union but was suppressed in 2003.
2 'The EU and the issue of conflicts in Africa: peace-building, conflict prevention and beyond' (March 1996/SEC (1996) 332).
3 Its members are the Gulf Cooperation Council (GCC), namely Bahrain, Kuwait, Oman, Qatar, Saudi Arabia and the United Arab Emirates. Yemen, Iran and Iraq are also members.
4 Its members are Algeria, Egypt, Israel, Jordan, Lebanon, Morocco, Syria, Tunisia, Turkey and the Palestinian Authority; Libya.
5 Particularly to Yemen, the GCC, Iraq and Iran. Those countries were not to be covered by the ENPI.
6 The members of the MD are Egypt, Israel, Mauritania, Morocco, Tunisia, Jordan (since 1995) and Algeria (since 2000).
7 As a Commission working document clarifies, 'Subsidiarity and synergy between the different Northern Dimension actors are two concepts highlighted in the Action Plan. Both concepts ensure the full involvement of all stakeholders in the Action Plan implementation, including the partner states, the regional organizations, regional and local authorities, education and research institutions and civil society, as well as the Union itself'. Commission staff working document, 2004 Annual Progress Report on the Implementation of the Northern Dimension Action Plan, Brussels 20.5.2005 SEC (2005) 688.
8 An additional problem is that the tendency of the Union to play a more strategic role to the Eastern neighbourhood might be hampered by the fact that while some old EU Member States (especially France) favour it, others, particularly the new Member States of Central and Eastern Europe, seem reluctant to push ahead for a more autonomous European Defence disentangled from NATO coordination.

9 The September 2005 joint statement drafted on the occasion of the eighth bilateral summit in Beijing states that the EU side 'reaffirmed its willingness to continue to work towards lifting the embargo'.

10 Because the Chinese economy offers so many challenges and opportunities simultaneously in various sectors, economic interests in Europe have become extremely diversified across both business sectors and EU members: investors, exporters, importers, delocalising companies, consumers, all have distinct goals. The job of the EU institutions is thus particularly hard in trying to make consistent policy decisions.

7 The European Security Strategy and the continuing search for coherence

Jan Joel Andersson

Coherence, like coordination is a principle everyone in the EU agrees with – but only when it applies to someone else.

Senior EU official

The European Security Strategy (ESS) is a great achievement. For the first time ever, the European Union (EU) has agreed on a document that sets out what the threats to Europe are, what Europe's main interests and objectives are, and how the European Union will achieve them. However, for the ESS to be implemented in full will require far-reaching changes in how the European Union conducts its foreign and security policy in a coherent manner. Today, the Common Foreign and Security Policy (CFSP) and European Security and Defence Policy (ESDP) encompass enormous resources. In addition to the Member States' own military and civilian capabilities and assets, a number of other instruments have been created at the EU level, such as EU Special Representatives and the European Development Fund. Moreover, EU diplomatic initiatives, trade promotion, disarmament and non-proliferation efforts and environmental policies are all instruments that can be employed before, during, or after crises occur in order to prevent or manage the spread of such crises. The European Union's international relationships are also increasingly affected by its internal policies which play a vital part in the European Union's influence externally. For example, EU internal policies on the environment, energy, competition, agriculture and fisheries, transport, anti-terrorism and illegal migration have all affected the European Union's external relations. These external and internal capabilities, resources, instruments and policies each have their own structure, logic and rationale. While some of them work well together, many others do not and may even work counter to each other. In order to make Europe a more impelling and more effective actor, the European Union must develop a unity of purpose and achieve unity among its institutions as well as coherence among its many instruments, capabilities, and not least its Member States. As the ESS makes clear, this is a major challenge the European Union now faces.

The issue of coherence is complex, arising at many stages in the policy process and at several political levels. In this chapter, I will first discuss why Europe must become more skilled at coordinating and conjoining analyses and strategies both in the CFSP and ESDP, between EU institutions, and between EU institutions and Member States. I will then look at EU policy *vis-à-vis* Macedonia as an example of why greater coherence is required and discuss how such coherence might be achieved. As I will argue, the European Union ought to coordinate all elements of the CFSP and ESDP in order to effectively employ the instruments and capabilities it actually possesses. Since the Constitutional Treaty and its promising proposal of an EU Foreign Minister and an integrated External Action Service is all but dead, the chapter will proceed to discuss what can be done instead to improve coherence by reviewing some of the proposals for coherence and effectiveness that the Commission recently published in a paper entitled 'Europe in the World' (European Commission 2006).

What is coherence and why is it needed?

Although it is a fundamental guiding principle in the European Union, coherence has not been given a great deal of attention (Neuwahl 1994; Krenzler and Schneider 1997; Tietje 1997; Smith 2001). The term itself is not, in fact, used consistently in all EU translations. For example, in the English translation of the Treaty on European Union (TEU), 'consistency' (meaning absence of contradictions) is used, while many other languages favoured 'coherence' (meaning positive connections) which sets a higher standard for the European Union's various policies (Tietje 1997: 211–12). Nevertheless, the strong language in Article 3 of the Treaty on European Union indicates the drafters' concern that the European Union's pillar structure may make coherent and consistent external action difficult (Eeckhout 2004: 152). Article 3 of the TEU provides:

> The Union shall be served by a single institutional framework which shall ensure the consistency and the continuity in the activities carried out in order to attain its objectives while respecting and building upon the acquis communautaire.
>
> The Union shall in particular ensure the consistency of its external activities as a whole in the context of its external relations, security,

economic and development policies. The Council and the Commission shall be responsible for ensuring such consistency and shall co-operate to this end. They shall ensure the implementation of these policies, each in accordance with its respective powers.

In short, coherence means that the European Union should be able to pursue its external policy goals regardless of which institution and policy tool it chooses. For the purpose of this analysis, coherence can usefully be divided into two dimensions: horizontal and vertical. 'Horizontal coherence' concerns the extent to which the various external policies and activities of the European Union's institutions, agencies, and representatives are logically connected and mutually supportive. 'Vertical coherence' concerns the extent to which the external policies and activities of the Member States are logically connected and mutually supportive with those of the European Union's institutions, agencies and representatives (Tietje 1997: 211; Smith 2001: 173).

The ESS openly states that the 'point of the Common Foreign and Security Policy and European Security and Defence Policy is that we are stronger when we act together' (European Council 2003a: 19). Improving the effectiveness and coherence of the European Union's external capabilities has been on the agenda for many years. A major step in this process was the formalisation of the relationship between the European Community and the European Political Cooperation (EPC) in the 1986 Single European Act (SEA).[1] While the European Union's external coherence somewhat improved with the SEA, it was woefully inadequate to deal with the challenges of the fall of the Berlin Wall, the Persian Gulf War and the dissolutions of the Soviet Union and Yugoslavia. Uncertainty about the future role of the United States in the post-Cold War world served as another important reason to strengthen the coherence of EU external action. Arguably, then, a key motivation behind the 1991 Maastricht Treaty on the European Union was to improve external coherence by formally linking the economic and trade capabilities of the European Community in the first pillar to the foreign and security policy assets of the Member States in the second pillar, and to the justice and home affairs in the third pillar.[2] It was hoped that this new three-pillar structure would bridge the competing decision-making methods of supranational decision-making in the European Community and the intergovernmental negotiations in the political cooperation for foreign and security policy, and justice and home affairs (Smith 2004).

To ensure a more effective European Union, the Treaty on European Union explicitly emphasised the principle of coherence. Under Articles A and C, the European Union was tasked with ensuring 'the consistency of its external activities as a whole in the context of its external relations, security, economic, and development policies' (Article C). The principle of coherence was also to guide CFSP in general (Title V, Articles J.1 and J.8). However, while the new single 'EU' institutional framework that the Treaty on European Union established was an important step towards the goal of greater coherence, many outstanding issues remained. Some of these issues were resolved with the 1997 Amsterdam Treaty.[3] Two institutional innovations were especially important in improving coherence in the CFSP. The first was the creation of a new High Representative for the CFSP who would also serve as Secretary-General to the Council. The new post was to provide the 'one phone number to call' in Europe on foreign affairs that many outside the European Union had long asked for. The second institutional innovation was the creation of a Policy Planning and Early Warning Unit, bringing together members from the Council Secretariat, the Member States, the Commission, and the Western European Union. While far from being an 'EU foreign ministry', the new unit gave the CFSP a very much needed capacity for analysis independent of the Member States (Peterson and Bomberg 1999: 231).

How to achieve coherence: a first step

All the EU Member States and individual EU institutions pay lip service to the principle of coherence to improve coordination and avoid duplication of the European Union's external activities. The truth of the matter is that no Member State or institution has ever been prepared to give up completely its own role in this field. With a European Union consisting of 27 Member States and growing numbers of individual EU institutions, lack of coherence is quickly becoming a recipe for disaster. Given the background of different, sometimes overlapping, sometimes competing, objectives and capabilities of Member States, Council, Commission, and agencies, how much coherence can we expect to really achieve? Even if it is very difficult, most experts and policy makers agree that more can be done on improving both horizontal and vertical coherence in the European Union. The adoption of the European Security Strategy provides an interesting moment to take stock and discuss these obvious obstacles to more effective EU external action.

It is true that the European Union can be an inefficient and uncoordinated external actor. For example, the European Union's foreign economic policy has been heavily criticised for lacking in coherence. It is a well-known fact that the European Union is the largest aid donor in the world, but its overall foreign economic policy is torn between the promotion of multilateral trade liberalisation and the protection of least-developed countries.

These policies, in turn, work counter to the European Union's Common Agricultural Policy (CAP), which prevents farmers from poor countries from competing in the European market. The challenge, then, is to find a way to replace this multitude of ad-hoc policies with an overall global EU strategy for the many various EU policies that affect the CFSP and ESDP. However, while it is true that trade liberalisation and poverty reduction are not always compatible (at least in the short term) and that the protection of EU farmers by the CAP can act against the Union's external and security interests, this is a basic contradiction that exists in all the Member States' own foreign economic policies. It is therefore unrealistic, many EU officials argue, to expect the European Union to develop the right policy mix for all these goals on a supranational level when individual Member States have failed to do this on a national level. However, there are still a number of things that can be done.

Horizontal coherence must start at the level of policies. Horizontal coherence does not only concern the CFSP but should include all relevant policy areas and decision-making levels that can have an important impact on the Union's security. For example, the energy policy area must encompass not only energy security but also maritime protection of sea-lanes in the Persian Gulf region and pipeline security in Russia and the Caucasus. Justice and home affairs policies include issues of migration, border trafficking, organised crime, terrorism, as well as agriculture and foreign aid (impact of the CAP on farmers in the third world, economic development and stability in poor regions of the world). Horizontal coherence also requires the European Union to balance values, such as human rights and democracy with strategic interests, such as trade and security. For example, current EU policy towards Russia and Indonesia demonstrates lack of coherence in these areas and how hard such coherence can be to achieve.

At present, the European Union does not have the machinery to coordinate policies and instruments across the wide range of issues the European Union deals with. It is widely agreed that the General Affairs and External Relations Council (GAERC) cannot fulfil this role. A basic reason for failure of the GAERC to deliver more coherence is the institutional structure of the EU policy areas that affect external relations. First, there are external policy areas that are dominated by supranational institutions and decision-making procedures, and include EU trade, aid, and development. In these areas, economic interest is the driving force, the European Commission and the European Court of Justice are the main actors, and qualified majority voting dominates decision making. Second, there are external policy areas in which both supranational institutions and the Member States are active. Here, economic interests coexist with other goals such as political stability or promotion of human rights and democracy. Some of these policy areas are part of regional and political 'dialogues', part of the CFSP, and part of Justice and Home affairs, dealing with drug smuggling and combating terrorism outside the European Union. Finally, there are external policy areas in which intergovernmental institutions and decision-making procedures clearly dominate. These policy areas include the ESDP and other forms of 'hard' security and defence cooperation (Smith 2001: 174–75).

It is easy to complain about the duplication of EU representations in the field and the confusion that ensues when a multiplicity of actors representing the Union deliver multiple uncoordinated messages and demands. However, the problem of coherence is not only a problem for EU institutions and policies. A more coherent European Union in external affairs also requires more coherence between what is being done at the EU level and the Member States, i.e. vertical coherence. Vertical coherence demands greater coordination between EU institutions and Member States in both Brussels and in the field. This requirement has long been recognised by the Member States and at the informal meeting of Foreign Ministers in Evian in September 2000 – later endorsed by the European Council – it was agreed that more should be done about this. A natural focal point for better vertical and horizontal coordination of communication and representation in the field are the EU Special Representatives. The EUSRs would also be able to coordinate messages from the field to Brussels in order to avoid duplication and contradictory information. However, it would require more funding and a strong mandate from both Council and Commission before the EUSRs would be able to assume this role. Vertical coherence does not only require Member States' embassies and representatives to follow a coordinated EU line in the field, but also to coordinate external polices better in Brussels.

Coherence is also an issue between the European Union and various other different regional organisations in Europe and elsewhere. Accordingly, the ESS also points out that 'problems are rarely solved on a single country basis, or without regional support . . . ' (European Council 2003a:13). Today, there are three major organisations with a security-related agenda in Europe: the European Union, NATO and the OSCE. While each organisation was created for different reasons, at different times and with different agendas, more or less the same Member Countries are found in each, and they play an important role in minimising overlap and duplication between the European Union and these organisations. It is clear that EU Member States in these organisations could do more to aid them in avoiding duplication and overlap. For example, one country has been simultaneously pushing for the development of a civilian crisis management capability in both OSCE and the European Union. Other EU Member States have taken opposing views of the same issue in NATO and the European Union. The controversy of the possible overlap/duplication/incompatibility between the NATO Reaction Force and the EU Rapid Reaction Force is a case in point. As one senior EU official stated: 'The NRF concept didn't fall from the sky, it was agreed by NATO Member States – including the 11 current EU members who are also members of NATO'.[4]

However, coherence does exist in some policy areas. In the area of trade policy, the European Union has successfully negotiated its position as one voice for many years in bilateral talks with other countries and in multilateral negotiations in organisations such as the GATT/WTO. The emergence of the European Union as a global economic power has been made possible by an institutional structure that promotes coherent positions among the Member States. The Common Commercial Policy (CCP), which has been in effect since 1961, is the oldest and most potent manifestation of the European Union as a coherent actor (Bretherton and Vogler 2005: 49). While the responsibility for making the final decisions in the CCP rests with the Council of Ministers, it is the Commission that has the exclusive right to initiate policy and to propose negotiations. The granting of exclusive competence in trade to the Community is established in Article 113 [133] of the Treaty of Rome. In this article, the Member States transferred powers to create and implement trade policy to the supranational community level. As a result of the transfer of power, uniform principles and common policy could be forged by the Commission on tariff rates, international negotiations, liberalisation, exports and trade protection measures.

As the CCP has developed over the years, the Commission's autonomy *vis-à-vis* the Member States has increased. Today, the Commission plays an active role at every level in trade policy. The Commission generates new policy initiatives, is responsible for investigating and taking action against unfair trade practices, and proposes negotiations to the Council for new agreements with other countries and organisations. When the European Union negotiates trade agreements, it is the Commission that proposes the mandate which provides the brief from which the talks will be conducted and conducts the talks. In any negotiations in which representatives from the Member States are present, they will remain silent while the Commission articulates the common EU/EC position. The Council, in turn, has the right to approve or disapprove Commission policies or proposals for negotiations by Qualified Majority Vote. Nevertheless, on issues in which national interests of Member States are severely threatened, a de facto consensus may be required (Bretherton and Vogler 2005: 49–50; McCormick 2002: 206).

The ceding of responsibility over trade to a supranational institution has allowed the European Union to act as a coherent actor, and as such, to become a key contestant in the often heated relations between the major trading blocks in the world economy. The Commission's role as negotiator and gatekeeper determining who gets preferential access to the Single Market has also made it a powerful actor in bilateral relations with many states in the world trading system. However, there has always been a certain tension between the Commission and the Member States. To mitigate this tension, the Member States and the Commission regularly meet in a committee consisting of senior national trade officials and their counterparts in the Commission. While the original function of the committee (a.k.a. the Article 113 Committee) was to monitor the Commission's negotiation activities, it has become a collegiate forum in which the Member States and the Commission can exchange views on a daily basis (Hayes-Renshaw and Wallace 1997: 90; Bretherton and Vogler 2005: 52).

Could the EU trade policy be a blueprint for a more coherent CFSP? Some would argue that ceding national responsibility to a supranational institution might be acceptable on matters of 'low politics' such as trade, but would be impossible on matters of 'high politics' such as security and defence. However, with the end of the Cold War, trade policy has become increasingly 'high politics' as national security is increasingly linked to international competitiveness (Strange 1994; Stopford and Strange 1991). The ability to produce high-technology products and generate trade surpluses is seen as fundamental to national security (Tyson 1992; Sandholtz *et al.* 1991). The increasing political salience of trade policy in the 1990s was demonstrated by the conflict between the European Commission and the EU Member States over who had exclusive competence in the 'new' areas of trade, particularly services and intellectual property (Peterson and Bomberg 1999). Conversely, some areas of defence and security have become more like traditional 'low politics'. The defence industry is a case in point. From having been an integral part of a country's defence policy, the defence industry has increasingly been linked instead to employment, industrial, and research, technology and development (RTD) policies (Andersson 2003b; Mörth 2003).

What, then, would a Common Foreign and Security Policy formed along the lines of the Common Commercial Policy look like? A CFSP patterned on the CCP would undoubtedly increase coherence. By transferring the formulation and implementation of foreign and security policy to the supranational community level, the problem of vertical coherence would be resolved. Similarly to the procedure in the CCP, in a reformed CFSP it would be the Commission that has the right to initiate policy and to propose negotiations, within the limits of Council mandates. In international negotiations, it would also be the Commission that proposed the mandate that provides the brief from which to conduct negotiations. In any talks in which representatives from the Member States were present, they would remain silent while the Commission argued the common EU position. The Council, in turn, would have the right to approve or reject policies or proposals for negotiations by Qualified Majority Vote. Nevertheless, similar to the CCP, a de facto consensus would be required on issues in which the national interests of Member States were severely threatened.

It is important to note, of course, that the majority of EU Member States are nowhere near the decision to cede responsibility over foreign and security policy to a supranational institution, nor is this a development that the Commission currently advocates.[5] Given this fact and that there is little hope for an EU Foreign Minister along the lines proposed in the Constitutional Treaty for the CFSP, how can more coherence be achieved? At least one step forward would be to increase the number of 'personal unions' in the field between EU Special Representatives who are appointed by the Council and Heads of Delegations appointed by the Commission. As the Macedonian example below suggests, the integration of Commission and Council representatives does increase coherence and facilitate work on the ground. While this does not address the fundamental issue of horizontal and vertical coherence in the CFSP it is a step in the right direction.

The case of Macedonia

The ESS argues that the European Union can have a greater impact by acting collectively, rather than as a sum of its component parts. Over the past few years the European Union has also developed more common – if not fully coherent – external policies towards many regions, including the Balkans. Currently, the European Union is the main promoter of peace and stability in this region. The European Union has been especially important in averting a threatening full scale Balkan civil war in Macedonia. The European Union was not only instrumental in ending the violent confrontation between Slav-Macedonian-dominated security forces and ethnic Albanian armed groups in 2001 but also put Macedonia back on track towards European and Euro-Atlantic integration. A sign of how successful this process has been is the fact that Macedonia submitted its membership application to the European Union in 2004.

Macedonia remained at peace throughout the break-up of former Yugoslavia in the early 1990s. The Kosovo War in 1999, however, destabilised the country. During the war an estimated 360,000 ethnic Albanians fled from Kosovo to Macedonia. While most of these refugees left after the war, Albanian radicals on both sides of the border took up arms in pursuit of autonomy or independence for the Albanian-populated areas of Macedonia. A short armed conflict broke out between the government and ethnic Albanian rebels in March–June 2001. This conflict ended with the intervention of a NATO ceasefire monitoring force. The following EU-led negotiations resulted in the Ohrid Framework Agreement, signed by the government of the Republic of Macedonia and Albanian representatives on 13 August 2001. The agreement ended fighting between the National Liberation Army and the Macedonian security forces and set the groundwork for improving the rights of ethnic Albanians in Macedonia that would guarantee peaceful coexistence between the ethnic groups (International Crisis Group 2001a, b). Among other things, the agreement included provisions for altering the official languages of the country, with any language spoken by over 20 per cent of the population becoming co-official with the Macedonian language. Currently only Albanian with approximately 25 per cent of the population fulfils this criterion (Whyte 2001; Brunnbauer 2002). In a further sign of progress, Macedonia submitted its application for EU membership in March 2004. The European Union formally granted the Republic of Macedonia candidate status on 17 December 2005. Moreover, in February 2006, the Republic of Macedonia became the fourth member of the Central European Free Trade Agreement (CEFTA), joining Croatia, Bulgaria and Romania.

In Macedonia, the European Union had for the first time at its disposal the full range of political, economic and military instruments in one country. Following the signing of the Stabilisation and Association Agreement (SAA) with the European Union in Luxembourg on 9 April 2001, Macedonia entered into an enhanced relationship with the European Union which included active EU assistance with the implementation of the Ohrid Agreement from August 2001. As part of this effort, the Council has appointed an EU Special Representative for Macedonia since 2001 to contribute to the consolidation of the peaceful political process. In line with the objectives of the Ohrid Agreement and in close partnership with local authorities, the European Union also established a military operation, code name Concordia, in March 2003 to contribute to a stable secure environment, and a Police Mission, code-named EUPOL Proxima, in December 2003 to help fight organised crime as well as promoting European policing standards in Macedonia (Council of the European Union 2003b, c). Moreover, the European Union also made available increasing financial and technical assistance to Macedonia as it moves closer towards the Union. It is clear that all these instruments function more closely together, and more synergies have been found, than what would have been the case if the leading political representative, the major assistance provider, and the main security presence had represented different international actors. Arguably, even greater results could have been produced with more synergies and streamlining between the involved EU institutions, agencies representatives and Member States.

A major obstacle to a truly coherent approach to external action is the large number of different EU representatives in the field. Foreign leaders may at times encounter five or more representatives of the European Union, which risks blurring the message and confusing local authorities and population on the Union's strategy, priorities, and authority. Ultimately, this is a question of the distinction between the Member States, the Council and Commission and goes to the heart of both horizontal and vertical coherence. For example, in Macedonia the European Union and its Member States were at various times represented not only by the Delegation of the European Commission (opened in March 2000), but also by a civilian EU Monitoring Mission (EUMM), police mission (Proxima), military operation (Concordia), the European Agency for Reconstruction (EAR), the European Investment Bank (EIB), and the European Bank for Reconstruction and Development (EBRD). The main objective of each of these missions and agencies was to facilitate the development of political and economic relations between the European Union and Macedonia in the framework of the Stabilisation and Association process. They were also all formally separate from, or had only weak links with, the EU Special Representative who had been appointed in 2001 by the Council.

Adding to the coherence problem was the issue of vertical coherence between the Member States and the European Union. While the EU Member States, for example, rapidly found money for fielding Operation Concordia, the first ever EU-led military operation, they were less prepared to financially support the European Union's political presence in the country and it took months for the EU Member States to find suitable staff members for the office of the EU Special Representative in Macedonia.[6] Moreover, the country holding the rotating EU Presidency added another representative speaking on behalf of the European Union. In the Macedonian case, for example, Swedish, Greek and Italian presidencies all took a particular interest. While these national initiatives were welcome in some regards, they also created problems for EU coherence since each rotating EU presidency had its own foreign policy priorities.

However, the opportunity for coherence improved considerably in November 2005 when the leadership of the European Commission Delegation and the EU Special Representative office were merged. In an unusual 'personal union', Ambassador Erwan Fouéré was concurrently appointed EU Special Representative by the Council and Head of Delegation by the Commission. This 'personal union' was the first ever joint external representation of the European Union (Council of the European Union 2005b, European Union Mission to FYROM 2006). In its dual role of representing both the Council of Ministers and the European Commission, the EU Mission in Skopje has been able to interact in a more coherent manner with the authorities, institutions, media and citizens of Macedonia about the pre-accession process and about the EU institutions and policies. Since the granting of candidate status in 2005 the work of the EU Mission has focused increasingly on monitoring and reporting on compliance with the political and economic criteria for membership of the European Union, and alignment of legislation with EU legislation as well as capacity to implement and enforce it (European Union Mission to FYROM 2006). The double-hatting of Mr Fouéré allows the EU Mission to serve as the single contact point channel for day-to-day communication between national authorities in Macedonia and the Council and the Commission decision-makers in Brussels with little risk of confusion or mixing of messages.

What more can be done for better coherence?

The fact that the European Union consists of 27 Member States, each with its own national interests and priorities, poses a significant coherence challenge to the CFSP that some may believe is impossible to solve. However, the proposed Constitutional Treaty went very far in addressing this issue. In the Constitutional Treaty, the main institutional innovation was the creation of the post of Union Minister of Foreign Affairs (Constitutional Treaty Article I-28). This position would merge the present tasks of the High Representative for the Common Foreign and Security Policy with those of the Commissioner for External Relations. In addition to being appointed by the Council and being a full member and a Vice-President of the Commission, the Foreign Affairs Minister would also be chairman of the External Relations Council. This new single legal personality would be responsible for representing the European Union on the international scene and play a more visible role in world affairs. The Foreign Minister would represent the European Union in matters concerning the CFSP, conduct political dialogue on the European Union's behalf and speak for the European Union in international organisations and conferences, as well as coordinating the Member States' actions in international fora (Constitutional Treaty Article III-305).

The Constitutional Treaty would further strengthen coherence by appointing a President of the European Council for a term of two and a half years who would represent the Union on CFSP issues at his or her level. Moreover, the Constitutional Treaty also provided for the establishment of a European External Action Service, drawn from Commission and Council as well as staff seconded from Member States' national diplomatic services, with delegations in 125 countries to assist the Foreign Minister (Constitutional Treaty Article III-296). The Union Foreign Minister and an integrated External Action Service would not only make it possible for the European Union to play a more visible role in world affairs but also provide for much improved horizontal and vertical coherence. However, at present the Constitutional Treaty and the plans for an EU Foreign Minister and integrated External Action Service are all but dead after the 'No' vote in France and the Netherlands. Nevertheless, the requirement for more coherence expressed in the ESS remains. Given this fact, what other alternatives are there to improve coherence in the CFSP?

The objectives of the Constitutional Treaty to improve coherence, effectiveness and visibility remain valid. Despite the rejection of the Treaty, there are still a number of steps that can be taken within the limits of existing treaties. At an informal meeting in October 2005, the EU Heads of State and Government decided that the European Union should improve its external action, including the link between internal and external policies, despite the setback to the Constitutional Treaty. In response to this call, the European Commission published a communication in June 2006 in which a number of practical steps were proposed to improve both horizontal and vertical coherence that can be summarised under the headings of 'Better Strategic Planning', 'Better Delivery' and 'Better Co-operation' (European Commission 2006).

While there is wide agreement that greater coherence is needed, one should not overstate the lack of coherence in the European Union's external policies. In fact, there is a high level of consensus on the broad framework of the European Union's external objectives in the Treaties. The broad goals set in the Treaties and in the European Security Strategy are then developed in more detail in documents such as Council conclusions, strategy papers, and instructions for financial assistance programmes. In addition, reports and resolutions from the European Parliament also feed into this process. While there is a high level of consensus on the broad framework, there is considerable scope for a more systematic approach for the European Union to setting its strategic objectives and political priorities. For example, in order to improve its internal coherence and effectiveness, the Commission proposes to strengthen the role of the External Relations Group of Commissioners under the authority of the President in identifying strategic priorities. This Group of Commissioners is proposed to be enlarged to include other Commissioners with relevant portfolios on specific geographic and thematic issues. The EU High Representative for the CFSP could also be invited to be associated with the strategic planning work of the External Relations Group of Commissioners. To further improve internal coherence, the Commission plans to strengthen its reporting and analytical capacities in Brussels and in its overseas delegations (European Commission 2006: 7).

There are also many things that could be done to improve coherence between the Commission, the Council and the High Representative for the CFSP in their strategic planning, assessment and action. For example, the incoming president of the Council and his/her foreign minister, the president of the Commission and the External Relations Commissioner, and the High Representative for the CFSP could all meet every six months to jointly review the Union's external action. Intensified cooperation and contacts between the Commission Services and the Council Policy Unit could also lead to a principle of joint papers for policy discussions in the Council and its working groups. Improving the information exchange between Commission and Council could also include sharing information and analyses from Commission Delegations and EU Special Representatives' offices in the field as well as the sharing of reporting and analytical resources between the Council Secretariat's Situation Centre and the Commission's Crisis Room in Brussels. The Commission has also undertaken to enter into a regular dialogue with the European Parliament on draft strategy papers (European Commission 2006: 7–8). If closer coordination and cooperation between the Council Secretariat and the Commission staff in these areas could be achieved, a more solid base for Member States to define a coherent strategy in the Council would be in place.

However, improving coherence is not only a question of better strategic planning. Even when the European Union has clear goals and strategies, impact and effectiveness is often hampered by mixed messages and poor implementation. To become a more effective external actor, the European Union also needs to ensure that any policy decision taken by the European Union is rapidly integrated by all EU institutions into both internal policy development and external messages. It is therefore very important for Commission Delegations, EU Special Representatives and Member States' Embassies to send coherent messages to partners and other international actors. This requires close cooperation between EU Institutions and Member States and the establishment of a shared diplomatic culture between the different actors in EU external policy. To this end, the Commission is proposing to launch an enhanced exchange programme of personnel with diplomatic services of the Member States and the staff of the Commission and Council Secretariat (European Commission 2006: 9). Member States could also open up national diplomatic training schemes to staff in EU institutions working on external relations. Similarly, the Commission and

Council could invite diplomats from the Member States into their training programmes. Much can also be done on practical matters. As mentioned earlier, the successful experience of double-hatting the Head of Commission Delegation and EU Special Representative in Macedonia, for example, shows the advantages of integrating EU representation in the field. Such arrangements could become far more prevalent. In multilateral institutions, Member States and EU Institutions could also coordinate positions and initiatives to better promote common interests. Member States and the Commission could also develop cooperation in the area of consular assistance, particularly in crisis situations (ibid.).

The proposals for greater coherence, effectiveness and visibility made by the Commission in the paper 'Europe in the World' were presented to the Council and Member States at the European Council summit in Brussels in June 2006. The paper was welcomed by the European Council, which supported the internal measures being implemented by the Commission. The European Council also invited the Presidency, the Council, the High Representative and the Commission, on the basis of existing treaties, to examine the proposals in the paper to improve strategic planning and coherence between the Union's many external policy instruments as well as cooperation between the EU institutions and between the EU institutions and the Member States. At the European Council in Brussels in June 2006, it was agreed that a first stocktaking of the implementation of these measures would be made at the end of the Finnish Presidency in December 2006 (European Council 2006: 12–13).

Conclusion: the continuing search for coherence

The fact that the European Union consists of 27 Member States, each with its own national interests and priorities, poses a significant coherence challenge to the CFSP that some believe is impossible to solve. However, the approval of the European Security Strategy (ESS) by the European Council on 12 December 2003 was a crucial step towards a more coherent European Union. The ESS serves two main functions. First, it provides a common, EU-wide, frame of reference for both long-term strategies and for current political problems. Second, the document provides a common base for negotiations with other countries and organisations on issues of strategic importance.

According to the ESS, in order for the European Union to be actively engaged in crisis management on a global scale, it has to be 'more active, more capable and more coherent' (European Council 2003a: 17). In order to be more active and capable, the European Union has begun to develop a range of new instruments and policies. For example, the European Security and Defence Policy (ESDP) is strengthened by the establishment of the European Defence Agency (EDA), the creation of European Battlegroups consisting of rapidly deployable contingents of 1,500 soldiers including support elements, and the establishment of a Civil–Military Planning Cell and Operations Centre for the conduct of autonomous EU operations. The European Union is also strengthening its civilian capabilities as it accumulates resources aimed at institution building, reinforcing the rule of law and increasing police and civil protection. Activity and capabilities alone, however, do not make the European Union an effective global actor. If the European Union is going to be successful in its global role, it must be more coherent. The Iraq crisis of 2002–3 exposed the European Union's lack of both horizontal and vertical coherence in its external policies. The European Union's open disarray during the crisis undermined its identity, credibility, and institutional structures, as well as hurting the trust between the Member States. If it wishes to make a contribution to global security that matches its potential, the European Union must be able to conjoin all of the military and civilian instruments and capabilities of its Member States and unite these with existing EU instruments such as the European Development Fund and the European assistance programmes.

When the European Union speaks with one voice, as it does in international trade negotiations, it carries great weight. When the European Union fails to act in a coherent manner, as it did during the Balkan conflicts of the 1990s and the Iraq crisis of 2002–3, it loses influence as well as credibility. If the European Union wishes to be a major international actor, it must meet the challenge of coherence. The adoption of the European Security Strategy and the strong support shown by both the Member States and European Institutions for the creation of an EU Foreign Minister are two steps towards meeting this challenge. Both are very promising signs that a more coherent future Common Foreign and Security Policy for Europe is conceivable and may also one day be achievable.

Notes

I would like to thank Stephanie Buus for helpful comments and suggestions and Stefan Borg for able research assistance.

1 The Single European Act was agreed in 1986 and came into force in July 1987.
2 The Treaty on European Union was agreed in Maastricht in December 1991, formally signed on February 1992 and entered into force in November 1993.
3 The Treaty of Amsterdam amending the Treaty on European Union, the Treaties establishing the European Communities and certain related acts, commonly

known as the Amsterdam Treaty, was signed in October 1997 and entered into force in May 1999.

4 Personal communication with a senior EU official.

5 One EU Member State that strongly supports the application of the Community method to EU foreign policy is Belgium. See, for example, a recent paper by Belgian Foreign Minister Karel De Gucht (2006: 3).

6 Personal communication with a senior EU official.

8 The European Security Strategy and the United States

The past as prologue

Catherine Kelleher

Analysis of the impact of the ESS on American views of transatlantic relations and the European Union's role within them must begin at the beginning: Washington's differential reactions to the ESS in its initial months in 2003. This is in part because of the general hubris of the Bush administration about Washington's centrality to all events and developments. As seen from Washington in June 2003, the United States was the target audience for development of the ESS. Washington had not only been Europe's sparring partner in the extremely painful transatlantic confrontations over the Iraq war in late 2002 and early 2003 (Gordon and Shapiro 2004; Shawcross 2004). It was also the principal sceptic to be persuaded regarding the emerging ESDP and the European Union's new status as a strategic actor with a vision and a broad strategic doctrine to guide its efforts. At least, Washington was to see and understand the carefully crafted ESS vocabulary that invoked the general words and thrust of Bush's own National Security Strategy (NSS) of 2002.

As was so often the case in the Bush administration's first term, this view unquestionably overstated Washington's centrality. The ESS was focused as much on the deep rifts within Europe that the Iraq debate had revealed, between those Donald Rumsfeld had labelled the 'Old' (France, Germany, and Belgium) and the 'New' (essentially every other European state).[1] Bush's team may have been the fine Italian hand behind several of the more acrimonious and public European disputes, but the core disagreements – European and transatlantic – were real. A number of alliance members and all of the candidate states saw the choice for war in Iraq differently from Paris, Berlin, and Brussels. Discussion of a new European constitution made it imperative to heal these wounds and find a forward-looking plan to anchor a security consensus to support the new structures and division of powers envisaged for the future.

But the ESS did prove, and continues to prove, an important facilitator in the attempts on both sides to rebuild the frayed, if not frozen, transatlantic dialogue on collaborative security. The tale of American reactions to the ESS in 2003 turned on core issues that persist in the present and foreseeable European–American security debates: (1) the nature of security in the twenty-first century and its requirements, (2) the need for a global perspective and an intense collaboration, and (3) the broad scope of instruments necessary – soft and hard power, conventional and unconventional means, diplomatic and military responses.

Moreover, the timing and message of the ESS were both critical. Although not actually the stuff of conversion, it quietened a number of important critics in the administration and on Capitol Hill and provided new stuff for the intra-administration defenders of the significant role of allies and multilateral security organisations. Finally, the launch of the ESS offered a key opening in the slow transatlantic accord that culminated by 2005–6 in a mutual understanding to 'agree to disagree' over Iraq and to reaffirm the broad alliance commitment. The broad principles embedded in the ESS and the associated strategies allowed, and still allow, the United States and willing European states to proceed cooperatively on issues important to both the administration and its critics: the fight against global WMD proliferation and active operations against terrorism, inside and outside of Europe.

It is important and useful to look first at the critical strands and the broad context against which the dialogue on 2003 occurred to define the general category of Washington actors and calculations involved, and then to evaluate the longer-lasting policy impacts of the ESS on American perspectives on a global strategy and the European Union's role within it that can be deduced.

The context of the American reactions to the ESS

To understand American perspectives on the ESS, it is necessary to realise that American reaction to the integration of European defence policies and capabilities has always been ambivalent at best. Americans pride themselves as having been among the first supporters of the integrationist ideas and plans of Jean Monnet for a strong, united Europe. They found in them not only a validation of their own nation-building experience but also the solution to the problems of the control of a revived Germany and defence against an aggressive Soviet Union. American diplomats and officers were intensely involved in the drawing up of the abortive European Defence Community (EDC) treaty and in anchoring it firmly in the broad Kennan–Nitze strategy of containment in Europe.

Eisenhower and Dulles threatened in 1954 that if the EDC were not ratified there would be an 'agonizing reappraisal' of American–European relations and an immediate military withdrawal from Europe (Aron and Lerner 1957). The French passive defeat of EDC led, of course, to another outcome – the restructuring of NATO to provide a clamp to (and for) the United States in the safeguarding of European security.

Even for the early supporters of an integrated European defence arrangement, the inherent gains for the United States were clear. If Europe integrated and therefore strengthened its capabilities, the United States could count on a strong burden-sharing partner, eventually willing and able to pay for much of its own defence. The US effort and its military presence could be drawn down; perhaps the United States could, then, even return to an expeditionary strategy for Europe and leave, in order to attend to its other global commitments and responsibilities. Moreover, true to Monnet's neofunctionalist vision, the internecine rivalries that had twice drawn the United States into European battle would be overcome and daily bested through operational cooperation, coordinated planning, and intra-European transparency and trust.

With almost equal intensity, however, successive American administrations have also manifested profound suspicion about or direct opposition to an integrated European security approach. From this perspective, Washington would find itself at a disadvantage faced with a European consensus or a demand for equal voice in security decision making. United, with the one telephone number made famous by Henry Kissinger, Europeans would form a caucus – with disastrous consequences within the alliance. Washington would not be able to use its full influence through either its military predominance inside the alliance or its cross-cutting channels of bilateral agreements and commitments. With France the likely leader, this argument stressed, Europeans would first bargain among themselves about the distribution of tasks, the carving-up of the procurement pie, and the nature of intelligence requirements. A single European voice would then be a powerful 'other' in policy debate. This would be true on issues within the alliance space and, more importantly, outside of Europe. It would have far more potential for success in demanding more forceful American action (as it had done in Bosnia), set its own global limits (as in its attempts to avoid involvement alongside the United States in Vietnam), or push for concessions or even appeasement over confrontation and military action (as it had tried to do in its efforts at *détente* with the Soviet Union in the 1970s) (Kelleher 1995).

Worse yet would be an autonomous European defence capacity within the European Union that would come to SHAPE and other operational/

planning organisations with a fully developed posture of Europe's own. Some American pessimists feared that in the end a united Europe might falter or fail. Europeans, weary of war and the costs of maintaining a cold peace after a century of combat, might just choose a lowest common denominator defence effort or simply go 'soft' – spending less, choosing ineffective capabilities and status quo 'national champions' to produce them, and lacking the domestic political will necessary to authorise the use of force.

The terms of debate

The Solana strategy initiators and drafters in 2003 were well aware of these arguments and their contradictions. The form and language of ESS were purposely shaped to meet most of the questions and issues raised in the abstract sense. Javier Solana, Robert Cooper, Christoph Heusgen, and their colleagues in Solana's office consulted widely and travelled to Washington themselves for informal soundings and tactical discussions. Officials from all parts of the Bush administration – particularly State Department officials and National Security Council professionals – welcomed the Solana strategy in formal and informal discussions in part as a new offset in an increasingly bitter transatlantic and domestic debate over Iraq. Solana and his associates used their long-established personal reputations and prestige in the United States to maximum advantage across most of the elite security-political spectrum. In a relatively short time, the ESS initiative also met with largely positive responses within American think-tanks and among expert analysts in Washington. As will be discussed in more detail below, perhaps only the die-hard 'NATO firsters' and extreme neocons in the Pentagon insisted on more doctrinal and operational proof immediately.

But the ESS initiative also confronted more than a decade of fundamental American disappointments with Europe over how to devise new transatlantic responses to the post-Cold War era. For military officials and political figures alike, the key questions turned less on a specific EU–NATO arrangement, as long as there was no fatal harm done to NATO or to the basic transatlantic bargain, than on the specific security priorities, operational requirements, and defence costs that European states were now willing to take on, in the face of the range of new threats the West confronted. If ESDP meant the Europeans would finally do more and spend more, it was worth it.

This was true across the political spectrum and on the Hill as well as in the executive departments and agencies. Most of the American elite still preferred NATO to all other possible arrangements but also were interested in defence savings, emerging Asian priorities, and a respite from the primary burdens they believed the United States had shouldered for Europe throughout the Cold War. By the time of Clinton's second term, the broad Washington consensus had accepted the inevitability of a more or less independent European security identity and an ESDP; its final shape and scope were forthcoming. Until the Iraq debate, their focus was most often not on specific European declarations or rhetoric or even – notwithstanding the seemingly perpetual verbal battles with France in Brussels – on the details of US–European decision-making processes.

The lessons of Bosnia and Kosovo

The historical hook on which many in Washington hung their concerns, however, was what they saw as the lessons of Bosnia, especially and increasingly the lessons of Kosovo. The broader Yugoslav conflict involved more than enough blame to be shared by Americans and Europeans. From 1991 to 1995, the Bush–Baker team, then the Clinton–Christopher partnership, had sought to maintain distance or demonstrated core ambivalence over US involvement. Europe – particularly Kohl's Germany – flush with unification euphoria, had overestimated its ability to stop the conflict or indeed to engage the warring factions in negotiations toward peace and had then lurched from political tactic to tactic. NATO found itself by 1995 in its first shooting war, suffering from limited organisational and functional capabilities, outdated planning infrastructure, and coordinating an unforeseen set of other involved institutions and actors, state and non-state. In the end, the Yugoslav outcome – stability but at the cost of more or less permanent ethnic division – was something no one had wished and some found not worth the cost. Both Americans and Europeans had struggled painfully to master the tasks of mounting a defence against irregular armies, quelling ethnic unrest and conflict, and the stabilising/recreating of an imploded state.

But Kosovo put transatlantic differences and the gap in fundamental security capabilities into even sharper relief. The short engagement, with precision strikes planned and approved by Clinton, Madeline Albright, and William Cohen, became a protracted three-month war producing thousands of refugees. American forces remained largely high in the air while Europeans posted higher-risk ground troops for peacekeeping goals. American political figures wanted military 'compellance' and escalation strategies to force negotiations on Serbian withdrawals but confronted strategic disagreements and inadequate capacities within the alliance. For the first time, they were impressed, often dramatically and negatively, by the basic European military dependence on the United States. Clinton estimated that with the exception of Britain, France, and perhaps Germany, none of the European contributors had the budget, forces, modern equipment, or secondary support capabilities (intelligence, transport, communications, and reconnaissance functions) needed for the new warfare or for effective humanitarian intervention. Further, there seemed to be little to indicate that these states would pay for or acquire the needed capabilities, given the continuing overall downward spirals in the numbers and funding of European military establishments.

The judgements of the American military were even sharper (Clark 2001). For many in the leadership, Kosovo had proved the impossibility of military action with even the closest NATO allies without a commonly accepted strategic concept and set of planned operational priorities and congruent rules of engagement (ROE) that had been previously or were immediately agreed to. Target selection was in many ways the focal point of serious discomfort. There were fundamental disagreements over targeting choice and tempo between the United States and the United Kingdom, between various NATO authorities, and even between field commanders and their national political leaderships, highlighted in the relationship between the Supreme Allied Commander Europe, Wesley Clark, and Washington. More importantly, the requirement of consensual political control meant that the allies exercised a *droit de regard* over 99 per cent of Washington's target choices, a time-consuming and often fractious process.[2]

It is interesting that these disagreements assumed even greater virulence in American military lore after the relatively successful (however protracted) conclusion of the Kosovo campaign and despite the very different lessons drawn by others. For many Europeans, again more strongly in retrospect than observable at the time, European weakness and overweening American military superiority had led to demands to accept American priorities, military estimates, and ROE without comment or discussion. Too often Americans had pushed for action while Europeans were assigned to the mopping up and the costly, risky peace-building missions on the ground.

A broad range of American support for ESDP and an ESDI, therefore, was increasingly 'preconditioned' – upon what would produce not just new European defence architecture or organisational diagrams but also capabilities and operational taskings for the strengthened forces within Europe. This had essentially been set in place beginning in 1998, when the British–French Summit at St-Malo launched ESDP and a major political initiative. The emphasis thereafter was on a Britain supporting European defence autonomy and a defence process (within limits), and on a France acknowledging NATO as the usual framework for Europe. Madeline Albright as secretary of state had cautiously summed up American support for this in the formulaic three 'Ds' for which there was general bipartisan, centrist support on the Hill as well as within the executive branch:[3] a European security programme would be supported by the United States so long as it did not 'discriminate' against non-EU NATO states, 'decouple' Europe's security from that of the United States, or lead to 'duplication' of NATO's command structure and planning system. EU–NATO meetings spent the next several years in debate about the definition of these fairly imprecise terms, with a formal institutional channel and relationship established in January 2001 and a comprehensive joint declaration on ESDP only in December 2002.

Transformation urgency post-9/11

Broadly categorised, the second hook for American circles was the stark conclusions about defence capability and readiness in the twenty-first century that the Bush administration drew from the 9/11 attacks. These views and the impact these attacks had on the evolution of the first Bush National Security Strategy (NSS), then nearing finalisation, have been well described elsewhere (Dombrowski and Payne 2006; Nichols 2005). Included here on the critical counter-proliferation terrorism nexus is Spear's (2003) depiction of the attributes reflected in the NSS in comparison with the prescriptions of the ESS. Table 8.1 provides an overview of the basic orientations of the NSS and the ESS.

It is perhaps enough here to note that in at least the first year after 9/11 and for some well beyond, these Bush prescriptions and the subsequent actions taken in Afghanistan and then in Iraq met with almost unquestioning congressional, elite, and popular approval. Obvious throughout the NSS is the very different American sense of context and timing for action than had been heard before – strikingly different from that prevalent in Europe in 2002 or even that eventually reflected in the ESS itself. The United States, the NSS intoned, was now 'at war', and so were its allies, and the war was global and unconventional. The threat was not just radical ideological terrorists, who cannot be deterred or won over by past strategies of political recognition, but more importantly, their access to WMD or to advanced conventional weaponry, which must be countered. The threat was immediate and pressing and would require immediate response or preemption/prevention by the United States acting together with its allies or alone, if necessary. The usual international rules and the conventions of existing institutions, including the UN and even NATO, faded in relevance in the face of the urgent task of confronting this primary challenge; waiting for its

Table 8.1 How US and EU national security strategies differ

On ...	US National Security Strategy	EU Basic Principles
The perceived threat	We will not permit the world's most dangerous regimes and terrorists to threaten us with the world's most destructive weapons. We must accord the highest priority to the protection of the United States, our forces, and our friends and allies from the existing and growing WMD threat.	The proliferation of all weapons of mass destruction ... and means of delivery such as ballistic missiles constitutes a threat to international peace and security. These weapons are different from other weapons not only because of their capacity to cause death on a large scale but also because they could destabilize the international system.
The use of force	While the United States will constantly strive to enlist the support of the international community, we will not hesitate to act alone, if necessary, to exercise our right of self-defense by acting preemptively against such terrorists, to prevent them from doing harm against our people and our country ... [T]he United States can no longer solely rely on a reactive posture as we have in the past.	To address the new threats, a broad approach is needed. Political and diplomatic preventative measures ... and resort to the competent international organizations ... form the first line of defence. When these measures ... have failed, coercive measures under Chapter VII of the UN Charter and international law (sanctions, selective or global, interceptions of shipments and, as appropriate, the use of force) could be envisioned. The UN Security Council should play a central role.
Fundamental principles	Our National Strategy to Combat Weapons of Mass Destruction has three principal pillars: Counterproliferation to Combat WMD Use ... Strengthened Nonproliferation to Combat WMD Proliferation ... [and] Consequence Management to Respond to WMD Use ... The three pillars of the US national strategy to combat WMD are seamless elements of a comprehensive approach.	The EU is committed to the multilateral system. We will pursue the implementation and universalisation of the existing disarmament and non-proliferation norms. With regard to biological and chemical weapons, we will work towards declaring the bans on these weapons to be universally binding rules of international law.

| Stopping the spread of WMD | One of the most difficult challenges we face is to prevent, deter, and defend against the acquisition and use of WMD by terrorist groups. The current and potential future linkages between terrorist groups and state sponsors of terrorism are particularly dangerous and require priority attention. The full range of counterproliferation, nonproliferation, and consequence management measures must be brought to bear against the WMD terrorist threat … | The best solution to the problem of proliferation of WMD is that countries should no longer feel they need them. If possible, political solutions should be found to the problems which lead them to seek WMD. The more secure countries feel, the more likely they are to abandon programmes: disarmament measures can lead to a virtuous circle just as weapons programmes can lead to an arms race. |

Excerpts taken from Basic Principles for *An EU Strategy against Proliferation of Weapons of Mass Destruction* (June 2003), *National Strategy to Combat Weapons of Mass Destruction* (December 2002), and *National Security Strategy* (September 2002).

first strike was no longer acceptable. Moreover, Washington argued, present capabilities – especially military and intelligence capabilities at home and abroad – were inadequate for the new task. It would take massive new efforts and hard political tradeoffs among all like-minded and allied states to protect the populations and the democratic heritage of the West.

Most American elites saw as predictable the 'soft' or 'antiwar' public reactions in Europe to the NSS and the stress that Europe's elites placed on American 'rampant isolationism'. But large numbers of those in Washington expected and confidently predicted that European governments and elites would in the end acknowledge the same sense of threat and the need for a direct American response to the 9/11 outrage.[4] There had to be a *national* retaliation for a national outrage, a territorial attack. The administration and its conservative supporters scarcely acknowledged the NATO invocation of Article V, the first-ever assertion of the cooperative defence clause, in the days following 9/11. The campaign in Afghanistan was deliberately conceived and planned as an American response to 9/11, with minimal dependence on allied contributions or allied political legitimisation until well after the first phases of conflict had been concluded.[5]

The most conservative military and political circles took their criticism of America's European allies many steps farther. The failure of the allies to conceive of a global threat requiring more numerous, more capable, and more deployable forces meant that the United States might be better off fighting alone (Gompert, Kugler and Libicki 1999). Beginning in the late 1980s, these critics and some defence analysts began arguing about an unbridgeable gap in transatlantic capabilities, a gap reinforced by the experiences in the first Gulf war. By 2003, the theme had sharpened – the gap in the level of capability was continuously increasing and was now irreversible, with the United States in the throes of defence transformation and the shift to a network-centric warfare strategy. Few if any of the allies were allocating the same kind of investments, thus making a sham of even the minimal standards of interoperability that NATO had set. Arguments about ways to reduce the gap, share equipment, or even find technical fixes were swept aside. Huge deficits in command and control, communications, and intelligence, these critics now concluded, meant that US forces would probably be safer operating on their own.

Geopolitical ideologies

The third and perhaps most debatable hook was an assertion heard on both the far left and the far right of the American elite spectrum, namely, the political–military judgement that Europe and the Atlantic alliance would not be central arenas for Americans in the twenty-first century. Asia or the war on terror would be far more important to American domestic and international stability interests. The assertion was familiar; it had been heard not only historically but also with increasing frequency during the immediate post-Cold War years and as the Clinton administration wore on. Popular magazines as well as seasoned analysts pointed to Asia's emerging power, particularly in the economic sphere. The Bush NSS raised this assertion to new levels: Europe and the European Union received scant mention, China and (for the first time) India loomed large. In informal but government-related Washington circles, China was routinely discussed as a near-peer competitor, India as a great democracy and an advanced technological power, with interests in prosperity and security that converged with those of the United States perhaps more closely than did those of the traditional European allies.

Capping these judgements, the concept of Europe as a strategic backwater was given new dimensions by Kagan's (2002, 2003) Mars–Venus analogy, which conservatives routinely trumpeted as the primary explanation for Europe's failure to follow America's lead in Iraq.[6] Europe as self-indulgent Venus was culturally and politically unable to take security seriously, especially in the new post-Soviet security context, and would never step up to the new challenges with the required forces or the necessary political will. Kagan's somewhat facile analysis seemed primarily influenced by (and was largely a reaction to) Germany's brand of multilateralism in the 1990s and what he saw as wimpish behaviour regarding the use of force (e.g. the debate on the use of force in Kosovo, particularly among the Greens). Kagan ignored much of NATO's hard-wrought record in Bosnia and Kosovo, discarded or dismissed previous instances of European (and particularly, the increasing numbers of German) forces involved in out-of-area interventions, and downplayed French and British determination to retain and, if necessary, use their national nuclear forces. He also overlooked or seemed unaware of broad similarities in European and American popular opinion – as demonstrated, for example, in Bailes's (2005a) striking comparison of public opinion trends in 2003.

But as with all popular 'bumper sticker' arguments, and with the megaphone handed to him by conservatives, Kagan soon shaped much of the transient Washington mood and the inside-the-beltway chatter on Europe's deficiencies. In the absence of competing explanations, it was easy to fasten onto the idea that Venus might be nice but would never be a partner worthy to take into battle.

For the rest of the American elites outside of Washington and outside of government, Europe seemed increasingly far away. Most European states were focused inward, with weak governments (Blair's Britain was the exception) concerned primarily with domestic welfare and prosperity. Most of Europe's dynamism as perceived by Americans was involved in furthering the European project itself. The principal debates, in which Americans were largely irrelevant or unwelcome, centred on the eastward enlargement of the Union or the new European constitution and the development of organisations and processes for the future. They were not about substantive new military contributions or achievements in security for the present. Public opinion trends demonstrated this: US distancing from Europe seemed more than matched by European distancing from the United States and from, above all, the increasingly reviled Bush administration and the emerging war in Iraq.

American decision-makers and the ESS

Initial reactions

The announcement of the ESS in June 2003 thus came as a welcome surprise to most in the American policy elite. There were few headlines, even in the newspapers of record; few noted, for example, that the text had only been 'taken note of' by the foreign ministers. Even fewer, according to several interviewees, understood that it was a 'living text', presaging changes and that would only thereafter be formally accepted. The reception was generally favourable among 'insiders' and in most Washington circles, within the administration and outside of it. It was one more sign that the reconciliation with the European allies for which the president now wished, and that domestic critics now demanded, was progressing. The administration itself was already feeling somewhat vulnerable on the issue of dividing Europe over Iraq and was beginning to sense that the capability that had won the war in Iraq was not sufficient to win the peace.

Seasoned actors on both sides of the Atlantic had also been looking for ways to knit together some of the more obvious holes in the transatlantic fabric. Solana himself (2003a, b) had given a notable Harvard speech in April about reconciling Mars and Venus; the stream of European visitors had been constant. Moreover, there had already been a number of EU–US compromises on the much-debated European Security and Defence Policy, most notably the agreements in December 2002 and March 2003 on organic NATO–EU planning links and EU access to NATO's assets. Indeed, with little explicit notice in the United States, the European Union was beginning its first two military operations, Operation Artemisin the Democratic Republic of the Congo, and Operation Concordia in Macedonia.[7]

More importantly, the ESS's language and its focus on a threat-based assessment made it, in the words of one figure in the Office of the Secretary of Defense, 'something we could work with, something that had some handles'. The tone was pro-active and forward-looking, with optimism about the potential to transform the international environment in ways consistent with Western democratic values and political traditions. The analysis of threats was new and almost identical to that proclaimed in the NSS and presidential speeches throughout 2002 and 2003: proliferation, terrorism, and the nexus of the two; extremism, regional instability; and transborder crime. The scope was global, with recognition that most threats would have to be addressed outside of Europe, despite the emphasis on Europe's regional roles and the reference to internal social and economic concerns (crime, immigration). There was a call for both robust and speedy responses, including a new sense of urgency that matched in critical ways that so keenly felt in Washington.[8]

Not all were, of course, equally surprised. Just before Thessaloniki, some in the White House and at State had seen a draft and been able to comment. (But as one Washington interviewee remarked, 'We didn't get much more of a chance than most European foreign ministries did before the roll-out'.)[9] Several had applauded the surprisingly short, direct statement and its emphasis on 'concrete problems we all now faced after 9/11' as being 'right for the American ear'. These individuals were instrumental in shoring up the other, broadly favourable, reactions and in answering questions on, for example, what was meant by the Solana draft's language regarding 'preemptive engagement'. One or two American interviewees remarked later that they had themselves pondered this particularly, since in at least some drafts they saw, or as they had been told, the words 'preemptive' had been inserted in the text by hand.

Prominent in the welcoming response was also the generally high regard that most in Washington felt for Solana and his team and for this ESS having been achieved so quickly after its initial conception earlier in the spring. Solana had been the Clinton candidate for Secretary-General of NATO, especially favoured by then secretary of state Warren Christopher and National Security Advisor Anthony Lake. He won the admiration of the secretary of defence, William Perry, and his Pentagon team, as well as kudos from some of the American right as well, through his strong, fair leadership during campaigns in the former Yugoslavia. Kosovo had proved more trying, but his stature had not diminished.

Solana's voice and push behind the June draft thus increased the document's credibility and attraction. His rapport and easy access had continued even after he joined the European Commission. For most in Washington, Solana was one of the few 'known quantities' in the evolving EU mix focused on the new constitution, and he was thought the natural choice for European foreign minister. He was still a frequent visitor and speaker, and he worked at good relations across the American political spectrum. The members of his team, especially the legendary Robert Cooper, were equally well connected and enjoyed direct continuing links to most of the East and West Coast think-tank world and the high-level transatlantic policy circuit of public intellectuals.

The Washington process

The June draft generated an internal debate of some proportions, one that played out over the next six months. The political lineup is interesting not only because it reflects that actions regarding Iraq itself were perhaps less productive of tension and division than was the spiral of bitterness, perceived betrayals, and the resulting domestic political fallout that characterised calculations and miscalculations on both sides of the endless arguments in 2002–3. The push for the ESS confronted a basic division of the relevant Washington policy community into three somewhat fluid groups, each with its own agenda and its own approach to the future use of the Solana draft.[10] Events and the onrush of events in Iraq and in the Bush reelection campaign meant that the possibilities for intergroup compromise were never really tested. By 2006, the balance had clearly shifted, but the self-definition of each group reveals characteristics and trends that persist in American thinking about Europe and the European Union's role in global security.

The unconvinceables

Perhaps the easiest to describe were the small number of consistent adversaries of any reconciliation with the Europeans. Located as always within parts of the Pentagon and on both the right and the far left on the Hill, they tended to focus on the strategic agenda of the NSS: the Asia theatre, the need for new strategic partnerships, and coalitions of the willing rather than restrictive alliances tied to the pace of the slowest – the primacy of national control in the defence of national interest.

Their principal proximate anger arose from what they saw as European – primarily French but with also (and with particular anger) German – treachery in the Iraq crisis. French actions were the traditional target; Germany's behaviour prompted more outrage, as new and somehow more treacherous and 'ungrateful'. The majority of the group was often self-described as 'NATO-firsters', those who saw NATO as the last best hope for cooperative defence to which any EU security arrangement was a prima facie provocation and evidence of an attempt to thwart American dominance. Their mistrust of European intentions and rejection had been given new energy by the Franco-German (with Belgium) decision to break NATO's first cardinal rule, the invocation by a Member State of Article V, when the three blocked NATO preventive action requested by Turkey in January 2003 before the actual attack in Iraq.[11] The simultaneous climbdown from that opposition and the cresting of disagreements at the UN had been bitter on all sides. The final straw for this group was perhaps the April 2003 Tervuren meeting (dismissed by several interviewees as 'The Chocolate Summit') to consider breaking NATO's second cardinal precept – by establishing a European headquarters and planning cell physically and conceptually separate from SHAPE.[12]

ESS, in their eyes, was just one more stone in this pile. There was 'nothing there', 'just words' and 'clever British drafting', or 'the old French ploy wrapped up in new clothes'. The ESS did not solve the problems that 9/11 and Iraq had highlighted about different European and American conceptions of threat. Moreover, they did not indicate that the Europeans had changed their views about the necessity of rapid military force to combat the intersecting challenges of terrorism and WMD proliferation. There was no specification of follow-through, and questions to the relevant European national authorities had not produced any concrete answers on new military capabilities or monies.

Nor, most concluded, would there ever be. There was no need for protracted opposition to the ESS beyond the initial discussions; the Europeans would do themselves in by themselves, 'just like always', one concluded later. These actors largely bought Kagan's argument as ground truth – that there was an almost inevitable, culturally driven European tendency toward protracted ineffective diplomacy, and an aversion to conflict *per se*. European pacification after World War II, largely through US agency, was now complete. Europeans would no longer fight one another or require American intervention or mediation. But they also could not and would not confront the issue of the legitimate use of force against new challenges, including some that forced preemption to anticipate and thereby blunt horrendous effects. Deterrence no longer worked in those instances; as the Bush administration repeatedly proclaimed, only rapid, decisive, prestrike action would. Bush neocons claimed that the United States must therefore now pursue its own vital interests and leave the Europeans to their words and organisation building.

The 'yes . . . but' faction

Some of this scepticism and pessimism characterised the second group – elements primarily in State, several in the Senate, and policy groups within the Pentagon who might be termed the 'yes . . . but' actors on general European policy. Over the summer and fall months of 2003, they tried to laud the ESS at home and in Europe as a 'breakthrough' in the recent transatlantic debacles. But they simultaneously probed or lobbied for ideas on next steps, mechanisms, and budget implications at both the European and the national levels.

The biggest concern for a number in this group was how the ESS would affect the EU plans for future interactions with NATO. Would NATO still be the place of first resort for crisis decisions? How would the new EU structures foreseen for planning and decisions on rapid action mesh with those on SHAPE and the North Atlantic Council? What would be the cumulative impact, if any, of the various European strategies that were being produced with some regularity in the run-up to the European constitution – on counter-terrorism, against proliferation, on good governance and stability in the European neighbourhood, as well as the ESS itself? Which new entities in the European Union would exercise authority – the Commission, the Council, or varying coalitions of the national institutions?

Most worried too that the ESS represented at most a bold move forward by Solana and the Commission, but one not supported by the Member States, at the time of inception or conceivably in the future. Several watched the process of revision for the December document with considerable care and saw this as a test of Europe's real intentions and ability to move ahead along the lines the ESS spelled out. They were on the whole reassured by the small number of changes demanded by the EU states and surprised that most came from the smaller members, not the imagined French or German barrage. In contrast to the first group, they also tended to downplay as 'predictable in terms of German domestic politics' the one major change in the final version – the change to 'preventive' rather than 'preemptive' engagement in cases 'when the signs of proliferation are detected'.

But the stalemates that brought a suspension of the EU constitutional negotiations brought new fears about Europe's real stability and fundamental political will. Some in the end found themselves in basic agreement with Nicholas Burns, then ambassador to NATO, who returned again and again to NATO's strategic priority and the restraint of other duplicative organisational structures. As he had argued in September 2003 in a press conference,

NATO and the European Union negotiated seven agreements in March of this year (2003). Together they're called, in diplomatic parlance, Berlin Plus. Those seven agreements essentially come down to one objective: that NATO will support ESDP. NATO will support the evolution and growth of Europe's security and defense capabilities, of the European Union taking on new missions, as we've supported the European Union in Macedonia. But that it will be a cooperative and collaborative relationship, where the European Union will not seek to create duplicative institutions.

(Burns 2003)

Others joined the US ambassador to the European Union, Rockwell Schnabel, in his frustration over some dire options for Europe's future security policy. As he later expressed it:

We hope for a Europe that can make the tough decisions on how to face the very real threats that face us, including the spread of WMD, of terrorism and of organized crime networks that thrive off evil commerce in humans, drugs and arms. But let me repeat, it needs to be a Europe that can make the tough decisions. If the result of having a common European foreign policy means that policies on issues such as Iran's nuclear programme or North Korea's missiles degenerate into some sort of lowest common denominator . . . [W]ell, then, we'd prefer what help we can get from each Member State acting independently.

For this group more than the two others in Washington, the general downward spiral of transatlantic debate over Iraq intruded as 2004 progressed. Even the new efforts on both sides of the Atlantic to overcome these or to adopt more positive themes (e.g. collaboration in Afghanistan, the handover in the Balkans) tended to overshadow more policy emphasis on what had been achieved and what could be done cooperatively in follow-on steps. Iraq in a sense had absorbed all the oxygen, everything else was on muted hold.

By the midpoint of 2004 there remained major questions as to what specific operational implementation would actually happen and what next doctrine steps could and should be taken on both the side of Europe and by the United States. The 'battlegroups' initiative in November 2004 overcame some but not all of the disappointments that this group felt.

There had been no follow-up to the ESS; there was still the failure to produce new capabilities to meet the Headline Goals or to reverse the downward slide of national budgets. With functioning battle groups in 2006–7, Europe would have at least some projectable power assets that could be deployed in a crisis, even if still lacking in the strategic lift and communications infrastructure needed to support them.[13]

The restorers

The last group of American decision-makers reacting to the ESS is the most difficult to describe succinctly. All but a few were 'restorers' – they welcomed the ESS for its sake but perhaps more for their own. This was the group whose members were most discouraged by the Bush administration's disputes with the European allies, its willingness to downplay NATO to the benefit of coalitions of the willing or unilateral action, and its determination to lead even if the allies did not wish to follow. Many were centrist or Bush I Republicans and a handful of 'old' Democrats, but there were more than a few Bush II Republicans as well. Most had long valued the alliance and especially the American leadership it supported, but few were blind to its deficits or to European capability failures or unceasing commitment to diplomacy above any other form of action. All were convinced, however, that the 9/11 world required more international cooperation rather than less; all saw the European allies as 'those whom you went to first' and who saw the world 'in the end, the way we do'.

To this group, the tone and language of the ESS suggested the beginning of a new strategic dialogue among the allies. It was the beginning of a new concept that would guard against a repeat, at least in the near term, of the breakdown of the Atlantic consensus and of the 2002–3 divisions over Iraq.[14] Their welcome for the ESS was rooted less in Atlantic idealism or old transatlantic bargains than in a realist or instrumental approach to the present American agenda. The problems of unilateralism in Iraq were increasingly obvious. But more critically over the longer term, the United States could not and should not act alone if it wanted to transform the international community or effectively fight either terrorism or proliferation. Europe was the primary place to find specific, effective contributions to these missions – militarily, politically, and economically – first because of common values and perspectives, but secondly because of the patterns and habits of cooperation well practised over four decades.

This group saw the ESS as decisively reinstating strategic partnership with the United States. Discussions about the replacement of the word 'preemption' in the second Solana iteration flared up but then almost as quickly subsided. So too did speculation about the motives of the European critics of the initiative and the watering down of what were seen as key commitments in terms of timetable and rapid action. Certainly, the mood at the end of 2003 was generally positive. Indeed, the ESS gave a new impetus to both bilateral and multilateral planning, again especially within State.

It signalled that increased European contributions could be mobilised and legitimised in the relatively near future on terms acceptable to both American public opinion and European public opinion still roiling or highly charged from the fallout of the Iraq debates. Informal discussions could begin almost immediately, with the specific needs in Afghanistan first on the agenda. Europeans were already voicing some willingness to take on new responsibilities and leadership in former Yugoslavia, including the Bosnia mission. There were also crisis needs in Africa – East, West, and South; there was the continuing surveillance need in the Gulf and in Operation Enduring Freedom. Also there was still the need to give Europe the 'first-responder role' in stabilising and securing the new Europe – in its neighbourhood, in the Caucasus, and in terms of integrating and socialising Russia and Ukraine.

Moreover, the ESS could be a mechanism to allow construction of a bridge to the new European institutions that the constitution would empower. The protracted NATO–EU organisational battles could be put aside and replaced eventually, it was argued in State, by direct policy planning talks even at the US–EU level. These would still parallel the national 'bilaterals' in which the Policy Planning Staff took the lead, but (reportedly in Secretary Colin Powell's words) these were mechanisms 'worth exploring'.

They would also ensure greater EU political engagement in the United States as well as far greater understanding of the domestic political forces that figure into security decisions on both sides of the Atlantic. In this view, Kagan had it wrong; his dichotomy was too simple. During the Iraq debates of 2002, Powell had reportedly complained privately about 'misplaced European help'. His analysis implied to some who heard it a suggestion that France and Germany believed their progressively more strident opposition to a war against Iraq or in rapid, American-led action at the United Nations would strengthen Powell and the pro-diplomacy/anti-war forces active within the administration. Powell reportedly indicated that, on the contrary, this had made his own position more difficult, with his opponents accusing him not only of disagreement but of disloyalty and responsiveness to 'external' interests as well.[15] Ultimately this had proven even more damaging for the US–European discourse and had led to the spread of broad anti-European rhetoric in Washington and more importantly, throughout the country (at its most absurd, the 'freedom fries' campaign).

What this group feared, however, was that the European Union would never get there. By December 2003 and the breakdown of the constitutional talks, it was by no means clear for whom Solana was speaking or how even formal acceptance of the ESS in December would translate into operational realities. The resolution of the constitutional crisis in March 2004 was progress, but as eventually was proven, it still did not guarantee acceptance by all the Member States.

Conclusion

By 2006, analysts from either side of the Atlantic but particularly in Washington could be impressed with how much had been done in the intervening three years to advance operationally the basic themes and purposes addressed by the ESS. Global strategic partnership across the Atlantic now seems the norm or the usual expectation, even if the specifics are still rocky or agreements case by case. Both sides of the Atlantic have worked to advance specific, positive programmes of security cooperation. To mention only the obvious, there has been evolving collaboration in the efforts to persuade Iran not to acquire nuclear weapons, cooperation in both peacemaking and peacekeeping in Afghanistan, the successful handover to EU command in the Balkans, the emerging settlement in Kosovo, the relatively peaceful and successful 'colour revolutions' in Eastern Europe, and wave-off of Russian oil blackmail in Ukraine. Both the parameters of the transatlantic debate and the amplitude of the public-opinion wave in the United States supporting the president's choice to attack and criticise French and German 'infidelity' have changed decisively.

As argued at the outset, the ESS and its associated strategies on terrorism and counter-proliferation contributed directly to this change in atmospherics and in policy. They provoked and reinforced interesting speculation in insider executive-branch circles in 2004 about how to change the approaches to Europe and the European Union if Bush won a second term. These efforts met with considerable success even in the first months of 2005, with Bush's first visit to the European Union and his several speeches stressing cooperation and unity in global security. It also provided a context for persuading the sceptical Bush team finally of the merits of the diplomatic approach of the European Three toward Iran and of a framework for a common public story for those seeking alternatives.

Interested American specialists and the group of congressional politicians sensitive to Europe still raise the major outstanding questions as to what the specific operational implementation of the ESS will be, when it will actually happen, and what next steps in doctrine and means to make it operational can and should be taken. At the moment neither Europe nor the United States seems to have definitive answers. The Bush National Security Strategy document issued early in 2006 was decidedly gentler and less overtly nationalistic in tone than its immediate predecessors. It was also more specific and inclusive in its emphasis on global partnerships and attention to Europe. It highlighted the concerns of integrating the instruments of power that the ESS envisioned across the spectrum. There was less rigidity regarding the choice of instruments and less drama surrounding the need for a credible threat of preemptive action, although the assertion of the threat itself remained. Capabilities and transformation through new technology were also still the keystones.

Compared to the 2003 lineup that confronted the ESS, the balance in the Washington policy arena looks critically changed, largely because of developments in Iraq and the resulting fall in the Bush poll numbers. But the majority of Washington officials and experts remain broadly sceptical and demanding of specifics about European follow-through. There is far more consensus on the need to have the Europeans 'inside' in global enterprises of all kinds, in part due to an emerging transatlantic agreement that Europe is a global player in security as well as across the board. The traditional 'out of area' debate seems long past. Broad popular concerns in Europe about out-of-area commitments are seen as subsumed in case-by-case decisions, and the steadily rising numbers of European coalition deaths is thought still small enough not to have further inflamed domestic opinion.

Few of the old American neocon sceptics are as powerful within the Pentagon, the executive branch, or *vis-à-vis* the Congress as they were in 2003. Vice President Dick Cheney remains a force always to be reckoned with, but he faces more frequent and more direct contradiction from within State and within the Congress. To a number of observers, including in the attentive foreign policy public, the neocon view that 'Europeans don't count' seems foolhardy or at least a sign of fatal hubris. The campaign of 'transatlantic smiles' continues, even if the perspective from Washington is largely instrumental – how Europe can help in this or that crisis.

But there is also much about which to be pessimistic. The shift in dominant American governmental opinion has been to the 'yes . . . but' group, with many of the 'restorers' now prepared to accept operational cooperation and surface comity as enough to get by with for now. The present military leadership rhetorically stresses global partnership and allied solidarity – such as the new concept of an active integration of allied and partner navies in a thousand-ship navy. But most seemingly have not changed their pessimism about Europe's global role or, in the press of Iraq, even given it much detailed thought of late. They do not as yet seem prepared to trust the new types of cooperation developing in Afghanistan or in the several areas outside of Iraq itself, areas where European and Americans together are confronting precisely the new challenges both the NSS and the ESS specified. Those interviewed are fairly dismissive of the EU missions so far. Cooperation in Africa, East and West, is rarely highlighted in public or private. Even the complex division of labour in Afghanistan is seen principally through the lens of the urgent need of the United States to shift some of its burden in order to reinforce the forces in Iraq.

NATO – not necessarily in the best of health and itself struggling with the fallout of expansion on decision making – remains the principal preferred forum for discussion and planning. The disagreements and difficulties of 2002–3 are not discussed; Americans and Europeans have moved on to more specific issues – Darfur, Afghanistan, and the requirements of force transformation. The European Union is most often seen as mired in constitutional crisis and not soon able to move forward again, even though few understand what the constitutional crisis really is about. Some know of the progress with the first steps of the European Defence Agency, but all argue that few serious coordinating institutions exist in Europe or have the right experience to push forward at the transatlantic level. Beyond NATO, the US–EU channels are still not seen as appropriate mechanisms for operational coordination, let alone brainstorming before policies congeal on national levels.

The security sector seems in particularly bad shape. Europe appears less capable in 2007 than it did in 2003, and with even weaker governments, recently elected or about to undergo electoral tests, even less able to take up expanded missions, create new capabilities, or preserve those that had existed. Beyond those of the Big Three – France, Britain, and Germany – the acts of European governments regarding doctrine and force transformation in particular remain less than impressive. Poland may yet come through, but the path for cooperation no longer seems certain in a revived nationalist environment and after withdrawal from Iraq. European defence budgets continue to spiral downward except in France and Britain, and the force numbers now deployed outside of Europe are seen as essentially representing the maximum that Europe can now sustain from the base of over a million men under arms. The EU battlegroup numbers and goals have slipped again, and the rapid reaction forces of both NATO and the European Union are less numerous and operational than their supporters had fervently hoped in 2003.

But if the outward traces are hard to discern, the impact of the ESS in terms of policy context is still considerable. A number of Americans have noticed that the ESS is still invoked in Europe and occasionally in Washington public discussions, if not explained or necessarily practised.[16] A summary judgement offered on the ESS by one of those interviewed in 2006 reflected the opinion of the majority – implementation of the ESS as a moment that could never have been but was well worth the ripple effect. The ESS and policy changes in Europe and the United States since 2004 have facilitated and smoothed the path for many specific improvements in critical areas: they have reinforced counter-proliferation (including the Proliferation Security Initiative) efforts, improved counter-terrorism evolution after Madrid and London, and provided opportunity and framework for needed discussion in both transatlantic and bilateral channels.

If the ESS itself were formally introduced today, a number of interviewees were asked in 2006, would the American reaction, and indeed the critical first reactions in Europe, be any different? Most of those American decision makers interviewed who gave the ESS any credence at all thought yes, with the optimistic conclusion that the ESS would do at least as well today and probably better in the long run. Interestingly enough most reached that conclusion not because they observed changes in American judgements or political calculus but because they saw more evidence of European interest in, and push behind, a potentially expanded and deepened ESS. The strategy's theme of global involvement, the need for joint vigilance against new challenges, the nexus of non-proliferation and counter-terrorism policies were deemed more acceptable to European national publics after the horrors of Madrid and London, and the emotional upheavals over the anti-Muslim cartoons. These events brought to Europeans a greater sense of vulnerability and a support for more direct, effective responses. The terrorist threat at home and the uncontrolled spiralling of violence in the Middle East made the search for transatlantic cooperation even more significant. A few believed that American and European agreement would be strengthened by the experience of dealing with Iran, almost whatever the final outcome.

Perhaps, one expert mused, the ESS and the European and transatlantic partnerships it foresees prevail as a totem, a set of benchmarks, or (in a way familiar to American domestic politics) as a hostage to the future. Serious policy changes in the United States often take place in two phases, he argued: an initial effort that is praiseworthy but fails, followed by a second, later effort that builds deliberately on the first incomplete phase. It carries the policy consensus and eventually popular sentiment with it.

All but a very few saw Germany again as key factor. Some wondered whether Chancellor Merkel's election victory really did represent enough change to carry the day with respect to constitutional changes in the European Union that are needed and to legitimise more specific operational moves toward security integration. But the intervening years of German–American discussions were judged by the majority to have seen a renewal of old habits of cooperation. No matter who was chancellor, Germany certainly has had far more experience in military missions outside of Europe than would have been thought possible even ten years ago. Merkel's Berlin has developed a far better understanding of global issues at stake and a willingness to define force as a necessary and legitimate response in some cases. This means the end of German diffidence and practised timidity in Berlin, to be replaced with more assertive, if also somewhat more tactical and conciliatory, German tone.

One or two also pondered the increased significance of the ESS, new or expanded, in the global order and the new NATO roles that various groups in Washington foresee for the future. Among the initiatives designed for NATO's November 2006 Riga Summit, a number among the Bush administration 'restorers', especially in State, are arguing for the transformation of some of NATO's political functions into an expanded global consultation scheme, something along the lines of the forum of democracies Madeline Albright once discussed in the late 1990s, or perhaps a multilateral PSI-like coalition of the willing.[17] There will be not a new alliance but rather new channels for consultation between the United States, the European Union, and such like-minded governments as Japan, Australia, and New Zealand. But the watchwords will be a NATO/EU-centred web; in the words of Assistant Secretary of State for Europe Dan Fried,

> Unilateralism is out. Effective multilateralism is in. We are working to make NATO the centerpiece alliance through which the transatlantic democratic community deals with security challenges around the world. This is not a global NATO but it is a NATO capable and actually, in fact, dealing with global challenges.
>
> (Fried 2006)

A quite different (although not mutually exclusive) view is the counterpoint advanced by Vice President Cheney in a speech in May 2006. NATO in this perspective is to expand as far east as possible, certainly including Ukraine and Georgia, and perhaps more of the borderlands of Russia, the states once called the 'FSU' or the Russian 'near abroad'. Certainly, for the NATO-firsters, the European Union is not expected to follow, nor is it wished, as a first priority, for the urgent security tasks in this region. A still larger NATO would form the right structure for rapidly implementing critically expanded cooperation on non-proliferation, counter-terrorism, and items of common concern from infectious diseases to preventing drugs, thugs, and human trafficking.

Only a small minority, it seems, wants NATO to remain much as it is and to have time to both sharpen its capabilities and digest the cumulative changes it has undergone in the last decade. The agenda is less interesting and perhaps even less in America's short-term interest, one of the former 'yes . . . but' group observed. But it is necessary for the next big challenges – the post-post Iraq, if it ever comes, and the foreseeable challenges around Russia's borders or in the still boiling Middle East.

But the context may well be different then, not least because of the pressures that ultimately drove American disappointment with the initial ESS effort. Any future option presupposes a European Union willing and able to take up global partnership in security, still not totally assured. Renationalisation of defence – in other words, the capabilities of the Big Three plus putatively Italy, Spain, and Poland may be all that there is. Concrete implementation is what most interviewed in Washington say they want, and soon – a set of new capabilities, guidelines, structured discussions, or eventually some other new form of cooperative decision-making structures. While the formation of the battlegroups may itself become the driving force for force transformation in a number of European militaries, there is no short-term solution to Europe's inability to field more than 60,000 to 70,000 troops.

This scepticism would seem particularly probable in most conceivable post-Iraq scenarios. As the United States begins to draw down its own forces or confronts the economic burden involved in long-term deployments in Iraq, Afghanistan, or somewhere else outside of Europe, most decision makers of either American party will ask, 'What is Europe doing?', 'Doesn't it have the power/the responsibility/the moral obligation to provide for stability in the face of continuing violence?'. Democrats would seem to be especially prone to this kind of thinking. They are themselves still divided on the outcomes they see as possible for the Iraq war. If they are electorally successful in 2008, they may yet have to confront the challenge – akin to that faced by Eisenhower regarding Korea in the early 1950s – of having to withdraw American forces and bring Iraq to a conclusion, however unsatisfactory.

And in the end, one overriding policy assumption seems remarkably persistent in some parts of the political spectrum, and it may characterise a new Democratic administration or Republicans who succeed the Bush–Cheney team. It is that Europe should and perhaps must be a global security partner to the United States in pursuit of its own European interests but also amenable to or mindful of American leadership. Iraq has challenged majority American confidence in its overweening power and its belief in the centrality of its beliefs and values to global outcomes, but these verities have not yet been shattered.

In the meantime, Iraq and the domestic agenda of immigration, budget overruns, abortion, gay marriage, and future elections dominate. A shooting war and the complaints of generals on the American side of the Atlantic focus attention on the specifics, on present capabilities, on practical contributions rather than idealised potential or future promise. The principal mode in election-year Washington is still one of waiting – in part for Iraq, in part for Iran, in part for Europe, but mostly for itself.

Notes

1 See Pond (2004) on the broad sweep of the discord and on what should be called the 'battle of the letters' in January and February 2003. See also the innovative content analysis of the specific arguments between France and the United States at the United Nations in Marfleet and Miller (2005).
2 Haine (2004: 42) cites a Rand study of 2001 documenting that Europeans flew only 40 per cent of the total sorties yet exercised approval of 807 of 976 targets beyond those initially planned by SHAPE. Several of those interviewed remembered the capability contributions of Europeans as far lower, one asserting that they had flown only 15 per cent of the sorties.
3 *Financial Times*, 7 December 1998. A knowledgeable source interviewed in 2004 in Washington stated that it should be stressed that while alliterative, the 'Ds' posed numerous hurdles in internal American discussions. A good deal of time in State was consumed in attempting to specify exactly what was or was not meant. Most military involved in transatlantic discussions with their counterparts found them either unhelpful or vague, to the point of clouding a firm American policy line on no independent European command or planning instance.
4 Most in interviews in 2004 mentioned two familiar refrains heard from Bush loyalists about the Europeans in 2001–2: (1) the Europeans will complain, stay fixated on rhetoric, and not act if left on their own, whereas if the United States shows leadership and resolve, they will eventually come around and stand beside us/follow us; and (2) the far harsher 'Where else do they have to go?'.
5 See Woodward's (2004) account of the cabinet discussion on 12 and 13 September about the sequence and the form of the American response and the intensity of the emotions behind branding this as an American undertaking. Indeed, the most dramatic conflict images favoured by Secretary of Defense Donald Rumsfeld stressed American symbols and American dominance across the spectrum of military capabilities. Who else, he seemed to argue, could have special forces on horseback with laptops calling down air strikes targeted in real time and launched from aircraft carriers virtually an ocean's width away?
6 Kagan himself seemed occasionally mystified at the instant 'inside the beltway' traction that his characterisation achieved and has since repeatedly said in public discussions that he wishes he had not approached the subject from this particular 'astrological' direction.
7 Followed in 2004 by Operation Althea, taking over responsibilities in Bosnia from NATO.
8 'Conflict prevention and threat prevention cannot start too early'.
9 The words in quotes that follow are either drawn directly from the interviews of 2004 and 2006 or are careful paraphrases designed to obscure identities.
10 Howorth (2005) sees four groups, but in this case I observe only three.

11 One source from outside the administration interviewed reminded that the Turkish 'invocation of Article V' had had at least something of a Washington flavour – that the Turks had not really considered the matter so urgent but had been 'encouraged' by American friends to take a principled stand. This source, quite hostile to the Bush administration, also noted the embarrassing dilemma several of the neocons believed the Turkish request had created for the Germans in particular. See related comments in Everts *et al.* (2004).

12 The Tervuren Summit had a number of names in the press accounts but also in Washington's chatter – 'Praline Summit', 'Summit of the Chocolate Makers'. In Washington terms at least, these were hardly complimentary.

13 Several cited Schake's (2002) paper as summing up their wish lists for European priorities in redressing their capabilities deficit. See also Everts *et al.* (2004).

14 They, for example, would share Pond's (2004) characterisation of the dispute as 'a near-death experience' for the transatlantic alliance.

15 This story was recounted by two otherwise unconnected interviewees.

16 Two recent articles are good examples. Kaldor and Salmon (2006) argue for the development of a new European strategic culture to support the ESS. Grant and Leonard (2006) assert the need to expand the ESS to forge coherent policies or approaches to such issues as 'East Asian security, Russia, promoting democracy in the Middle East', or the 'European Neighbourhood Policy'.

17 See the speeches and testimony in the run-up to the Riga 2006 NATO Summit given by Assistant Secretary Daniel Fried and his principal deputy, Deputy Assistant Secretary Kurt Volker, during March, April, and May 2006, available on the State Department website, www.state.gov/p/eur/rls/rm/66175.htm (accessed 31 May 2006).

Conclusion

Jan Joel Andersson and Sven Biscop

In the early 1970s, the European Communities (EC) began to be referred to as a new superpower in the making. Some analysts even foresaw a future in which a European superpower would try to impose a 'Pax Bruxelliana' on the world. Indeed peace research professor Johan Galtung was so concerned about this prospect that he outlined possible counter-strategies for the potential victims of this emerging superpower (Galtung 1973). While Galtung was in the minority, many scholars nonetheless agreed that a highly integrated Europe would be a formidable force in the international system. Among other things, a 'united Europe' would be a central actor in the international economic arena and the world's third strongest military power (Mally 1974). Despite its great power in terms of overall economic size, trade, and foreign aid, however, few analysts of the time actually considered the EC to be a 'real' actor with real effect in the international arena. Many argued that due to the fact that all the EC Member States were old nation-states with basically different ambitions, interests and traditions they were inevitably forced to choose diverging, if not contradictory lines of action (Hoffmann 1966). Lack of a common monetary system and a unified military in combination with Member States' prioritisation of policies aimed at strengthening their national independence was all taken as proof that the EC was not yet a fully fledged international actor. Nevertheless, in the international arena of the 1960s and 1970s, the EC was able to act as a 'real' actor with real effect in relation to other nations – at least some of the time and under certain conditions (Sjöstedt 1977).

Today, few would question that the European Union is a real actor. The European Union is not only the world's largest trading block, with over 490 million people who produce a quarter of the world's GNP, but it also has a wide range of civil and military instruments at its disposal. The European Union has, for example, adopted a common currency and an EU-wide solidarity clause and has set up a European Defence Agency. Yet despite these attributes of real 'actorness', many still question the extent to which the European Union is able to act as a 'real' actor with significant effect in the international security arena. While the European Union has strengthened its role as a key actor in international trade and finance, it has failed to do so sufficiently in foreign affairs and, most notably, in the military arena.

The emergence of a common foreign policy has been one of the most contentious issues in the history of the development of the European Union. For years, the failure of attempts such as the European Political Community (EPC) of the 1950s and the Fouchet Plan of the 1960s were taken as evidence of Europe's inability to act as a unified entity in the area of international diplomacy. Today, the Common Foreign and Security Policy (CFSP) has achieved some real success since its humble beginnings as the European Political Cooperation of the early 1970s. In the last few years, the European Union has developed common policies toward many regions, including the Balkans and the Middle East. In addition, the European Union has gradually developed a military and civil crisis management capability and launched police missions and military operations in countries such as Bosnia, Macedonia, and the Democratic Republic of Congo. However, while the European Union may now rightfully be called a 'real' actor, this does not mean that it is an effective actor.

The wide array of challenges facing the European Union from beyond its extending borders has led to an extraordinary growth in European foreign and security policy cooperation. Still, despite its great resources and many instruments, including trade, foreign aid, diplomacy and defence, the European Union has frequently found itself ill-equipped to manage foreign and security policy challenges. For example, the Council, the Commission, and the Member States often fail to coordinate their various instruments and policies for the common good. The fact that the European Union is represented in external affairs by the six-month rotating presidency, the High Representative for the CFSP, and the Commissioner for External Relations is but one of the ways in which the European Union's effectiveness is curtailed. As recent events have also demonstrated, there are many challenges involved in forging an effective foreign policy. The Iraq war, for one, revealed deep divisions between some of its 'old' and 'new' members. Such intra-European conflicts have in turn led certain critics to dismiss the idea that a genuine common foreign policy will be achieved anytime soon. Equally important, the enlargement of the Union to 27 Member States cannot help but have an impact on the effectiveness of the European Union as an actor *vis-à-vis* other major international actors such as the United States and China.

The European failure on Iraq again demonstrated the need for a more effective Common Foreign and Security Policy. In an effort to show the world that the European Union could function as a strategic actor, European leaders gave High Representative/Secretary General Javier Solana the task of drafting a European Security Strategy (ESS) in the spring of 2003. Following a consultation process that included European diplomats and politicians as well as experts and academics, the document was adopted with minor changes at the European Council meeting in Brussels in December 2003. This strategy paper outlined five major threats to European security – international terrorism, WMD proliferation, regional conflicts, failed states and organised crime – and pledged a more robust European response to these threats. While the wording of the ESS was viewed as rather ambiguous and therefore open to interpretation as well as disagreement, the document articulated a general vision of the European Union's role in the world and provided a strategic framework for the formulation of all subsequent European foreign and security policies. Given the amount of attention that the ESS received when it was presented in December 2003, it seems only reasonable to discuss what sort of impact this document has had – and will have – on EU foreign and security policy in the future.

The previous chapters in this volume have analysed the European Security Strategy and its impact on Europe and the world from various angles and with different approaches. While all of the contributors to this volume are impressed by the speed and skill with which the ESS document was produced, assessments of its impact remain somewhat mixed. Perhaps the mixed verdict is a reaction to the fact that the ESS was not representing a major new orientation but rather, as Sven Biscop argues in Chapter 1 of this volume, a codification of already existing European foreign policy guidelines established over many years of collaboration in the CFSP and EPC. One of the fundamental aspects of this distinctly European foreign policy tradition is the 'holistic approach' to security and its long-term perspective. A holistic or comprehensive approach that wants to integrate all dimensions of foreign policy, including aid, trade, diplomacy and defence, in an integrated way across the EU pillars is desirable in theory but difficult to execute in practice. This challenge is also discussed more in depth by several of the authors in this volume. Moreover, although the ESS achieves a holistic foreign policy approach on paper, the document is vague on several important points and avoids making a number of difficult choices on key issues because of lack of consensus among EU Member States. For example, the ESS does not adopt a clear stance on the nature of the transatlantic relationship nor does it stipulate how much latitude the European Union should have as an independent actor. However, the failure of US-led foreign policy approaches emphasising politico-military action, most notably in Iraq and in the 'Global War on Terror', have strengthened the European Union's more holistic and long-term approach to security. Despite its weaknesses, Biscop therefore argues that the ESS represents not only a key contribution to the growing trend of more comprehensive approaches to security, but may also serve as an inspiration and a blueprint for alternative holistic or comprehensive foreign and security policies of the future.

While it may have its flaws, the ESS is also a unique EU document in that it clearly states that there are real threats to the Union, a point rarely made in such explicit terms. While the ESS is clear about what the threats to Europe are, it does not want to rank or prioritise between them. Nevertheless, the five listed security threats – international terrorism, WMD proliferation, regional conflicts, failed states and organised crime – mix old and new threats to form a common ground between the Member States' divergent threat perceptions and strategic posture. At the same time, the ESS makes clear that the traditional form of border defence is a thing of the past and that the first line of defence now lies abroad. In Chapter 2, Jean-Yves Haine argues that the ESS, by stressing the notion that the European Union's 'first line of defence now lies abroad', implies a projection of both soft and hard power in a way previously unknown in the European Union. At the same time, the document's call for a more extrovert and active role for the European Union in the world is also directed towards an increasingly inward-looking Europe in which growing national protectionism and competition among EU Member States have made collective action more difficult. The management of old and new risks and threats must be collective, however, and requires a unity of diplomacy and military capabilities that does not yet exist.

While the ESS may have been clear about the threats facing Europe, it has been less clear in its call for 'an international order based on effective multilateralism'. Following the Iraq war, the concept of 'effective multilateralism' was very much in vogue but ill-defined. Some have understood the term to mean the strengthening of the United Nations, while others have focused instead on the European Union, NATO, the G8 and other types of multilateral initiatives. Despite these competing understandings of multilateralism, the ESS strongly emphasised the importance of the UN and stated that an effective UN 'must be a European priority'. However, some promoters of the European Union as a foreign policy actor hold that the Union's value lies in its difference from the UN, not its similarities. It remains therefore unclear how the European Union, as one type of multilateral organisation, can act effectively *vis-à-vis* and within another type of multilateral organisation such as the UN. In Chapter 3, Richard Gowan shows that the European

Union has a diffuse set of ad hoc forms of cooperation with various elements of the UN System. Despite how difficult it is to organise global multilateralism effectively, there has nonetheless been significant EU–UN collaboration on such important areas as state failure and the anti-proliferation of weapons of mass destruction. However, effective multilateralism also requires the ability to form and sustain broad-based coalitions across various issue areas in the UN. Unfortunately, the European Union is not a coherent actor in the UN and the failure of the EU Member States to fully coordinate causes great frustration as the Union could carry immense weight within the UN System. In the face of a crisis, the European Union often finds itself losing coherence and so far the ESS has not been able to improve the situation.

If the policy outcomes on the issue of effective multilateralism are still uncertain, the ESS has perhaps been more successful on the issue of the European Union's neighbourhood policies. Although the promotion of the European Neighbourhood Policy (ENP) was not the direct result of the ESS, it was certainly influenced by it. In Chapter 4, Ronald Dannreuther argues that the ENP was, at least in part, an attempt by the European Union to turn the ESS's focus on building security in the neighbourhood into substance. The principal targets of the ENP are the western Newly Independent States and the countries of the Southern Mediterranean. These countries have never been offered the prospect of future membership but the European Union seeks to encourage regional stability and integration through partnership with the Union. While the ESS is a document of broad objectives and principles, the ENP provides more details and policies on how to promote democracy and economic reform as a way to resolve existing insecurities and conflicts. However, for the ENP to succeed, democracy and economic reform issues must be integrated with other security-driven interests such as immigration, energy and counter-terrorism. According to Dannreuther, the ENP could potentially articulate a new vision and comprehensive policy framework for the European Union's relationship with its eastern and southern neighbours. If the ENP can and does develop in this way, the ESS can be said to have contributed to the provision of greater strategic coherence and policy capacity to the European Union in its relationship with its neighbouring regions.

A more capable Europe does not only involve more effective policies but also requires improving the military capabilities of the Union. Although it would take time, the ESS called for the transformation of the Member States' militaries into more flexible and mobile forces that could address the new threats facing the Union. To achieve this goal, more resources for defence and more effective use of existing resources are necessary. Jolyon

Howorth argues in Chapter 5 that European military capability has come a long way in a few short years. After almost a decade of stagnation after the end of the Cold War, progress in procurement, planning, rationalisation, force transformation and general 'usability' has greatly improved. However, there is still a long way to go before the European Union is a fully credible and coordinated actor that is able to undertake the full range of Petersberg tasks. While the European Union does not aim to become a military actor at the level of the United States, it still needs to invest heavily in R&D and personnel in order to succeed in the new type of 'security fire-fighting' it wants to do. Collectively, the EU Member States spend large amounts of money on defence but get very little useful capability out of it. A major rationalisation of the European Union's defence spending is overdue but some things have been done. The newly created Battlegroups, rapidly deployable units of 1,500 men with combat support, and the establishment of a European Defence Agency are good examples. Both of these examples can at least partly be traced back to formulations in the ESS.

The European Union has always known that it can not run the world by itself and must rely on partners. The ESS therefore emphasises a partnership approach to security. To realise the goals set in the ESS, the European Union must work with partners such as the United States but also other key actors and organisations. In Chapter 6, Roberto Menotti and Maria Francesca Vencato analyse the wide variety of partnerships described in the ESS and find four main types. In the first type of partnership, the European Union leads a policy effort by offering a framework for potential partners but acts in autonomy. In the second type, the European Union plays a supporting role by virtue of its expertise or particular value added. In the third type, the European Union 'inter-operates' within the framework of a US-led effort. The final type of relationship is a kind of great power concert. As the authors point out, in reality these types will sometimes overlap but the ESS seems to point to different situations in which one of the four types of partnership will be predominant. However, Menotti and Vencato argue that when the European Union finds itself having to team up with 'key actors' to share risks, costs and responsibilities, the ESS has been and will remain insufficient in providing guidance on how to do it. The European Union has to reconcile multiple interests in its relations to established and new partners. While we should not expect to find all the solutions to these problems in a general policy document such at the ESS, more can be done to apply the Strategy's principles to specific regional settings.

A recurring theme in the discussion on European foreign policy-making is the Union's lack of coherence. The ESS is explicit about the need to bring together the many different instruments and capabilities of the Union.

Indeed, both the CFSP and ESDP operate according to the notion that Europe is stronger when it acts together. As Jan Joel Andersson points out in Chapter 7, coherence is not only a question of better coordination between EU institutions but also an issue of coherence between EU instruments and the external activities of individual Member States. However, improving the effectiveness and coherence of the European Union's external capabilities has been on the agenda for many years. While all EU Member States and EU institutions agree on the need to improve coordination and avoid duplication when the European Union is acting externally, no Member State or institution has ever been willing to relinquish its own role in this area entirely. With a European Union consisting of 27 Member States, Council, Commission and agencies, how much coherence can really be achieved? Some analysts, however, argue that we should not be obsessed with the myth of the European Union as an inefficient and uncoordinated external actor. If most Member States cannot achieve coherence among their national policies internally, how can we expect the European Union to achieve such coherence across national boundaries?

Improving coherence is difficult. However, the ESS serves as a constant reminder of the need for more coherence. There are also things that can be done. For example, in an effort to better coordinate EU external action in Macedonia, the European Union merged the leadership of the European Commission delegation and the EU Special Representative office in Skopje in November 2005. In an unusual 'double-hatting', Ambassador Erwan Fouéré was concurrently appointed EU Special Representative by the Council and Head of Delegation by the Commission. In this first ever joint external representation of the European Union, the EU Mission is able to provide a single point of contact to the authorities in Macedonia and the various decision-making bodies in Brussels with little risk for confusion or mixing of messages.

Despite its shortcomings, one thing is clear: the ESS had an important role to play in healing the transatlantic rift over Iraq. Although the ESS never became a centrepiece of discussion in Washington, its timing and message were critical. As Catherine Kelleher argues in Chapter 8, the ESS did not only silence some of the administration and Capitol Hill critics of the importance of allies but also provided key support for those who argued for the significant role of multilateral security organisations. Even more importantly, the ESS offered an opening in the transatlantic relationship that culminated in 2005–6 with the agreement to disagree over Iraq but with an intact broad alliance commitment. It remains perhaps less clear, however, what sort of relevance the ESS will have for the transatlantic relationship in the future. Nevertheless, the broad principles embedded in the ESS and its associated strategies allow the United States and willing European states to cooperate on pressing issues that face both the United States and Europe such as the fight against WMD proliferation and global terrorism.

If the ESS has played an important role in convincing both Europeans and others that the European Union can be an actor and not only a reactor in international affairs in the aftermath of the Iraq war, its continued relevance may perhaps depend on factors beyond the strategy paper itself. The number of foreign policy challenges to the European Union is ever increasing. The continuing uncertainty of the future of the Western Balkans, the Union's deteriorating relationship with Russia, the continuing wars in Afghanistan and Iraq, the nuclear challenge from Iran, the Israeli–Palestinian conflict and unrest in the wider Middle East all demand a more active EU involvement. Ultimately it is the political will of the Member States that will determine what kind of global actor the European Union is and will become. In this volume, each author has addressed how and to what extent the ESS has contributed to a more active and more effective EU foreign and security policy. While the verdict is somewhat mixed on the direct effects of the document and the extent to which it has helped shaping a European 'strategic culture', the fact remains that the European Security Strategy has been and continues to be the reference framework in the forging of a Global Europe.

Bibliography

Albright, D. and Hinderstein, C. (2003) 'Iran, Player or Rogue?', *Bulletin of the Atomic Scientists*, 59(5): 52–58.

Allison, G. (2004) *Nuclear Terrorism, The Ultimate Preventable Catastrophe*, New York: Times Books.

Andersson, J.J. (2003a) 'The European Union Security Strategy: Coherence and Capabilities', Discussion Paper. Stockholm: Swedish Institute of International Affairs.

—— (2003b) *Guns and Butter. A Neoliberal Statist Analysis of Cross-border Defense Industry Collaboration in Western Europe, 1950–2001*, Ann Arbor, MI: UMI.

—— (2006) *Armed and Ready? The EU Battlegroup Concept and the Nordic Battlegroup*, Stockholm: SIEPS.

Andrews-Speed, P., Liao, X. and Dannreuther, R. (2002) *The Strategic Implications of China's Energy Needs*, Adelphi Paper, No. 346, Oxford: Oxford University Press.

Annan, K. (2005) *In Larger Freedom – Towards Development, Security and Human Rights for All*, Report of the Secretary-General for Decision by Heads of State and Government in September 2005, New York: UN.

Aron, R. and Lerner, D. (eds) (1957) *France Defeats EDC*, New York: Praeger.

Arquilla, J. and Ronfeldt, D. (2001) *Networks and Netwars: The Future of Terror, Crime, and Militancy*, Santa Monica, CA: RAND.

Bailes, A.J.K. (2005a) *The European Security Strategy. An Evolutionary History*, Policy Paper No. 10, Stockholm: SIPRI.

—— (2005b) 'The Role of the EU in Fighting Proliferation: An Assessment of the Iran Case and its Consequences', text of a lecture given in Paris, 9 December 2005.

Batt, J. (2004) 'The Enlarged EU and its new "Neighbourhood Policy"', *Transatlantic Internationale Politik*, 2: 19–27.

Baun, M. (2005) *A Common Strategic Culture for Europe*. Online, available at: www.yes-dk.dk/YES/index.php?option = content&task = view&id = 157&Itemid = 173 (accessed 6 January 2006).

Betts, R.K. (2006) 'The Osirak Fallacy', *The National Interest*, 83(Spring): 22–25.

Biscop, S. (2002) 'In Search of a Strategic Concept for the ESDP', *European Foreign Affairs Review*, 7(4): 473–90.

—— (2005) *The European Security Strategy. A Global Agenda for Positive Power*, Aldershot: Ashgate Publishing.

—— and Drieskens, E. (2006) 'Effective Multilateralism and Collective Security: Empowering the UN', in K.V. Laatikainen and K.E. Smith (eds) *The European Union at the United Nations: Intersecting Multilateralisms*, Basingstoke: Palgrave Macmillan.

Blair, A. and Bush, G.W. (2003) 'Effective Multilateralism To Build a Better World: Joint Statement by President George W. Bush and Prime Minister Tony Blair', 20 November.

Bobbitt, P. (2003) *The Shield of Achilles, War, Peace and the Course of History*, London: Penguin Books.

Boureston, J. and Ferguson, C.D. (2005) 'Keep Your Enemy Closer', *Bulletin of the Atomic Scientists*, 61(6): 25.

Boswell, C. (2003) 'The "External Dimension" of EU Immigration and Asylum Policy', *International Affairs*, 79(3): 619–38.

Bozo, F. (2003) 'The Effects of Kosovo and the Danger of Decoupling', in J. Howorth and J. Keeler (eds) *Defending Europe*, New York: Palgrave.

Brawley, M.R. and Martin, P. (eds) (2000) *Alliance Politics, Kosovo, and NATO's War: Allied Force or Forced Allies?*, New York: Palgrave.

Brenner, M. and Parmentier, G. (2002) *Reconcilable Differences: US–French Relations in the New Era*, Washington, DC: Brookings.

Bretherton, C. and Vogler, J. (2005) *The European Union as a Global Actor*, 2nd edn, Abingdon: Taylor & Francis.

Broad, W.J. and Sanger, D.E. (2005) 'Worries Deepen over Nuclear Ring: Kahn Was Selling a Complete Package', *The New York Times*, 22 March.

Brunnbauer, U. (2002) 'The Implementation of the Ohrid Agreement: Ethnic Macedonian Resentments', *Journal on Ethnopolitics and Minority Issues in Europe,* January. Special focus: The Ohrid Agreement and After: Forging a Political Settlement in Macedonia. Online, available at: http://www.ecmi.de/jemie/download/Focus1-2002Brunnbauer.pdf

Bures, O. (2006) 'EU Counterterrorism Policy: A Paper Tiger?', *Terrorism and Political Violence*, 18(1): 57–78.

Burke, J. (2004) 'Think Again: Al-Qaeda', *Foreign Policy*, May/June: 18–24.

Burns, N. (2003) *Press Briefing by the Ambassador 30 September 2003*. Online, available at: http://nato.usmission.gov/ambassador.html (accessed 19 March 2006).

Bush, G.W. (2004) 'President Discusses Strong Relationship With Canada', text of a speech given at Halifax, 1 December.

Centre for Defence Studies (2001) *Achieving the Helsinki Headline Goal*, Centre for Defence Studies Discussion Paper, London: Kings College.

Cerny, P.G. (2005) 'Terrorism and the New Security Dilemma', *Naval War College Review*, 58(1): 11–33.

Clark, W.K. (2001) *Waging Modern War*, New York: Public Affairs.

Clay, M.J., Orlov, V.A. and Stulberg, A.N. (2004) *Preventing Nuclear Meltdown, Managing Decentralization of Russia's Nuclear Complex*, Aldershot: Ashgate.

Cohen, A. (2003) *Hizb Ut-Tahrir: An Emerging Threat to US Interests in Central Asia*, Washington, DC: The Heritage Foundation.

Coll, S. (2006) 'The Nuclear Edge', *The New Yorker*, 2 February.

Coolsaet, R. and Biscop, S. (2003) *A European Security Concept for the 21st Century*, Egmont Paper No. 1, Brussels: Royal Institute for International Relations.

Cornish, P. (2004) *Artemis and Coral: British Perspectives on European Union Crisis Management Operations in the Democratic Republic of Congo*, Unpublished report, London: Kings College.

Council of the European Union (2003a) *Joint Action/423/CFSP: On the European Union Operation in the Democratic Republic of Congo (Artemis)*, Brussels, 5 June 2003.

—— (2003b) *Council Joint Action 2003/92/CFSP: On the European Union Military Operation in the Former Yugoslav Republic of Macedonia*, Brussels: Council of the European Union.

—— (2003c) *Council Joint Action 2003/681/CFSP: On the European Union Police Mission in the Former Yugoslav Republic of Macedonia (EUPOL 'Proxima')*, Brussels: Council of the European Union.

—— (2004) *Headline Goal 2010*, Brussels: Council of the European Union.

—— (2004a) *Council Joint Action 2004/847/CFSP: On the European Union Police Mission in Kinshasa (DRC) Regarding the Integrated Police Unit (EUPOL 'Kinshasa')*, Brussels: Council of the European Union.

—— (2004b) *Council Joint Action 2004/495/CFSP: On Support for IAEA Activities under its Nuclear Security Programme and in the Framework of the Implementation of the Strategy Against Weapons of Mass Destruction*, Brussels: Council of the European Union.

—— (2004c) *Paper for Submission to the High-level Panel on Threats, Challenges and Change*, Brussels: Council of the European Union.

—— (2005a) *Council Joint Action 2005/355/CFSP: On the European Union Mission to Provide Advice and Assistance for Security Sector Reform in the Democratic Republic of Congo (DRC)*, Brussels: Council of the European Union.

—— (2005b) *Council Joint Action 2005/724/CFSP: Appointing the European Union Special Representative in the Former Yugoslav Republic of Macedonia and Repealing Joint Action 2005/589/CFSP*, Brussels: Council of the European Union.

—— (2005c) *European Union Counter-Terrorism Strategy*, Brussels: Council of the European Union.

—— (2006a) *Council Joint Action 2006/319/CFSP: On the European Union Military Operation in Support of the United Nations Organization Mission in the Democratic Republic of Congo (MONUC) During the Election Process*, Brussels: Council of the European Union.

—— (2006b) *Council Conclusions on Lebanon*, Brussels: Council of the European Union.

Cronin, A.K. (2002) 'Behind the Curve: Globalization and International Terrorism', *International Security*, 27(3): 30–58.

Culpeper, R. (2005) *Human Security, Equitable and Sustainable Development: Foundations for Canada's International Policy*, NSI Paper on the International Policy Review, Ottawa: The North-South Institute.

Daalder, I.H. and O'Hanlon, M. (2006) *Winning Ugly*, Washington, DC: Brookings.

Dassù, M. and Menotti, R. (2005) 'Europe and America in the Age of Bush', *Survival*, 47(1): 105–22.

de Barochez, L. (2006) 'Paris Accuse l'Iran de Préparer l'Arme Nucléaire', *Le Figaro*, 17 February.

De Gucht, K. (2006) 'Shifting EU Foreign Policy into Higher Gear', *EU Diplomacy Papers* 1/2006, Bruges: College of Europe.

Deighton, A. (ed.) (1997) *Western European Union 1954–1997: Defence, Security, Integration*, Oxford: St. Antony's.

De Wijk, R. (2002) 'The Limits of Military Power', *Washington Quarterly*, 25(1): 75–92.

DFID (2005) *Fighting Poverty to Build a Safer World. A Strategy for Security and Development*, London: Department for International Development.

Dombrowski, P. and Payne, R. (2006) 'The Emerging Consensus for Preventive War', *Survival*, 48(2): 115–36.

Duchêne, F. (1994) *Jean Monnet: The First Statesman of Independence*, New York: W.W. Norton & Company.

Duffield, M. (2002) *Global Governance and the New Wars*, London: Zed Books.

Dunay, P. (2004) 'Strategy with Fast-Moving Targets', in R. Dannreuther (ed.) *European Union Foreign and Security Policy: Towards a Neighbourhood Strategy*, London: Routledge.

Duyvestein, I. (2004) 'How New is the New Terrorism?', *Studies in Conflict and Terrorism*, 27: 439–54.

Eeckhout, P. (2004) *External Relations of the European Union. Legal and Constitutional Foundations*, Oxford: Oxford University Press.

Eide, E.B. (ed.) (2004) *Global Europe Report 1: Effective Multilateralism: Europe, Regional Security and a Revitalized UN*, London: Foreign Policy Centre and British Council Brussels.

EUISS (2004) *European Defence. A Proposal for a White Paper*, Paris: EU Institute for Security Studies.

European Commission (2000) *Green Paper: Towards a European Strategy for Security of Energy Supply*, COM (2000) 769 final, Brussels: European Commission.

—— (2001) *Conflict Prevention*, COM (2001) 211 final, Brussels: European Commission.

—— (2003a) *Wider Europe – Neighbourhood: A New Framework for Relations with our Eastern and Southern Neighbours*, COM (2003) 104 final, Brussels: European Commission.

—— (2003b) *A Maturing Partnership – Shared Interests and Challenges in EU-China Relations*, COM (2003) 533 final, Brussels: European Commission.

—— (2003c) *The European Union and the United Nations: The Choice of Multilateralism*, COM (2003) 526 final, Brussels: European Commission.

—— (2004) *European Neighbourhood Policy: Strategy Paper*, COM (2004) 373 final, Brussels: European Commission.

—— (2005a) *Speeding up Progress Towards the Millennium Development Goals. The European Union's Contribution*, COM (2005) 132 final, Brussels: European Commission.

—— (2005b) *Policy Coherence for Development. Accelerating Progress Towards Attaining the Millennium Development Goals*, COM (2005) 134 final, Brussels: European Commission.

—— (2005c) *Proposal for a Joint Declaration by the Council, the European Parliament and the Commission on the European Union Development Policy. 'The European Consensus'*, COM (2005) 311 final, Brussels: European Commission.

European Commission (2006) *Communication from the Commission to the European Council of June 2006. Europe in the World – Some Practical Proposals for Greater Coherence, Effectiveness and Visibility,* COM (2006) 278 final, Brussels: European Commission.

European Council (2003a) *A Secure Europe in a Better World – European Security Strategy,* Brussels: European Council.

—— (2003b) *European Strategy Against the Proliferation of WMD,* Brussels: European Council.

—— (2004) *Declaration on Combating Terrorism,* Brussels: European Council.

—— (2005) *Presidency Conclusions,* 16–17 June, Brussels: European Council.

—— (2006) *Presidency Conclusions,* 15–16 June, Brussels: European Council.

European Union Mission to FYROM (2006) online, available at: www.delmkd. ec.europa.eu/en/index.htm (accessed 7 December 2006).

Everts, S. and Keohane, D. (2003) 'The European Convention and EU Foreign Policy: Learning from Failure', *Survival,* 45(3): 167–86.

—— and Missiroli, A. (2004) 'Beyond the "Big Three"', *International Herald Tribune,* 10 March.

——, Freedman, L., Grant, C., Heisbourg, F., Keohane, D. and O'Hanlon, M. (2004) *The European Way of War,* London: Centre for European Reform.

Fearon, J.D. and Laitin, D.D. (2004) 'Neo-trusteeship and the Problem of Weak States', *International Security,* 28(4): 5–43.

Ferguson, C.D. and Potter, W.C. (2004) *The Four Faces of Nuclear Terrorism,* Monterey, CA: Center for Non-proliferation Studies.

Foot, R. (2006) 'Chinese Strategies in a US-hegemonic Global Order: Accommodating and Hedging', *International Affairs,* 82(1): 77–94.

Forman, S. and Segaar, D. (2006) 'New Coalitions for Global Governance: The Changing Dynamics of Multilateralism', *Global Governance,* 12(2): 205–25.

Fried, D. (2006) Remarks at the National Conference of Editorial Writers, Washington, DC, 2 May 2006. Online, available at: www.state.gov/p/eur/rls/ rm/6816.htm (accessed 31 May 2006).

Galtung, J. (1973) *The European Community: A Superpower in the Making,* Oslo: Universitetsforlaget.

Gault, J. (2004) 'EU Energy Security and its Periphery', in R. Dannreuther (ed.) *European Union Foreign and Security Policy: Towards a Neighbourhood Strategy,* London: Routledge.

Gavin, F.J. (2006) 'Thinking Through Nuclear Proliferation in an Age Of Globalization', in R.A. Epstein and P. Vennesson (eds) *Globalization and Transatlantic Security,* Florence: European University Institute.

Geddes, A. (2000) *Immigration and European Integration: Towards a Fortress Europe?,* Manchester: Manchester University Press.

General Assembly (2005) *2005 World Summit Outcome,* General Assembly A/60/L.1.

Giegerich, B. and Wallace, W. (2004) 'Not Such a Soft Power: The External Deployment of European Forces', *Survival,* 46(2): 163–82.

Gillespie, R and Youngs, R. (eds) (2002) *The European Union and Democracy Promotion: The Case of North Africa,* London: Frank Cass.

Gnesotto, N. (1998) *La Puissance et l'Europe,* Paris: FNSP.

—— (2003) 'Strategie de Securite de l'Union Européenne: Compte rendu du séminaire sur les objectifs stratégiques', Paris: EU Institute for Security Studies.

—— (ed.) (2004) *European Security and Defence Policy: The First Five Years (1999–2004)*, Paris: EU Institute for Security Studies.

Goldberg, A. (1964) 'The Atomic Origins of the British Nuclear Deterrent', *International Affairs*, 40(3): 411.

Gompert, D., Kugler, R. and Libicki, M. (1999) *Mind the Gap: Promoting a Transatlantic Revolution in Military Affairs*, Washington, DC: INSS/NDU Press.

Gordon, P.H. (1997) 'Europe's Uncommon Foreign Policy', *International Security*, 22(3): 27–74.

—— (2000) 'Their Own Army?', *Foreign Affairs*, 79(4): 12–17.

—— (2006) 'The End of the Bush Revolution', *Foreign Affairs*, 85(4): 75–86.

—— and Shapiro, J. (2004) *Allies at War*, New York: McGraw-Hill.

Gowan, R. (2005) 'The Battlegroups: A Concept in Search of a Strategy?', in S. Biscop (ed.) *E Pluribus Unum? Military Integration in the European Union*, Ghent: Academia Press.

Grant, C. (2001) 'A European View of CFSP', text of a speech to the IISS/CEPS European Security Forum, 10 September.

—— and Leonard, M. (2006) *How to Strengthen EU Foreign Policy*, CER Policy Brief, London: Centre for European Reform.

Greco, E. (2004) 'South-Eastern Europe: The Expanding EU Role', in R. Dannreuther (ed.) *European Union Foreign and Security Policy: Towards a Neighbourhood Strategy*, London: Routledge.

Group of Personalities (2004) *Research for a Secure Europe*, Report of the Group of Personalities in the Field of Security Research, Brussels: European Commission.

Haass, R.N. (2005) 'The Case for "Integration"', *The National Interest*, 81: 22–29.

Haine, J.-Y. (2003) *From Laeken to Copenhagen: European Defence: Core Documents 3*, Chaillot Paper 57, Paris: EU Institute for Security Studies.

—— (2004) 'An Historical Perspective', in N. Gnesotto (ed.) *European Security and Defence Policy: The First Five Years (1999–2004)*, Paris: EU Institute for Security Studies.

Halaby, J. (2005) 'Suspects in Jordan Chemical Plot Had Instructions for Attack, Witnesses Say at Trial', *Associated Press*, 20 April.

Hannay, D. (2005) *Assessing the UN Millennium Review Summit*, Speech at the Royal Institute for International Relations, Brussels, 7 October.

Haukkala, H. (2004) 'Northern Dimension', in O. Antonenko and K. Pinnick (eds) *Russia and the European Union*, London: Routledge.

Hayes-Renshaw, F. and Wallace, H. (1997) *The Council of Ministers*, Basingstoke: Macmillan.

Hegghammer, T. (2006) 'Global Jihadism after Iraq War', *Middle East Journal*, 60(1): 11–32.

Heisbourg, F. (2003) *Hyperterrorisme, la nouvelle guerre*, Paris: Odile Jacob.

—— (2004) 'The "European Security Strategy" Is Not a Security Strategy', in S. Everts (ed.) *A European Way of War*, London: Centre for European Reform.

Helly, D. (2006) 'EU Just Themis in Georgia: An Ambitious Bet on the Rule of Law', in A. Nowak (ed.) *Civilian Crisis Management: the EU Way*, Chaillot Paper 90, Paris: EU Institute for Security Studies.

Henry, C.M., and Springborg, R. (2001) *Globalization and the Politics of Development in the Middle East*, Cambridge: Cambridge University Press.

High-Level Panel (2004) *A More Secure World – Our Shared Responsibility*, Report of the High-Level Panel on Threats, Challenges and Change, New York: UN.

Hill, C. (1993) 'The Capability-Expectations Gap, or Conceptualising Europe's International Role', *Journal of Common Market Studies*, 31(3): 305–28.

Hoffmann, B. (2004) 'The Changing Face of Al-Qaeda and the Global War on Terrorism', *Studies in Conflict and Terrorism*, 27: 551.

—— and McCormick, G.H. (2004) 'Terrorism, Signaling and Suicide Attack', *Studies in Conflict and Terrorism*, 27: 247.

Hoffmann, S. (1966) 'Obstinate or Obsolete? The Fate of the Nation State and the Case of Western Europe', *Daedalus*, 95(3): 892–908.

—— (2006) 'The Foreign Policy the US Needs', *The New York Review of Books*, 53(13): 60–64.

Howorth, J. (1998) 'French Defence Reforms: National Tactics for a European Strategy?', in *Brassey's Defence Yearbook 1998*, London: Brassey's.

—— (2005) 'Transatlantic Perspectives on European Security in the Coming Decade', *Yale Journal of International Relations*, 1(1): 8–22.

—— and Keeler, J. (eds) (2003) *Defending Europe: The EU, NATO and the Quest for European Autonomy*, New York: Palgrave.

Hurwitz, A. and Peake, G. (2004) *Strengthening the Security-Development Nexus: Assessing International Policy and Practice Since the 1990s*, Conference Report, New York: International Peace Academy.

Huysmans, J. (2000) 'The European Union and the Securitization of Migration', *Journal of Common Market Studies*, 38(5): 751–77.

Ignatius, D. (2004) 'Are the Terrorists Failing?', *The Washington Post*, 28 September.

International Atomic Energy Authority (2005) *Communication dated 8 August 2005 received from the Resident Representatives of France, Germany and the United Kingdom to the Agency*, Vienna: IAEA.

International Crisis Group (2001a) *The Macedonian Question: Reform or Rebellion*, Balkans Report 109, Brussels: ICG.

—— (2001b) *Macedonia: The Last Chance for Peace*, Balkans Report 113, Brussels: ICG.

—— (2005) *Darfur: The Failure To Protect*, Africa Report 89, Brussels: ICG.

International Energy Agency (2002) *World Energy Outlook 2002*, Paris: International Energy Agency.

International Institute for Strategic Studies (1989) *The Military Balance 1989–1990*, London: Brasseys.

—— (2001) 'The European Rapid Reaction Force', in *The Military Balance 2001–2002*, Oxford: Oxford University Press.

—— (2003) 'EU Operational Planning: The Politics of Defence', *Strategic Comments*, 9(10).

Jeesee, D.D. (2006) 'Tactical Means, Strategic Ends: Al-Qaeda's Use of Denial and Deception', *Terrorism and Political Violence*, 18: 367–88.

Joffe, G. (ed.) (1999) *Perspectives on Development: The Euro-Mediterranean Partnership*, London: Frank Cass.

Jørgensen, K.E. and Laatikainen, K. (2004) 'The EU at the UN: Multilateralism in a New Key', paper presented at Second Pan-European Conference on EU Politics, Bologna, 24–26 June.

Kagan, R. (2002) 'Power and Weakness: Why the United States and Europe See the World Differently', *Policy Review*, 113: 3–28..

—— (2003) *Of Paradise and Power*, New York: Alfred A. Knopf.

—— (2006) 'It's the Regime, Stupid', *The Washington Post*, 29 January.

Kaldor, M. (2004) A *Human Security Doctrine for Europe: The Barcelona Report of the Study Group on Europe's Security Capabilities*. Online, available at: http://www.lse.ac.uk/Depts/global/Publications/HumanSecurityDoctrine.pdf

—— and Salmon, A. (2006) 'Military Force and European Strategy', *Survival*, 48(1): 19–34.

Kelleher, C. (1995) *The Future of European Security*, Washington, DC: Brookings.

Keohane, R.O. (2002) 'Ironies of Sovereignty: The European Union and the United States', *Journal of Common Market Studies*, 40(4): 743–65.

—— (2005) *The EU and Counter-Terrorism*, London: Centre for European Reform.

Kepel, G. (2004) *The War for Muslim Minds: Islam and the West*, Cambridge, MA: Belknap Press.

Keukeleire, S. (2003) 'The European Union as a Diplomatic Actor: Internal, Traditional, and Structural Diplomacy', *Diplomacy and Statecraft*, 14(3): 31–56.

Kile, S.N. (2006) 'Nuclear Arms Control and Non-proliferation', in *SIPRI Yearbook 2006: Armaments, Disarmament and International Security*, Oxford: Oxford University Press.

Kissinger, H. (2006) 'Universal Values, Specific Policies', *The National Interest*, 84: 13–15.

Korb, L.J. and Boorstin, R.O. (2005) *Integrated Power. A National Security Strategy for the 21st Century*, Washington, DC: Center for American Progress.

Krenzler, H-G. and Schneider, H.C. (1997) 'The Question of Consistency', in E. Regelsberger, P. de Schoutheete de Tervarent and W. Wessels (eds) *Foreign Policy of the European Union: From EPC to CFSP and Beyond*, Boulder, CO: Lynne Rienner.

Leiken, R. (2004) *Bearers of Global Jihad? Immigration and National Security after 9/11*, Washington, DC: Nixon Center.

Leonard, M. (2004) 'One Year Later: Europe's Debt to Rumsfeld', *International Herald Tribune*, 28 February.

—— (2005) *Why Europe Will Run the 21st Century*, London: 4th Estate.

Loisel, S (2004) 'Les leçons d'Artémis: vers une approche européenne de la gestion militaire des crises', *Les Champs de Mars*, 16, Paris: C2SD.

McCormick, J. (2002) *Understanding the European Union: A Concise Introduction*, New York: Palgrave.

MacFarlane, S.N. (2004) 'The Caucasus and Central Asia', in R. Dannreuther (ed.) *European Union Foreign and Security Policy: Towards a Neighbourhood Strategy*, London: Routledge.

Mally, G. (1973) *The European Community in Perspective. The New Europe of Ten, the United States and World*, Lexington, MA: D.C. Heath.

—— (ed.) (1974) *The New Europe and the United States: Partners or Rivals?*, Lexington, MA: D.C. Heath for the Atlantic Council of the United States.

Manners, I. (2002) 'Normative Power Europe – A Contradiction in Terms', *Journal of Common Market Studies*, 40(2): 235–58.

Marfleet, B.G. and Miller, C. (2005) 'Failure after 1441: Bush and Chirac in the UN Security Council', *Foreign Policy Analysis*, 1(3): 333–60.

Maull, H.W. (2005) 'Europe and the New Balance of Global Order', *International Affairs*, 81(4): 775–99.

Menkhaus, K. (2004) *Somalia: State Collapse and the Threat of Terrorism*, Adelphi Paper 364, London: International Institute for Strategic Studies.

Messervy-Whiting, G. (2003) 'The Politico-Military Structure in Brussels: Capabilities and Limits', discussion paper for the Geneva Centre for Security Policy, Workshop on the EU and Peace Operations, 22–23 September.

Ministry of Defence of the UK (1994) *Front Line First: The Defence Costs Study*, London: HMSO.

—— (1995) *Statement on the Defence Estimates: Stable Forces in a Strong Britain*, London: HMSO.

—— (1998) *The Strategic Defence Review*, London: HMSO.

Ministry of Foreign Affairs of the People's Republic of China (2005) *Position Paper of the People's Republic of China on the United Nations Reforms*, 7 June.

Missiroli, A. (2003) *From Copenhagen to Brussels, European Defence: Core Documents 4*, Chaillot Paper 67, Paris: EU Institute for Security Studies.

Moghadam, A. (2003) 'Palestinian Suicide Terrorism in the Second Intifada: Motivations and Organizational Aspects', *Studies in Conflict and Terrorism*, 26(2): 65–92.

Mörth, U. (2003) *Organizing European Cooperation: The Case of Armaments*, Lanham, MD: Rowman & Littlefield.

Mueller, J. (2005) 'Six Rather Unusual Propositions about Terrorism', *Terrorism and Political Violence*, 17: 487–505.

Müller, H. (2003) *Terrorism, Proliferation: A European Assessment*, Chaillot Paper 58, Paris: EU Institute for Security Studies.

NATO (1991) *The Alliance's Strategic Concept agreed by the Heads of State and Government Participating in the Meeting of the North Atlantic Council*, Rome, 8 November.

—— (2004) *Strategic Vision: The Military Challenge*, By NATO's Strategic Commanders, Mons – Norfolk: ACO – ACT.

Nesser, P. (2006) 'Jihadism in Western Europe After the Invasion of Iraq: Tracing Motivational Influences from the Iraq War on Jihadist Terrorism in Western Europe', *Studies in Conflict and Terrorism*, 29(4): 323–42.

Neumann, P.R. (2006) 'Europe's Jihadist Dilemma', *Survival*, 48(2): 71–84.

Neuwahl, N. (1994) 'Foreign and Security Policy and the Implementation of the Requirement for "Consistency" Under the Treaty on European Union', in D. O'Keeffe and P.M. Twomey (eds) *Legal Issues of the Maastricht Treaty*, London: Wiley Chancery Law.

Nichols, T. (2005) 'Anarchy and Order in this New Age of Prevention', *World Policy Journal*, Fall.

Nye, J.S. (2002) *The Paradox of American Power: Why the World's Only Superpower Can't Go it Alone*, Oxford: Oxford University Press.

Ojanen, H. (2000) 'The EU and its "Northern Dimension": An Actor in Search of a Policy, or a Policy in Search of an Actor', *European Foreign Affairs Review*, 5: 370–87.

—— (2006) *The EU and the UN: A Shared Future*, Helsinki: Finnish Institute of International Affairs.

Oman, D. (2005) 'Countering International Terrorism: The Use of Strategy', *Survival*, 47(4): 107–16.

Ortega, M. (2004) 'The EU and UN: Strengthening Global Security', in E.B. Eide (ed.) *Global Europe Report 1: Effective Multilateralism: Europe, Regional Security and a Revitalized UN*, London: Foreign Policy Centre and British Council Brussels.

—— (ed.) (2005a) *The European Union and the United Nations: Partners in Effective Multilateralism*, Paris: EU Institute for Security Studies.

—— (2005b) 'Introduction' in M. Ortega (ed.) *The European Union and the United Nations: Partners in Effective Multilateralism*, Paris: EU Institute for Security Studies.

Pailhe, C. (2003) *L'engagement de l'OTAN en Iraq: la fracture transatlantique*, Note d'Analyse, Brussels: Groupe de Recherche et d'Information sur la Paix et la Sécurité (GRIP).

Pape, R. (2003) 'The Strategic Logic of Suicide Terrorism', *American Political Science Review*, 97(3): 1–19.

Patten, C. (2001) 'Common Strategies for the Mediterranean and Reinvigorating the Barcelona Process', Speech to the Europeran Parliament, 31 January 2001. Online, available at: www.europe.int/comm/external_relations/news/patten/speech _01_49.htm

—— (2003) 'Wider Europe-Neighbourhood: Proposed New Framework for Relations with the EU's Eastern and Southern Neighbours', IP/03/358, 11 March.

Perkovich, G., Cirincione, J., Gottermoeeler, R., Wolfsthal, J.B. and Mathews, J.T. (2004) *Universal Compliance: A Strategy for Nuclear Security*, Washington, DC: Carnegie Endowment for International Peace.

Peters, I. and Bittner, J. (2006) 'EU-US Risk Policy in the European Neighbourhood: The Cases of Moldova and Georgia', paper presented at the ISA Annual Conference, San Francisco, March.

Peterson, J. and Bomberg, E. (1999) *Decision-making in the European Union*, New York: St Martin's Press.

Phillipart, E. (2003) 'The Euro-Mediterranean Partnership: A Critical Evaluation of an Ambitious Scheme', *European Foreign Affairs Review*, 8: 201–20.

Phillips, J. (2006) 'The Evolving Al-Qaeda Threat', *Heritage Lectures*, 16 February.

Pippan, C. (2004) 'The Rocky Road to Europe: The EU's Stabilisation and Association Process for the Western Balkans and the Principle of Conditionality', *European Foreign Affairs Review*, 9: 219–45.

Pollack, K.M. (2006) *The Iranian Nuclear Program: Motivations And Priorities*, Senate Foreign Relations Committee, 17 May.

Pond, E. (2004) *Friendly Fire: The Near-Death of the Transatlantic Alliance*, Washington, DC: Brookings for the European Studies Association.

Posh, W. (2006) 'The EU and Iran: A Tangled Web of Negotiations', in W. Posh (ed.) *Iranian Challenges*, Chaillot Paper 89, Paris: EU Institute for Security Studies.

Power, D. (2006) 'Mixed Reaction to "Battlegroup" Decision', *The Post IE*, 12 February.

Preston, C. (1977) *Enlargement and Integration in the European Union*, London: Routledge.

Rapoport, D.C. (2004) 'The Four Waves of Modern Terrorism', in A.K. Cronin and J. Ludes (eds) *Attacking Terrorism: Elements of a Grand Strategy*, Washington, DC: Georgetown University Press.

Richards, A. (2003) '"Modernity and Economic Development": The New "American" Messianism', *Middle East Policy*, 10(3): 56–78.

Robinson, C. (2005) *Whose Security?*, Brussels: APRODEV.

Roland, P. (2001) 'Human Security: Paradigm Shift or Hot Air?', *International Security*, 26(2): 87–102.

Rosecrance, R.N. (1987) *The Rise of the Trading State: Commerce and Conquest in the Modern World*, New York: Basic Books.

Rotberg, R.I. (2002) 'Failed States and State Building in a World of Terror', *Foreign Affairs*, 81(4): 1–17.

—— (2003) *States Failure and State Weakness in a Time of Terror*, Cambridge: Brookings Institution Press.

—— (2004) 'Strengthening Governance: Ranking Countries Would Help', *The Washington Quarterly*, 28(1): 71–81.

Roy, O. (2003) 'EuroIslam: The Jihad Within?', *The National Interest*, 71(Spring): 63–74.

Ruppe, D. (2006) 'Iran Should Receive Security Guarantee, Blix Says', *Global Security Newswire*, 28 January.

Sageman, M. (2004) *Understanding Terror Networks*, Philadelphia: University of Pennsylvania Press.

Sandholtz, W. et al. (1991) *The Highest Stakes: The Economic Foundations of the Next Security System*, Oxford: Oxford University Press.

Schake, K. (2002) *Constructive Duplication Reducing EU reliance on US Military Assets*, London: Centre for European Reform.

Schimmelfennig, F. (2001) 'The Community Trap: Liberal Norms, Rhetorical Action and the Eastern Enlargement of the EU', *International Organization*, 55(1): 47–80.

Schmitt, B. (2004) 'Progress Towards the European Defence Agency', *EUISS Analyses*, Winter.

Schnabel, R. (2003) *The Future of Transatlantic Relations*, Speech to the Konrad Adenauer Foundation in Brussels, Belgium, 5 November 2003.

Sedgwick, M. (2004) 'Al Qaeda and the Nature of Religious Terrorism', *Terrorism and Political Violence*, 16(4): 795–814.

Sen, N. (2006) Nonstate Threats and the Principled Reform of the UN, *Ethics and International Affairs*, 20(2): 229–34.

Shawcross, W. (2004) *Allies*, New York: Public Affairs.

Sjöstedt, G. (1977) *The External Role of the European Community*, Farnborough: Saxon House.

Sjursen, H. (2002) 'Why Expand? The Question of Legitimacy and Justification in the EU's Enlargement Policy', *Journal of Common Market Studies*, 40(3): 491–513.

Skeldon, R. (1997) *Migration and Development: A Global Perpsective*, Harlow: Longman.

Smith, K.E. (2004) *The Making of EU Foreign Policy: The Case of Eastern Europe*, Basingstoke: Palgrave.

—— (2005) 'The Outsiders: The European Neighbourhood Policy', *International Affairs*, 81(4): 757–73.

Smith, M.E. (2001) 'The Quest for Coherence: Institutional Dilemmas of External Action from Maastricht to Amsterdam', in A. Stone, W. Sandhotz, and N. Fliegsten (eds) *The Institutionalization of Europe*, Oxford: Oxford university Press.

—— (2004) *Europe's Foreign and Security Policy. The Institutionalization of Cooperation*, Cambridge: Cambridge University Press.

Solana, J. (2003a) *Mars and Venus Reconciled*, Albert Gordon Lecture, Kennedy School of Government, Harvard University, 7 April.

—— (2003b) *Europe and America: Partners of Choice*, Speech to Annual Meeting of the Foreign Policy Association, New York City, 7 May.

—— (2003c) *A Secure Europe in a Better World*, Thessaloniki, 20 June.

—— (2004) 'Address to the National Forum on Europe', Dublin, 8 January.

—— (2005) *Discours*, Speech to the Annual Conference of the European Union Institute for Security Studies, Paris, 25–26 September.

Spear, J. (2003) 'The Emergence of a European "Strategic Personality"', *Arms Control Today*, November. Online, available at: www.armscontrol.org/2003_11 (accessed on 17 January 2006).

Spring, B. (2006) *Assessing 'Rights' Under the Nuclear Non-Proliferation Treaty*, Washington, DC: Heritage Foundation.

Steinhäusler, F. and Zaitseva, L. (2005) *List of High-Reliability Incidents Involving HEU or Pu-239*, Salzburg: University of Salzburg.

Stern, J. (2003) 'The Protean Enemy', *Foreign Affairs*, 82(4): 27–40.

Stevenson, J. (2004) *Counter-Terrorism: Containment and Beyond*, Adelphi Paper 367, London: International Institute for Strategic Studies.

Stopford, J. and Strange, S. (1991) *Rival States, Rival Firms: Competition for World Market Shares*, Cambridge: Cambridge University Press.

Strange, S. (1994) *States and Market*, London: Pinter.

Suskind, R. (2006) *The One Percent Doctrine: Deep Inside America's Pursuit of Its Enemies Since 9/11*, New York: Simon & Schuster.

Taarnby, M. (2005) *Recruitment of Islamist Terrorists in Europe: Trends and Perspectives*, Aarhus: University of Aarhus.

Takeyh, R. and Gvosdev, N. (2002) 'Do Terrorist Networks Need a Home?', *The Washington Quarterly*, 25(3): 97–108.

Terriff, T. (2003) 'The CJTF Concept and the Limits of European Autonomy', in J. Howorth and J. Keeler (eds) *Defending Europe: The EU, NATO and the Quest for European Autonomy*, New York: Palgrave.

Tietje, C. (1997) 'The Concept of Coherence in the Treaty on European Union and the Common Foreign and Security Policy', *European Foreign Affairs Review*.

Toje, A. (2005) 'The 2003 European Union Security Strategy: A Critical Appraisal', *European Foreign Affairs Review*, 10: 117–33.

Tyson, L. (1992) *Who's Bashing Whom?: Trade Conflicts in High-Technology Industries*, London: Longman.

United Kingdom *et al.* (2004) 'The Battlegroups Concept – UK/France/Germany Food for Thought Paper', Brussels, 10 February.

Vakil, S. (2004) 'Iran: The Gridlock Between Demography and Democracy', *SAIS Review*, 24(2): 45–53.

Van Staden, A., Homan, K., Kreemers, B., Pijpers, A. and de Wijk, R. (2000) *Towards a European Strategic Concept*, The Hague: Netherlands Institute of International Relations 'Clingendael'.

Venusberg Group (2004) *A European Defence Strategy*, Gütersloh: Bertelsmann Foundation.

Vidino, L. (2005) *Al Qaeda in Europe*, Amherst, NY: Prometheus.

Weisman, S.R. (2006) 'Help With Reactor Included in European Offer to Iran', *The New York Times*, 17 May.

Wheeler, N.J. (2001) 'Humanitarian Intervention After Kosovo: Emergent Norm, Moral Duty or Coming Anarchy?', *International Affairs*, 77(1): 113–28.

Whyte, N. (2001) 'The Macedonian Framework Document and European Standards', *Europa South-East Monitor*, no. 26, August. Online, available at: http://neptune.spaceports.com/~ppd/CEPSCommentary.htm

Wiharta, S. (2006) 'Peace-building: The New International Focus on Africa', in *SIPRI Yearbook 2006: Armaments, Disarmament and International Security*, Oxford: Oxford University Press.

Williams, C. (2005) 'From Conscripts to Volunteers: NATO's Transitions to All Volunteer Forces', *Naval War College Review*, 58(1): 35–62.

Wolfers, A. (1962) *Discord and Collaboration, Essays in International Politics*, Baltimore, MA: The John Hopkins University Press.

Woodward, R. (2004) *Plan of Attack*, New York: Simon and Schuster.

Wu, K. (2002) 'Asia-Pacific Oil Dependence, Imports to Grow', *Oil and Gas Journal*, 15 April: 20–23.

Yglesias, M. (2006) 'Iran, Contra', *American Prospect*, 24 January. Online, available at: http://www.prospect.org/web/page.ww?section = root&name = ViewWeb&articleId = 10860

Youngs, R. (2004) *Europe and Iraq: From Stand-off to Engagement?*, London: Foreign Policy Centre.

Zakaria, F. (2003) *The Future of Freedom: Illiberal Democracy at Home and Abroad*, New York: W. W. Norton.

Zeyno, B. (2004) *The Challenge of Hizb ur-Tahrir: Deciphering and Combating Radical Islamist Ideology*, Washington, DC: Nixon Center.

Index

Note: page numbers in **bold** refer to illustrations

Routledge Advances in European Politics

Forthcoming Titles

The Politics of Slovakia
Voters, Parties and Democracy 1989-2004
Karen Henderson, University of Leicester, UK

This book presents detailed factual information about the Slovak political scene and explains the underlying domestic political dynamics in the Slovak Republic, which became an internationally recognized entity at the beginning of 1993.

June 2008: 234x156: 224pp
Hb: 978-0-415-33394-8: **£65.00**

The Northern Ireland Peace Process
Choreography and Theatrical Politics
Paul Dixon, University of Ulster, Northern Ireland

This innovative volume uses a theatrical metaphor to offer a clearer framework for capturing the complex and contradictory politics of peacemaking in Northern Ireland.

July 2008: 234x156: 240pp
Hb: 978-0-415-34860-7: **£65.00**

Poland Within the European Union
The New Awkward Partner?
Aleks Szczerbiak, University of Sussex, UK

The book covers the first three years of Polish EU membership, a key period for the development of Polish-EU relations

December 2008: 256x139: 240pp
Hb: 978-0-415-38073-7: **£65.00**

Unequal Europe
Social Divisions in an Old Continent
James Wickham, Trinity College, Dublin

A penetrating new study about what Europe means today, showing how 9/11 was a brief moment of trans-Atlantic solidarity that lit up the international scene, but was quick to fade. This book is about the rift that existed before this historic juncture and has developed since.

May 2009: 234x156: 256pp
Hb: 978-1-85728-551-2: **£65.00**

Nationalist Movements and European Integration
The Case of Catalonia
Elisa Roller, University of Manchester, UK

The major aim of the book is to examine the effect of the process of European integration on both regional governments and nationalist/regionalist governments in Western Europe.

May 2009: 234x156: 256pp
Hb: 978-0-415-34800-3: **£65.00**

The European Union's Mediterranean Enlargement
Cyprus and Malta
Roderick Pace

This book analyzes Cyprus and Malta's attempt to negotiate membership of the EU from a comparative and 'small state' perspective.

May 2009: 234x156: 256pp
Hb: 978-0-415-34790-7: **£65.00**

Ratifying European Union Treaties
Processes and Actors
Carlos Closa Montero, Centre for Political and Constitutional Studies, Madrid, Spain

This book focuses on the politics of ratification of EU Treaties and reviews the processes of ratification of EU primary legislation.

August 2009: 234x156:
Hb: 978-0-415-45489-6: **£70.00**

Email **politics@routledge.com** to order a copy of the new Politics and International Studies catalogue

Routledge
Taylor & Francis Group